Forced Endings in Psychot and Psychoanalysis

Forced Endings in Psychotherapy and Psychoanalysis: Attachment and loss in retirement explores the ambivalence the therapist may feel about letting go of a professional role which has sustained them. Anne Power explores the process of closing a private practice, from the first ethical decision-making, through to the last day when the door of the therapy room shuts. She draws on the personal accounts of retired therapists and others who had to impose an ending on clients due to illness, in order to move house, to take maternity leave or a sabbatical.

A forced ending is an intrusion of the clinician's own needs into the therapeutic space. Anne Power shows how this might compromise the work but may also be an opportunity for deeper engagement. Drawing on attachment theory to understand how the therapeutic couple cope with an imposed separation, Power includes interviews with therapists who took a temporary break and demonstrates the commonality of challenges faced by those who need to impose an ending on clients.

Forced Endings in Psychotherapy and Psychoanalysis opens up an area which has been considered taboo in the profession so that future cohorts can benefit from the reflections and insights of this earlier generation. It will assist clinicians making this transition and aims to support ethical practice so that clients are not exposed to unnecessary risks of the sudden termination of a long treatment. This book will be essential reading for practising psychotherapists and psychoanalysts, and to undergraduate and postgraduate students in clinical psychology, psychiatry and social work.

Anne Power is an attachment-based psychoanalytic psychotherapist working with individuals and couples. She teaches at Regent's University London. She is interested in retirement, both as a supervisor and as a middle-aged therapist wondering how she will manage this transition herself.

"This book is timely and thought-provoking. It grasps the nettle of therapists' retirement dilemmas firmly and skilfully. I found it very compelling reading, both because of its immediate relevance to therapists and supervisors today, and because the stories it traces in the retirees' own words are so rich and engaging. This book is a masterpiece of qualitative research, drawing on thirteen in-depth interviews, as well as a broad range of additional sources. Anne Power poses and explores a multitude of questions about when, how, why and with what support and with what in mind can therapists tackle the issue of ending their working life. I was deeply moved, sobered, intrigued and inspired."

Roz Carroll, MA Cantab, UKCP registered psychotherapist, trainer on the Minster Centre MA in Integrative Psychotherapy

"This is a wonderfully well written, sensitive and important book which examines, though interviews with therapists, the issues and challenges involved in the processes of retirement, ending and loss in a profession that has tended to avoid consideration of this significant aspect of life. An essential read for therapists of all ages in relation to their personal and professional journeys."

Dr Christine Driver, SAP and FPC Training Analyst, Supervisor, Director of Training, WPF Therapy

"A work of tremendous originality, Anne Power's new book tackles the vital but hitherto much neglected subject of retirement with the depth of a great investigator and with the breadth of creative thinker. Drawing upon extensive primary research and sensitive clinical understanding, the author allows us all – whether old or young – to engage with key questions about endings and mortality with admirable sensitivity and compassion. This volume fills a huge gap in the mental health literature by examining not only the vicissitudes of retirement but, also, the heaving subject of endings more generally – whether traumatic or ordinary – in such a useful way."

Professor Brett Kahr, Senior Clinical Research Fellow in Psychotherapy and Mental Health at the Centre for Child Mental Health in London; Honorary Visiting Professor in the School of Arts at the University of Roehampton; and Consultant in Psychology to The Bowlby Centre

"In a long term therapy the retirement of the therapist, be it from age, illness, sabbatical, maternity or relocation, is a challenge to both patient and therapist. This book shows how thirteen therapists met that challenge. The author makes good use of attachment theory which provides a fascinating and appropriate over-arching framework for her analysis."

Colin Murray Parkes

Forced Endings in Psychotherapy and Psychoanalysis

Attachment and loss in retirement

Anne Power

With a preface by Peter Fonagy

Routledge
Taylor & Francis Group

LONDON AND NEW YORK

First published 2016
by Routledge
27 Church Road, Hove, East Sussex, BN3 2FA

and by Routledge
711 Third Avenue, New York, NY 10017

*Routledge is an imprint of the Taylor & Francis Group,
an informa business*

British Library Cataloguing in Publication Data
A catalogue record for this book is available from the

Library of Congress Cataloging-in-Publication Data
Power, Anne.
    Forced endings in psychotherapy and psychoanalysis:
    attachment and loss in retirement/authored by Anne Power.
    – 1 Edition.
    pages cm
    1. Dependency (Psychology). 2. Attachment behavior.
    3. Psychologists – Retirement. 4. Psychotherapists –
    Retirement. I. Title.
    BF575.D34P69 2015
    attachment theory – dc23
    2015008184

ISBN: 978-0-415-52764-4 (hbk)
ISBN: 978-0-415-52765-1 (pbk)
ISBN: 978-1-315-71744-9 (ebk)

Typeset in Times New Roman and Gill Sans
by Florence Production Ltd, Stoodleigh, Devon, UK
Printed and bound in Great Britain by
Ashford Colour Press Ltd, Gospot, Hampshire

Cover Image by Florence Hendriks

To Jonathan, Edward and Richard

Contents

Note on language

I have chosen to use the female pronoun when one word is needed to stand for male or female.

The terms "client" and "patient" are used synonymously as I hope the book will speak to clinicians who prefer either of these words.

For the sake of variety I refer to the therapists who shared their stories as interviewees, contributors and participants. I use these terms interchangeably.

In the text when I mention that a contribution is located 'below' or 'above', I mean that it is within the same chapter. When the material is located in a separate chapter I give the chapter number.

Preface

In the process of talking to other therapists and thinking through the dilemmas of retirement, Anne Power has captured something of what it is to be a therapist – the particular achievement of emotional and intellectual reflectiveness characteristic of therapists who are working well, and responsibly. And Power also powerfully and sensitively reveals the complex emotional and intellectual demands and narcissistic challenges that confront a therapist who is considering retirement from practice.

The question of potentially intruding upon the therapeutic process via external regulation has long been a fraught one. The issue is particularly difficult in the context of considerations about retirement: how can you legislate about appropriate retirement age when ageing itself is such a variable process across individuals? But in the absence of any such external framework, how do we protect patients from the experience of working with a therapist who is no longer well enough to provide the treatment they need? Psychotherapists have always been able to work well beyond the statutory retirement age. Now that the statutory retirement age has gone for most professions, other groups will share the dilemma which psychotherapists have faced for many years: the conflict is one between wanting to impart the accumulation of decades of experience set against the subjective experience of the diminution of key competencies, for example the capacity to remember detail. Normally skills acquired through sheer number of repetitions mitigate against a slight decline in cognitive agility. I remember experienced teachers of mine were able to make what seemed to me to be remarkable shortcuts and to see through what, to a novice, seemed an impenetrable jungle of personal detail to get to the core difficulties that an individual brought to the consulting room. I saw this magical skill at work in senior colleagues who had genuine difficulty in recalling information that was not so personally relevant and who engaged in that hallmark trait of retelling the same anecdote without embarrassment on numerous occasions. Our profession, as well as others, is built upon and enriched by invaluable experience. Set against that is the plain fact that, to quote Freud, 'the ego is first and foremost a body ego' (Freud, 1923), and therefore the mind has to age along with the body, with its 'Bare ruin'd choirs, where late the sweet birds sang'.

And yet perhaps we sometimes irrationally expect wisdom to increase with age while we are far more ready to take on board our physical limitations. Our self-appraisal in relation to our clinical skills is notoriously inadequate. The motivation to obtain and use critical feedback to enhance experience declines rapidly and almost inversely to one's confidence in one's own competence (Tracey, Wampold, Lichtenberg and Goodyear, 2014). This justifies enforced retirement or at least forced monitoring of competence after a certain age. The medical profession in the UK is making a real and honest attempt at addressing this issue with the compulsory revalidation process. Should psychotherapy follow suit?

Power is careful not to be over-proscriptive about what therapists *should* do: this is a more reflective and discursive book than that. However, she convincingly describes how it is not always realistic to expect the therapist to make such a judgement via feedback from their patients, nor from colleagues or a supervisor. And as well as protecting the patient, consideration must also be given to the needs of the therapist: this work asks a lot of its practitioner, in terms of emotional and intellectual investment. The burden of the analyst is often borne with the help of the sense of identity that goes with it. As Power describes, many therapists are the children of depressed mothers; they are people who, to quote one therapist, make carrying the burden a way of life:

> my mother needed care, as it were, not my father, but I was definitely a parenting child. It's a sort of way of life really, and I think I just professionalised it.
>
> (Adams, M., 2014: 74)

It puts to mind the myth of Atlas carrying the celestial spheres – how is the therapist to be assisted in putting down their burden without fearing that the sky will fall on their own, or their patients', heads? Power is to be congratulated for interviewing Atlas directly and obtaining first-hand information about a decision-making process we all have to go through. Colleagues of mine whom I deeply admire and who have made the decision to retire all discuss this with mixed emotion. In my own informal survey, I'm not yet persuaded that I should stop at the earliest available opportunity. However, exceptions frequently prove the rule and a number of colleagues have made a real and genuine success of engaging with new challenges and obviously profiting from the changes that retirement brings. If I were to face up to this decision, careful reading of this book would obviously be of benefit. Reading the stories collected by Anne Power opens a window on the diversity of considerations presented by the dilemma of retirement. By reading about and identifying with other lives and other minds we can perhaps offset the significant risk of short-circuiting the process of decision making through premature closure and, even worse, prejudice.

Bowlby remarked that our attachment needs, as adults, are triggered 'especially in times of ill health, stress or old age'. Anne Power's work is important in its appreciation of the complexity of our psychic lives across life stages, and the thoughtful engagement of her interviews is an exercise in humanity and compassion. In creating a space for considering, with our colleagues, the meaning of retirement, Anne Power also creates a poignant meditation on what it means to be a therapist: what this particular life's work means to its many thoughtful practitioners. Anne Power and I, as well as sharing professions, shared a remarkable teacher – Shirley Pleydell, to whom, for her wisdom and compassion, we both owe a debt of gratitude. It seems fitting that Anne Power should have written such a sensitive and insightful book that speaks to the particular strengths and dilemmas of a caring profession.

*Peter Fonagy, Freud Memorial Professor of Psychoanalysis
and Head of the Department of Clinical, Educational and
Health Psychology at University College London*

References

Adams, M. (2014) *Myth of the untroubled therapist: Private life, professional practice*. London: Routledge.

Freud, S. (1923/1961). The ego and the id. In J. Strachey (ed.) *The standard edition of the complete psychological works of Sigmund Freud*, vol. 19. London: Hogarth Press, pp. 1–59.

Tracey, T.J., Wampold, B.E., Lichtenberg, J.W., & Goodyear, R.K. (2014). Expertise in psychotherapy: An elusive goal? *American Psychologist*, 69: 218–229.

Acknowledgements

Like most authors I am at a loss as to how I can appropriately thank so many people who helped me towards writing this book. I feel profound thanks to those who have encouraged me and in different ways enabled me to learn and to write. Even a long essay would not adequately convey the extent of what I owe so I have chosen to make a simple list.

Two teachers from my earlier life who gave me belief in myself when I most needed it – Shirley Pleydell and Sonia Poulson.

My original colleagues with whom I trained at the Bowlby Centre, and also my teachers there. I particularly wish to thank Linda Cundy, Jenny Riddell and Thea Thompson.

My colleagues at BAPPS Supervision Review, Chris Driver and Lynda Norton.

Colleagues at Wimbledon Guild.

Colleagues at Regents University London.

Supervisors and teachers who have helped me learn: Bernie Laschinger, Kate White and Brett Kahr. Joe Schwartz for the initial encouragement to write. Nick Midgley for supervision of this research.

My therapists who helped me at different stages of my life – they know who they are.

Peter Fonagy for his preface and for having previously put the subject of retirement on the agenda.

For their pioneering retirement workshops, Penny Kegerreis, Gill Barratt and Jean Wetherell.

Kate Hawes and Kirsten Buchanan at Routledge for believing in the project and facilitating it.

Colleagues who gave me time from their own busy lives to critique my drafts: Christina Patton, Debbie Vowles, Cynthia Ransley, Gillian Chapman, Mary Russell, Em Farrell, Angela Cotter, Marie Adams, Charlotte Wynn Parry and Angela Massucco.

My supervisee C, who retired and who provided the impetus for this study, and all my other supervisees and clients who have challenged and trained me over the years.

My interviewees who in a sense wrote the book for me.

Finally my family for fulfilling with love and protest most of the roles mentioned above.

Thank you.

I am grateful to the following individuals and organisations for permission to reproduce material in this book:

On page xxx The Collected Poems by Cavafy, translated by Hirst (2007) 27w from p.37. By permission of Oxford University Press, (URL www.oup.com).

'This last isn't something I actually saw, but what you end up remembering isn't always the same as what you have witnessed.' (2012: 3) Excerpted from *The Sense of an Ending* by Julian Barnes. Copyright © 2011 Julian Barnes. Published by Vintage. Reprinted by permission of The Random House Group Limited.

'This last isn't something I actually saw, but what you end up remembering isn't always the same as what you have witnessed.' (2012:3) Excerpted from *The Sense of an Ending* by Julian Barnes. Copyright © 2011 Julian Barnes. Reprinted by permission of Random House Canada, a division of Random House of Canada Limited, a Penguin Random House Company.

Excerpt from 'The Old Fools' from THE COMPLETE POEMS by Philip Larkin, Farrar, Straus and Giroux, 2012.

Excerpt from 'The Old Fools' from THE COMPLETE POEMS by Philip Larkin (electronic), Faber & Faber Ltd, 2012.

'When a supervisee retires' by Anne Power, published in *Psychodynamic Practice: Individuals, Groups and Organisations*, Vol. 18 (4): 441–455 (2012), http://www.tandfonline.com/. Reprinted with permission.

Introduction

I think there are some people who are able to mourn, to grieve, to be angry. And other people go on until far beyond they should be going on . . . It is incredibly hard work to retire.

(Celia)

In summer, when the windows are open, our cat has the pleasure of choosing when he comes and goes, but the route by which he makes his exit is audacious. As the house has a basement, the ground floor windows open onto a deep drop and the cat needs to jump across the area and pass through railings before landing safely on the pavement. He must gauge his trajectory to a very precise angle. The clearance between the railings is very slight and to miss would mean a fearful fall down the sheer cliff of the basement wall. Even for a cat, this undertaking requires special concentration and he seems to prefer to jump when no one is around. He is 12 years old. As each summer comes and the windows are left open I wonder if he will again make use of this route, and a small part of me worries about him attempting the jump and having a horrible accident. How will my cat know when he can no longer risk this leap? When his body is less agile, his eye less sure and his coordination less reliable, will he then have the sense to wait for us to open the front door? Another part of me trusts that it will be easy for him to give up this dangerous jumping because he does not have an ego to manage or a sense of loss or sacrifice. So he will not face the dilemma that many psychotherapists report in relation to retirement.

Why retirement matters

I hadn't anticipated – whether naively or defensively or omnipotently – even though I knew that these are big events – I didn't anticipate such a rollercoaster of feelings evoked in me. Because I actually feel very distant from some people as well. I have so many different feelings.

(Denise)

Age is not a precise indicator of the right time to retire. When we think in terms of quality control and duty of care, there are two main risks which need to be held in mind: first that an ageing therapist may lose capacity to do the work sufficiently well and second that as we age there is an increased chance of our dying, or of becoming seriously ill, and therefore abandoning patients in the midst of their process. Registering organisations are becoming aware of the large number of therapists who will be retiring in the next decade, but most have yet to evolve or implement procedures around retirement.

In a chapter looking back at her own retirement, Josephine Klein (2006) conveys the natural resentment felt by those whose strong sense of duty leads them to retire before those colleagues who take a more sanguine view of how age is affecting them. 'Anna Freud and Dorothy Burlingham, among others, practised into their nineties, said my more megalomaniac self, why could not I?' (2006: 66). This comment has slightly inflated the ages of these two pioneers, but several early analysts did work to a very advanced age and some died in harness. Freud himself continued working to within weeks of his death. The evidence of his later writing suggests that his mind remained enormously powerful and perhaps he was able to do good clinical work despite the appalling losses and the pain he was living with. The problem from a twenty-first-century perspective is that issues of continuity and attachment were overlooked. Freud did not consider it necessary to protect patients from the experience of an analysis cut short and the way he managed his practice through his years of illness raises some ethical questions (Klockars, 2013). Some months after arriving in London, and very weak following his final major operation, he took on three new patients at the age of 82. He was able to work with them for around 10 months before pain and weakness made it impossible to continue (Gay, 1988). It seems that the impact of his condition on others was denied and was most sharply brought home to him when his beloved dog cringed from the smell of his wound.

While the news that their therapist is leaving them is unwelcome for most clients and devastating for some, there will be clients for whom the imposed time frame turns out to be beneficial. Some of the literature on endings offers a positive view of the work which can be done under pressure. Kaplan, Weiss, Harris and Dick (1994) point out that, like any adjustment to the frame, the imposed ending provides a window onto parts of the unconscious which might otherwise not have been exposed and explored. All are agreed that the rupture will pose profound challenges to patients and therapists. Boyd-Carpenter (2010a) describes the sudden threat to the therapeutic alliance when the news was broken. She writes that once the approaching abandonment was known, in her clients' minds she was 'no longer a passably steadfast, predictable and safe "mother"; but had proved to be vulnerable, wilful, selfish and to have other loves and other "children"' (2010a: 91).

Stories we need to listen to

> I think it is a process which needs to be taken incredibly seriously. That's what I've come to feel – through experiencing it myself and watching other people go through it. Giving up of one's whole identity as a psychotherapist is mammoth, even if one may feel in some ways burnt-out, there is so much wrapped up in that identity.
>
> (Celia)

Five years ago, when I was 53, one of my supervisees began to speak of the possibility of retiring and I became aware of an aspect of clinical practice to which I had given little thought. I realised that the issues faced by a retiring therapist have much in common with those occurring in other imposed endings such as illness, maternity leave, relocation and sabbatical, where a therapist needs to close her practice. As I thought with my supervisee about her clients I became abruptly aware of what significant attachment issues this raised and how differently the experience of being left might play out for each of them. I realised I was becoming interested in retirement not only in order to fulfil my duties as a supervisor but also because in years to come this could be a challenging developmental stage for me. Until my supervisee mentioned retirement it had been a distant issue for me, but I now recognised that for those few clients who need a decade of therapy my own retirement could soon become a consideration. Like many therapists in peri-retirement I prefer not to put a figure on this but, if my health permits, 70 (or a bit beyond), seems the age I might close my practice. Of course sudden death and illness can arise at any age and from the first day of private practice all therapists should have in place a clinical will and an executor with access to all necessary contact details (Firestein, 1993; Despenser, 2008; O'Neil, 2013).

The lack of almost any research or commentary on retirement motivated me to set up my own study which aimed to discover what the process of retirement might involve. This book is based on my interviews with 13 retiring therapists, one who closed her practice to relocate, four who closed a practice temporarily for maternity or sabbatical leave and one who gave consideration to retirement but instead adopted a novel pattern of working. In the last few years the literature has been significantly expanded. A book by Junkers (2013) gives voice to psychoanalysts who have observed how hard their colleagues find it to make a timely retirement and how much harm may be done when the decision is postponed too long. A paper by Barratt, Kegerreis and Wetherell (2012) reflects on the pioneering retirement course which they ran in London for four years. Very recently a number of the registering bodies have begun to recognise the need for support in this area and to arrange workshops for therapists who are preparing to retire. In this book I particularly wanted to gather up the experience of retired therapists so that the next generation could benefit from what has already been digested and learned. My focus has been directed to two sets of questions: how hard is retirement for both therapists and their patients, and, how do they manage the challenges? The research was deeply enriching for me and I owe a profound debt to my anonymous interviewees.

A survey by Guy, Stark, Poelstra and Souder (1987) suggested that therapists who postpone retirement cite emotional satisfaction from the work as a reason for continuing regardless of age. In her research into therapists' personal challenges and tragedies, Adams (2014) explores this emotional need and the way, as therapists, we may be seeking to remedy the past through our work with clients. She concludes, 'in our work, many of us have also found an unconscious method of self-medicating' (2014: 8). Given my deep attachment to the work and the identity and meaning it gives me, I can recognise that I could fall into this group who are reluctant to let go. In this sense this study is part of my own extended preparation for retirement.

Psychoanalysis and ageing

Fonagy puts the matter squarely: 'Psychoanalysts took their time to catch on to ageing' (Fonagy, 2009: 212). In the early years of the profession, attention was naturally focused on childhood because it was recognised as formative for all that followed; old age was consequently left under-theorised. Freud's dismissive comments about the analysability of middle-aged people were famously made when he was 48 and wrote, 'psychotherapy is not possible near or above the age of fifty, the elasticity of the mental processes, on which treatment depends, is as a rule lacking

– old people are not educable' (1905: 264). These comments now sound ridiculous, particularly in the light of the three productive decades in Freud's life which followed, but Biggs (1999) explains Freud's statement in terms of context. A few years earlier he had been almost drummed out of town for his 'outrageous' ideas on child sexuality. This may have led him to be overcautious in his claims for the new treatment. Even if Freud himself was not as pessimistic as the 1905 statement can seem to imply, the negative attitude towards work with older people became embedded and only shifted towards the end of the century after pioneer papers by Segal (1958) and King (1974). This means that the cohort of therapists now coming into retirement will have been influenced by that earlier negative belief. If being older is taken as meaning 'not educable', no wonder there may be reluctance to own up to it. Biggs (1999) suggests that the Freudian legacy which privileges the importance of childhood has contributed to a negative discourse about old age and has meant that psychoanalysis has aligned itself with other ageist beliefs in our culture. It would be interesting to speculate whether elderly retired Jungians, supported by a theory which puts emphasis on later life development, might have a more positive self-image.

Attachment theory

I have chosen to look at the phenomenon of an imposed ending through the lens of attachment theory because this is the understanding at the heart of my own training and work, and because it offers an accessible way of thinking about loss. Each chapter opens with reflections on the attachment implications of the theme under discussion. Retirement involves loss and separation on many levels, and how we cope with this will owe much to our own attachment pattern and the defences with which we have managed earlier challenges. The patients are losing an attachment figure, a secure base and the person who carries (via projection) the unwieldy parts of the self until these can be integrated. The therapist is losing her clients, her colleagues and her identity as one who provides containment and meaning.

Attachment behaviour is most obviously triggered by separation. However, many states of reduced vitality can prompt us to draw close to a trusted other. Loneliness may evoke attachment needs and is often present to some degree in retirement. One retiree, older than her partner, spoke poignantly of going ahead of her attachment figure, saying, 'I feel daunted by doing it alone'. My hope is that this book can offer some sense of accompaniment by enabling the voices of an earlier cohort of retirees to speak to the next generation.

Scope of the book

This book explores the experience of therapists who closed a private practice in which they were working with long-term individual clients. I hope the book will have relevance to a wide range of therapists and counsellors, as well as to supervisors working with retiring supervisees. I focused my study on people who draw on psychodynamic ideas because the significance of imposing an ending may have particular repercussions for the therapeutic couple who have worked with the interplay of their unconscious worlds. I have used the terms patient and client interchangeably, hoping to speak to the wide range of clinicians who value psychodynamic principles. The papers I have drawn on tend towards more mainstream psychoanalytic pieces because the small literature that exists on imposed endings has mostly been written by analysts.

The psychoanalytic frame was developed to provide containment for a complex relationship with different levels of meaning. Disruptions to the frame have significant impact and the imposition of an ending cuts right into the 'as if' relationship as well as the more 'real' attachment relationship. Sherby sums up why the announcement of an ending is such a challenge, 'as if everything the analyst had explicitly or implicitly promised – security, safety, consistency, trust – has now been destroyed' (2004: 74).

Some of the interviewees worked once a week with clients and others more frequently, while two participants were analysts seeing patients up to five times a week. In order to maintain confidentiality I have not clarified to which of these three groups each contributor belongs, but there are some points where this is implicit in what they say. The participants were all working long term and some of them were working very long term – well beyond 10 years. Some of them had additional qualifications to work with groups, couples or children but, again to preserve anonymity, I have not made this clear. The special issues which arise in imposing an ending on groups or couples are outlined in Chapter 2, which also looks very briefly at retirement from an organisation. Child psychotherapy is not covered.

Chapters 1 to 8 focus on the contributions of the 13 retired or retiring therapists as well as the one who relocated. These therapists were all making a full and permanent closure of a practice. Each chapter addresses a question about the process, beginning with the enquiry, 'Why retire?' and leading through to Chapter 8 on life after retirement. While a staged model is always an oversimplification, it is interesting how the experience of closing a practice does chart the familiar stages of grief. The themes addressed in each chapter follow the familiar sequence quite closely:

ambivalence; uncertainty; abandonment; challenge; guilt; hoping for help; sadness; relief.

Chapter 1 asks contributors how they came to the decision to retire. Chapter 2 reports on how they set about the task and then two long chapters – 3 and 4 – cover the clinical stories of working with patients when the guillotine has been set. Chapter 3 focuses on how patients responded and the material here is circumscribed by therapists' obvious need to maintain confidentiality for patients. Chapter 4 continues to look at the clinical tasks of closing a practice and referring on. In Chapter 5 retirees speak about their countertransference. Chapter 6 asks what role supervision played in the process of retirement and considers the supervisor's own retirement. In Chapter 7 therapists speak about the different types of loss they faced and in Chapter 8 they share their experience in the period after retiring. Each of these eight central chapters opens with reflection on the attachment implications of this stage, followed by verbatim quotations from different participants and comments from the literature. The Introduction to the Contributors is placed in a section of its own before Chapter 1.

The eight chapters which describe the process of permanently closing a practice for retirement or relocation are followed by a single chapter looking at temporary closures. This chapter draws on interviews with two therapists who took maternity leave, two who took a sabbatical and one who made an innovative adaptation to his working schedule when he turned 60. These temporary endings are distinct from retirement and relocation but there is considerable overlap in the issues faced by patients and therapists. In all cases therapists are facing a dilemma as to how to balance their need to leave the work versus the clients' needs for care. This dilemma can be acute when patients are in long-term work, are invested in a challenging transference and have an early history of loss and abandonment. The appendices at the end of the book provide a checklist of the challenges relating to each type of ending.

Relocation

I have drawn heavily on papers about relocation because of the dearth of writing on retirement itself and because the two kinds of imposed ending are in many ways similar. In an early paper on relocation, Aarons (1975) is forthright about the enormity for some patients: 'For the analyst to move away is akin to the loss of a loved one in whom there has been great emotional investment' (1975: 303). Papers by Dewald (1965), Weiss (1972), Schwarz (1974), Martinez (1989) and Sherby (2004) also illustrate a personal record of relocation and their articles provide a basis for thinking about each stage of retirement. Although I see similarities in the experience of retirement and relocation and I have included the story of one interviewee who relocated, it is important to acknowledge that there are differences and so where the issues concerning relocation are more distinct I have included a specific paragraph on this. A key practical issue which distinguishes the two experiences is the pace of the change. Most therapists who are in good health are able (if not willing) to see their retirement when it is still a few years distant whereas the need to move home may arise much more suddenly. The most significant difference may be the emotional meaning of the imposed closure. For both therapist and client, feelings and fantasies will be differently informed. In the case of relocation the therapist is pursuing a new venture and making an exciting-sounding choice to move to another town whereas in retirement she is usually responding to her own life cycle.

That this simplification is misleading is immediately illustrated by the story of my contributor Alice, whose relocation was necessitated by the long illness and eventual death of her partner. The story of Nicola also illustrates how experience of retirement or relocation may not accord with such a simple distinction. Her own retirement was brought forward because her husband stopped working and this pushed them towards moving house. For many therapists who relocate, the reason for moving arises out of their partner's needs rather than their own. This experience of relocating under pressure is described by Sherby (2004), whose paper shares the personal challenge of eventually placing her husband's health needs above her own wishes and the claims of her patients.

Uncertainty over fitness to practise

Fitness to practise is essentially about being able to provide the contract which we explicitly and implicitly have with patients. Where there is doubt about our being reliably and effectively available, it may be necessary to close our practice. This is an important allied area which cannot be explored fully in this book but is considered in Chapter 1 and in Chapter 6, which looks at the role of supervision. When a therapist is facing an uncertain prognosis, decisions about how to proceed will need a lot of thought in supervision, and possibly in negotiation with our registering body, to identify the best way forward. Sometimes it is appropriate to take a limited period of time off in which the therapist comes to a view as to whether they will be able to resume or whether, provided they are well enough, they need to meet with their patients to say goodbye and to think with them about referral on.

Although this book is focused on planning retirement with the aim of avoiding an emergency ending, one participant, Emma, did have to make an abrupt closure. She ended with half of her patients over a three-month period and a year later was obliged to retire from work with her remaining patients, with just two weeks' notice. Her story will provide some insight into this particular challenge.

Methodology: research with a supervisory stance

In selecting a methodology I was looking for an approach which would sustain and deepen my own curiosity as well as that of my readers. I considered using an 'off the shelf' qualitative research method as a way to achieve philosophical coherence and academic rigour, but I felt that my primary aim of sharing information between generations of therapists would be best achieved by evolving a pragmatic approach. I intend the book to be user friendly for the reader and I would like it to span the gap which has often existed between research and practice. Freshwater (2007) has drawn attention to the role of the reader in appraising research, and she reminds us that every reader is a critic. I hope this book will evoke this kind of critique from the reader, so that they are aware of being participators in the research and may choose to build on it.

Sample

My research has been based on a small sample, most of whom practised in London, and cannot hope to represent the full range of retirement experiences. Nonetheless I wished to achieve some breadth of cover – in particular to hear the stories of therapists who retired at different ages. In pursuing that aim I rather de-prioritised achieving a gender balance and so a limitation of my sample is its homogeneity: my contributors are mostly women, all white and mostly middle class. This of course is representative of this cohort of British therapists. It is also my identity. In addition to data from the formal participants, I have drawn on conversations with colleagues who have kindly given permission for use of their material.

I have focused on therapists who made a planned retirement from private practice, who worked with patients long term and with an orientation which was either psychoanalytic or integrative with psychodynamic under-standing. The point of commonality was that therapists were working in a way that meant the unexpected break in the frame would represent a serious challenge to the clinical relationship. I did not ask contributors to identify their place on the analytic spectrum, but their comments may give some clues as to whether they tend towards neutrality in the therapy relationships or whether they are interested in the intersubjectivity of the analytic encounter (Benjamin, 1990, 2004). My own theoretical base of attachment theory would have been more familiar to some participants than to others. Training was thus one factor which made me closer to some of the interviewees than to others and there will have been other less obvious factors that supported a deeper level of rapport with some contributors.

Confidentiality and ethics

When we write about researching the work of other therapists we are inevitably engaging with a triangle. As in writing about supervision, there are two levels of participants whose identity needs to be protected: the therapists and their clients. To provide anonymity for interviewees and patients I have been sparing with personal details and of course pseudonyms are used. Contributors gave permission for recording of interviews and as I wanted them to feel that their script represented them and their clients fairly, I offered several opportunities for revision of the transcript and the draft.

Data gathering through a supervision-interview

It was important to me that interviewees felt comfortable to share their experience and I think this was helped by my approaching all of them through personal introduction. The first two subjects were known to me directly and the subsequent ones were all known to colleagues who knew me. This meant that in each case there was an initial level of trust that enabled us to use the space productively. Interviews lasted about 90 minutes and I let the contributors know in advance the areas on which I would ask them to reflect. The fact that all interviews and transcription were done by me may contribute to a clear frame and possibly a degree of consistency, although I believe that my method was evolving as my data-gathering progressed.

As interviewees were generously agreeing to share their stories, I gave them control of confidentiality and built this into the process. Occasionally contributors censored themselves as they spoke, interjecting 'That shouldn't go in!'. They also had the assurance that when I transcribed the conversation I would remove any identifying details about clients and I would be asking specific permission before I quoted any sentences verbatim. When they received the transcript they had a chance to ask for amendments; typically participants spotted a few more personal details which needed to be excised or they added the odd clarification. Later I invited them to read the first draft of the book and to check that they were satisfied with the way I had used their stories.

I would argue that with this frame in place, once interviewees felt confidence in the quality of my listening it was natural for them to make significant use of the contained thinking space which we created between us. I think that the use they made of it was analogous to supervision. I would define supervision as a generative thinking space where reflection on work with clients is deepened. Contributors were all experienced in using free association to access deeper levels of the self and they took the opportunity to tune into their own unconscious process. This happened to differing degrees in different interviews, but the pattern that emerged was that of a quasi-supervisory meeting. I became aware that my stance in these sessions had considerable overlap with the way I listen and respond as a supervisor and that my interviewees were, to some extent, using me in that way. This evolution seemed to be a mutual process and helped to promote a kind of supervisory dynamic. As most meetings were held in the therapist's current or former therapy room, this also contributed to our sense of working together on understanding the retiree's clinical experience.

This claim that my interviews had a supervisory nature makes sense if we consider the research qualities that are already present in regular clinical supervision. We could say that the supervisory dyad is engaged in a study of the supervisee's work. As supervisor and supervisee construct a narrative about the therapist and her patients, data are amassed and analysed and there is also reflection on the way the supervisory dyad is handling that material and on how it is impacting on them (Frawley-O'Dea and Sarnat, 2001).

While I have emphasised the sense of a frame in my interviews, it is important to acknowledge that these meetings happened within a research contract; Midgley (2006) suggests researchers benefit from psychoanalytic skills, but warns that the research interview is not suited to the kinds of interaction we expect within a clinical relationship. The factor that made this process very distinct from clinical supervision was the different intention. As a supervisor I have the needs of both the client and the supervisee in mind. In these research interviews the aim was different: I was hoping for the interviewee to understand more of her own process, so that I could make use of that emerging story. For those contributors who were still working with clients, it is possible that our meeting did perform a direct supervisory function.

The subjectivity of the researcher

As a therapist I subscribe to the idea that there is no neutral position to which we can retreat (Mitchell, 1993). There are always two subjectivities in the consulting room, and equally I do not claim objectivity as a researcher. Through reflection on my subjectivity I hope to deepen the understanding which the study may offer readers. Through transparency about my process I aim to put the reader in a position to interpret my work.

Avis and Freshwater (2006: 221) assert that 'it is having a theory in mind that makes particular features of experience apparent'. We know this of course from the consulting room where we listen with a certain filter assembled from our theoretical and personal values; our clients certainly know it, with different levels of consciousness, and they soon learn what we will and won't pick up on. The conscious filter which I brought to this work was constructed from a combination of attachment and psycho-analytic theory. This template for my listening was further coloured by a personal agenda to prepare myself for my own retirement, as well as to address my concern about those cases where reluctance to retire leads to unplanned endings. As I listened to my interviewees it was inevitable that my own responses would to some extent be implicitly conveyed. This may have happened through my expression, my demeanour and my choice, or phrasing, of supplementary questions. Clearly my own identification with, or defensiveness against, parts of each story will have impacted on how the story was being told.

We know that transference operates in all human relationships and it may help us to make sense of the assumptions and projections being made by researcher and participants. In some conversations I was aware of being particularly warmly engaged and also sensing mutuality in that feeling. It was not difficult for me to recognise the kinds of qualities which I was appreciating in these senior therapists and to observe my wish to inspire their respect in me. In some cases I was relating to them as authority figures. From these comments it is very clear that I do not stand outside of my inquiry.

All therapists will approach retirement with their own blend of concerns. For many the overriding question is how they will know when to retire. I am chiefly concerned with how deeply I will feel the loss of my work. When I no longer have the opportunity to be so useful to people, to benefit from the very particular contained intimacy which therapy involves, how will I manage the parts of me which have been sustained by this role? This need in me to understand the challenge ahead has shaped the research and the book.

Interpretation of contributors' stories

Although the participants in this study were all, by definition of their profession, signed up to the significance of unconscious process, and although when we met I tried to elicit new layers of reflection from them, I have not felt it was my role as researcher to subject these stories to full-blooded interpretation. Yet all my participants were aware, and readers will expect, that motivation for retirement, like other motivations, will include a mix of conscious and unconscious elements. In some of the interviews these layers were more fully exposed and the interviewee herself comments on her unconscious process. The stories are therefore to some extent self-interpreted, but the contributors' gift is that they have made their stories available for the reader to make sense of. Doubtless each reader will identify more fully with some participants than with others and they will seek to understand the stories through their own theoretical lens. I have tried to present material in a way which is faithful to the differences between contributors without creating a narrative which feels too exposing to individuals whose former colleagues are likely to read this book. The framework for the book is chronological, following recognisable steps through a retirement process. This choice of structure reflects the strong narrative sequence in the accounts I heard, but it is also the case that I was, from the start, looking for stories. By choosing this familiar and accessible format, I have necessarily forgone other ways of presenting the material which would have emphasised and linked up different aspects of experience.

Critique of my methodology

There are downsides to being as close as I was to my contributors. A serious limitation is my bias towards being nice to my interviewees – I identified with them as colleagues and to different degrees I felt admiration of their careers. Although I felt able to pose some challenging questions, my respect may have been more constraining than if I had been interviewing distinguished retirees from a profession other than my own. After gaining their permission to use their story, I did not want to steer the conversation in a way which might 'show them up' or enhance the feelings of regret or guilt they might be carrying about their retirement.

As well as sparing my interviewees from discomfort I was perhaps anxious on my own account: if a transcript had showed the speaker in a poor light I would then have had the dilemma of either presenting or censoring that material. In her writing about the relationship between researcher and subject, Rizq (2008) explores the impact of unconscious dynamics and the temptation there may be for collusion. She refers to 'the research couple's jointly constructed unconscious agreement to abolish disagreement, to deny Oedipal difference' (2008: 46). There are points in my interviews where I was aware of this collusion and almost certainly others of which I was unconscious, but which readers may identify. In some other passages I have purposefully avoided comments which could appear judgemental; readers may develop their own thoughts about best practice, in terms of their own clinical experience and modality.

In support of my method I would point to the deeper engagement which may be possible when the researcher is experienced as a like-minded colleague. In the supervision-interview process the mostly silent listening of another is likely to evoke a process of remembering which is different from a regular interview. In the pauses where the speaker stops but the listener continues to listen and to expect, there is an invitation to dig deeper, to look again at what has been said, to add or to revise. The knowledge that the listener is attending, and is receiving and holding what is said with an analytic attitude, is an encouragement to the speaker to also enter into that reverie and to allow material to loosen and to come to the surface and for new connections to be made. The paradox is that the same trust which meant that I was privileged with confidences meant that I felt constrained in how I used them.

Imposed ending as opportunity

For the most part this book looks at challenges and losses but an imposed ending also brings opportunities: the intrusion of real life can bring forth the adult part of the client so that their resourcefulness can become more apparent. In a comment about transitions which might speak here to either the retiring therapist or the patient, Murray Parkes writes that 'Crisis can lead to the stars as well as to the grave' (1971: 102). In some ways the dilemma of working through an enforced ending is the dilemma of all therapy writ large: how to allow space for the young, disturbed parts of the client to be known and reintegrated, while also holding appropriate expectations of the adult in the room.

Introduction to the contributors

> As you write, you are aware of the people with whom you talked; you hesitate to give meanings to their words which they would wish to reject.
>
> (Thompson, 2000: 271)

The book will draw on interviews with 17 participants. In Chapters 1 to 8 we follow the process of those who closed their practice permanently; these are the stories of 13 retirees and one contributor who closed her practice to relocate. Chapter 9 considers temporary closure of a practice and draws on the stories of two women who took maternity breaks, two who took a sabbatical and one who, on turning 60, adopted an unusual working timetable. Pseudonyms have been used throughout.

The retirees

This list shows retirees in descending order of their age at the point of retirement. This also gives their stage in relation to retirement, with the six whom I interviewed prior to their retirement being marked with an asterisk.

88	Alan		interviewed two years after retiring
88	Beatrice	*	interviewed six months prior to retiring
75	Rosemary		interviewed nine years after retiring
74	Mary	*	interviewed six months prior to retiring
72	Annette		interviewed one month after retiring
71	Clementine		interviewed a year and a half after retiring
70	Celia	*	interviewed one year prior to retiring
70	Emma		interviewed two years after retiring
68	Hannah		interviewed six months after retiring

65 Patsy	interviewed two months after retiring
64 Denise	* interviewed two months prior to retiring
62 Nicola	* interviewed ten months prior to retiring
61 Carol	* interviewed six months prior to retiring

This chapter will provide a brief introduction to all those who generously contributed their stories to the study. As a whole this presents too many characters to take in at one sitting, and readers may find it more useful to skim this chapter and refer back to it when they want to clarify the age and stage of a particular speaker.

To make these 13 individuals more accessible, I will introduce them under the four headings which emerged as I worked on the data: the *younger*, the *older*, the *forced* and the *classic*. These headings reflect participants' reasons for retiring. My first question to my interviewees asked them *why* they decided to stop work, and it was the pattern which emerged from those initial responses around motivation to retire which led me to think in terms of these headings. This typology offered itself as the way I could best make sense of the 13 narratives: it describes the patterns which I see indicated in my interviewees' experiences. Of course like any typology there is much overlap between groups and the risk of using these labels is that it forecloses our thinking.

The classic group: Clementine, Annette and Mary (aged 71, 72 and 74, respectively, at the point of retirement)

Clementine, Annette and Mary shared a style of retirement which seems to be most common in the psychoanalytic community. They had all chosen a carefully planned retirement soon after the age of 70, taking a couple of years to complete the process. I see this as a 'classic' style of retirement for therapists who feel deeply attached to their work and are in many ways reluctant to let it go. In the end they are motivated to do so by a balance of both push and pull factors. For them the decision rests on a combination of their concern to protect their patients from the risks of an ageing therapist and their appetite for an active life in retirement. Clementine was interviewed a year and a half later and Annette one month after retiring. Mary was 74 when I met her six months prior to her retirement.

From informal conversations with older colleagues I have seen that this is a way of managing retirement which is widely followed by those whose health is good and who greatly enjoy their work but who feel it would be responsible to end around the age of 70. Therapists in this group tend to reduce their patient numbers very gradually through their late 60s and eventually set a deadline of around 18 months. Their dominant reasons for retiring are the duty of care to patients (wanting to avoid both reduced performance and actual collapse) and the wish for a pleasurable retirement while they still have the health to enjoy it.

Clementine was 72 when I interviewed her 18 months into her retirement, and her story is quite typical of a carefully planned retirement: she saw 70 as a watershed around which her plans developed and, once she had made up her mind to end, she gave patients about 18 months' notice. Clementine had eight patients at the point when she settled on a date for retirement and she describes a duty of care as one of her main reasons for closing her practice. As a former social worker accustomed to working in a team of colleagues, she was acutely aware of the particular responsibility of the single practitioner. She also expressed her wish to retire while she still had enough energy to develop and pursue her other interests.

Annette had ended with her final patient just weeks before we met. She was 72 and had had a few years of practising with a reduced caseload after treatment for cancer five years earlier. During her radiotherapy treatment she had been able to schedule appointments in a way that allowed her to carry on working, but she had stopped taking new patients. When she realised how much she enjoyed the free time she decided to keep her case load very light. After her earlier cancer, it felt particularly important to her that she was able to retire in good health rather than through an emergency ending. As she had given 18 months' warning she felt confident that patients could not, in reality, attribute her going to illness and she was glad they had been spared tangible grounds for that possible fantasy. As Annette had made the earlier reduction in patient numbers, her retirement was particularly gradual with the final guillotine affecting only her last two patients and two supervisees. She also mentioned two pull factors: the wish to visit grandchildren who lived at some distance and a desire for 'me time'.

Mary was due to retire six months after our meeting. She was 74 and particularly clear about her duty of care and her concern not to expose patients to unnecessary risks through her ageing. Mary had anticipated her retirement well in advance and prepared for the closure by not taking on new patients for many years. Eventually she had given her remaining patients 18 months' notice but had been working with the end in her own mind for much longer. She pondered to what degree her husband's retirement had prompted her, but she felt on the whole it had not. Her appetite for enjoying artistic pursuits and her extended family were also important but here again she was mindful of the paradox of this stage, looking forward to leisure but aware that 'there's a scary thing about stopping and knowing who you are'.

The younger group: Carol, Nicola, Denise, Patsy and Hannah (aged 61, 62, 64, 65 and 68, respectively, at the point of retirement)

Therapists in this group may be more motivated by pull factors – the needs of a partner and family or a wish to pursue their own creative interests – than by the push factor of duty of care. On the whole this group managed their retirement over a shorter period than the classic retirees, with Denise and Hannah each giving six months' notice to patients. There was more explicit evidence of ambivalence in this group. Out of all the contributor Patsy and Carol expressed the highest level of uncertainty about the decision, though some ambivalence was indicated by most participants. Nicola's decision was combined with a house move and she was leaving open the possibility that she might open a new practice once she was settled. This form of 'trial retirement' is also particular to this group as Carol's decision to retire had been partly been triggered by an inevitable gap in her practice at a point where she had moved house. This was not a homogeneous group. In contrast to Carol, Patsy and Nicola who expressed much doubt about the step, Hannah reported a particularly smooth process and did not convey conflict about the decision or the experience of retirement. Denise's experience was different again: she spoke of a very heavy clinical challenge as she made the whole transition in just six months rather than starting with a gradual preparatory reduction in patient numbers.

Carol was 61 when I met her some months before she intended to end with her final client. She experienced uncertainty about the retirement decision which had arisen as a result of her partner's recent redundancy and their consequent house move. At the time of the move her commitment to continuing had been demonstrated by her recreating her therapy room in the new house with exactly the same decoration and furnishings as the old one. However, she found herself tired in the evenings and sometimes forgetful. Carol also had conflicted feelings about her financial situation, which was comfortable enough to permit her to retire, and she experienced guilt about choosing a life of leisure. The chief pull factor in her case was a desire for a good quality of life in retirement and an explicit recognition that her remaining span of life was unknown. She felt she was getting a bit better at allowing herself to relax and was determined to enjoy the next 10 years.

Nicola's decision to close her practice was also timed around her husband's retirement. When I spoke to her she was 62, and 10 months from the date she had set for final sessions. Her husband's retirement had been known well in advance and she sometimes found his keen anticipation trying. She described a drawn-out process of ambivalence about closing her practice and the possibility that after their intended house move she might start a new practice in their new location. Her intention was to stop working and then make a final decision about whether this would be a retirement. She wondered whether she would enjoy not working or whether she would feel that she lacked intellectual stimulation. Nicola's process of reducing the size of her practice and setting an end date was a gradual one and, in this respect, she is similar to the older therapists who follow the classic pattern. In common with them she was poised between attachment to the work and a wish to enjoy retirement. Like the classic retirees, Nicola was also very clear about her duty of care to patients and her wish to reduce the risk of abandoning them suddenly. She also noticed that she was getting tired and sometimes questioned whether her afternoon clients were being short-changed by seeing her at the time of day when her energy dipped.

Denise was 64 when I spoke to her and was halfway through the six months' notice she had given her patients. She was living through the gruelling experience of a timetabled, rather than an organic, retirement. She was one of the youngest of my participants and she voiced the 'pull' factor vigorously, and this included two elements which were relevant to other younger retirees: the timing of her partner's retirement and an imminent house move. In voicing the desire to be well enough to enjoy retirement she cited her mother, whom she felt had left retirement too late. Like others whose practice was outside of their home, Denise listed the renewal of the contract on her therapy room as a practical factor in setting the end date. She had had this date in mind at least a year in advance and negotiated a contract to allow for that. She then made a separate clinical decision that in order to achieve a real engagement with the meaning of ending she would give the patients six months' notice. This was informed by her personal experience of an overly protracted ending to her own therapy which she felt had not been productive.

Patsy was 65 at the point of retiring and her story is in many respects akin to the younger pull-factor retirements, yet her very conflicted feelings and her deep reflections make her pathway to retirement exceptional. I met Patsy a few weeks after she had finally closed her practice and she shared her evolving thoughts about the circuitous route she had taken to reach that point. Her story gives us a particularly interesting window into the role of the unconscious in the decision to retire. She had thought much about her motivation for retirement and struggled with particularly painful ambivalence including an initial aborted retirement, where she rescinded her plans to close her practice and worked on for a few more years.

Hannah's story is the closest to Denise's, being fairly swift and largely motivated by the choice to spend time with a new partner. She had been 69 at her retirement two months prior to our meeting. It was clear that she was a very fit and active 69-year-old and she explained that it had been her original intention to work for another decade. She recalled that during her training she had been impressed by the paper which Strauss had written while still practising at the age of eighty (1996). Hannah described herself as a latecomer to the profession; her training as a therapist had itself been a retirement project which she had undertaken in the closing years of an earlier successful career in business. Hannah expressed some sadness about not having stayed long enough in the profession to achieve all she had hoped for. In common with another younger retiree, Nicola, she mentioned irritation with the proposed changes in registration of psychotherapists as an additional factor which had influenced her decision. She felt disinclined to jump through the further hoops which she anticipated might be required.

The group who were forced to retire: Emma, Celia and Rosemary (aged 70, 70 and 75, respectively, at the point of retirement)

Emma and Celia are part of a significant minority of therapists who are forced into retirement by illness and who have had the double loss of closing their practice while facing a reduced and uncertain future. Emma had been compelled by her cancer to give up work and Celia was facing an undiagnosed cognitive decline which meant that she was losing her capacity for the work and was taking steps to close her practice. While I owe a debt of gratitude to all the participants, I felt that those who had been forced into retirement were exceptionally generous in how they shared their stories and as a fellow therapist I was very moved by their loss. I have included Rosemary in this group as she also retired out of duty of care to her patients when she found that her memory was losing its power. Her case is different in that when she noticed that her memory was reducing she stopped taking on new patients, but she did not actually impose an ending on any of them.

Emma's retirement was triggered by her illness at the age of 69. After her first treatment for cancer she retired the majority of her patients over a three-month period. She was hoping to work through to normal endings with a core of patients but a year later she was compelled to make an emergency ending over a two-week period with these five. I interviewed Emma two years into retirement. She had evidently been a very healthy active 69-year-old, with a full practice of 13 patients coming two, three or four times a week, when cancer had been quite suddenly diagnosed. Her first treatment took place in a longer than usual holiday break. When she returned to work she realised that her health would not allow her to sustain such a heavy practice and she made the decision to end with the patients who came most frequently. These patients then had three months to work towards closure. There were five patients who were less intensive and with whom Emma 'didn't feel right about ending', to whom she gave the option of staying on. Work with these five continued for another year until a scan showed that the cancer had recurred and another operation would be needed within weeks. At that point Emma made the decision to make a final emergency ending before having surgery. She was prompted both by a duty of care to these remaining patients and by a tiredness which she voiced in a most heartfelt way.

Celia was 69 when I met her in the middle stages of a retirement which was being forced on her by a neurological condition. After more than three decades as a therapist she was facing the deep uncertainty of symptoms for which doctors were unable to give a diagnosis. The symptoms she noticed most clearly were difficulty in finding words and difficulty in handwriting. She reported that about 18 months earlier she had come to the view that the changes she was experiencing were not going to go away and she was therefore obliged to move towards retirement. Celia had had a very full professional life both in organisations and in her private practice. By the time I met her she had stepped back from what had been a very active engagement in teaching and speaking. She was also in the final stages of withdrawing from her work in an agency and, by virtue of not taking on new patients, had reduced the size of her private practice. I had the impression that the fact that scans and hospital appointments had offered no clear diagnosis or prognosis was adding to the loneliness of this pathway to retirement.

Rosemary's story has much in common with the classic stories, but I see her ending as a forced one because it was *wholly* motivated by duty of care. Her case is unique in my sample as she accomplished her retirement without imposing any forced endings on her patients. She arranged her retirement as an organic process, allowing each patient to come to the end of their work in their own time without any guillotine of a set retirement date. Rosemary was 75 when she saw her last patient and I spoke to her about 10 years after that. She had been in her mid-60s when she had noticed that her memory for details of patients' lives and of earlier sessions was not as strong as it had formerly been. When I asked how long this organic process had taken, Rosemary said she had no idea but thought it had been less than eight years.

The older group: Beatrice and Alan (both aged 88 at the point of retirement)

Beatrice and Alan were both aged 88 at the point of retirement but aside from this detail of chronology their stories are very different. It is possible that if I had met Alan two years earlier, just before he closed his practice, I would have seen a closer correspondence in their experience. Prior to meeting Beatrice I held the belief that working as a therapist to the age of 80 was likely to be irresponsible. However, her clarity and insight into the effects of her ageing on her work impressed me, and disturbed my assumption that if therapists continue working to such an age they are exposing their patients to unwarranted risk. In her case I did not have the feeling that at 88 she had left retirement too late. Beatrice's story showed me, not that retirement is any less pressing a problem, but what a complex issue this is to address. My intuitive assessment was that Beatrice in her 80s had a talent for the work that most of us continue to strive for throughout our careers.

Beatrice was 88 when I interviewed her about nine months prior to her retirement. The way she handled her retirement matches the classic pattern in every respect except for her age: her case is different by virtue of her being nearly 20 years older than most in the classic group. Beatrice had allowed her practice to reduce organically over several years so that at the time we spoke she was seeing a few supervisees and a handful of patients. We met in May and the endings with her remaining patients were due to happen in a staged process with one or two terminating at the summer break, one at Christmas and the final ones at Easter. She anticipated that she might continue to see supervisees further into the future. (The potential ethical dilemma about supervisors continuing their work after they stop seeing patients is explored in Chapter 6.) Like many participants, Beatrice spoke of a duty of care to her patients. She felt that her analytic capacity was reduced and described herself as being carried along by counter-transference in a way that formerly she would have resisted. Although her health was very good, she was also aware of being at increased risk of dying by virtue of being old. Although Beatrice did not name her wish for free time as a motivation for retiring, she speculated that she might enjoy it so much she might after all cease to work as a supervisor.

Alan was the oldest contributor and he was the only retired man in the study. He had been 88 when he had closed his practice and, when I met him two years later, his health had deteriorated considerably. Sadly this meant that his recall of his retirement was missing in parts and so my understanding of his experience was not as full as I would have wished. His account of his working life was very engaging, and he spoke with pathos and eloquence about the major losses which retirement had brought him. This meant that I was able to gather a profound sense of his emotional experience of retirement, but the details of timing and process were not available.

The contributor who had relocated

Alice was 61 when we met three years after she had closed her practice in order to move house. She had been working in private practice for 18 years, with short- and long-term clients seen weekly. She had 10 or 12 clients at the time of ending and one of these had been seeing her for 11 years. Alice had made the decision to relocate at a point when her partner was terminally ill and they wanted to be closer to family, then sadly her partner died before they were relocated. Alice moved after the death and she then established a new practice outside of London. Her story reflects the challenge of managing a closure while living through very sad and uncertain personal events.

The contributors who closed their practice temporarily

These experiences of maternity leave and sabbatical are explored in Chapter 9.

Flora was interviewed about 30 years after closing down her practice to start a family. She had become unwell towards the end of her pregnancy and her first baby tragically died. She went on to have another baby and resumed a small practice before taking a six-month break to have a third child. Her story reflects the unpredictability of pregnancy and the challenge of holding the frame in the face of medical uncertainties. Her story includes the experience of closing a practice (to have her first child) as well as that of a short maternity break (for her third child).

Susannah was interviewed two years after her second maternity leave. She had taken a break of four months for each of her two children, who were born two years apart. Like Flora, she experienced a perinatal emergency as her second child was critically ill following her birth, before making a full recovery. Susannah's story includes the challenge of making two maternity breaks in succession – a normal pattern for a mother but a difficult experience for long-term patients.

Issy was 54 when we met six months into her sabbatical. After a year of deliberating and planning, she had taken another year to close a busy practice. There were various factors which contributed to her decision to take time out, but the most specific trigger was a health scare which had amplified her questions about the meaning of her work. She had told her clients that she would not be seeing people for at least a year.

Paula was 65 when I interviewed her a year after a 10-week sabbatical which she had taken in the summer, giving it the sense of an unusually long annual break. The model she devised might be relevant to many therapists who feel they would benefit from time out. By dividing her sabbatical into two shorter breaks she effectively reduced the sense of abandonment for clients. She returned to work for one week in the middle of this period so that patients could check in for a session between the two five-week breaks. Her thinking around this, and how it worked, are described in Chapter 9.

Simon's story combines the experience of retirement and sabbatical. I went to interview Simon on the misunderstanding that he was in the process of retiring. It turned out that he had taken a very small step towards retirement, having devised a working schedule which gave him every fifth week off. I have placed his story with those of sabbatical as I came to see his personal solution as an alternative to both retirement and sabbatical. Through his reimagined frame he has achieved some of the benefits of both. Simon was 62 when I interviewed him two years after adapting his working hours to give him frequent short breaks.

Chapter 1

Why retire?

I want a life after work finishes and a good life with energy and creativity. I don't want to retire to die.

(Denise)

Gradually I began to find it too difficult to be constantly putting my centre of gravity into somebody else – that exquisite self-control.

(Emma)

I want to explore why therapists retire and also why they might sometimes neglect to do so. This book follows the stories of those who prepared for their retirement. The exception to this is Emma, whose sudden cancer diagnosis pushed her into imposing a hurried ending on some patients and later obliging the remaining ones to end extremely suddenly. In making the case for planning our retirement, this opening chapter will look briefly at the consequences of not planning and the impact on patients when an emergency ending is imposed. As in each of the subsequent chapters I will begin by referring to attachment theory to reflect on the question in hand.

Attachment implications

Can attachment theory help us to understand the reluctance which many therapists feel about closing a practice? The losses at the end of a career could be very significant, but does it make any sense to think of this an attachment wound? The therapist is clearly not losing her own attachment figure as, unless something has gone very wrong, patients do not function as attachment figures for their therapists. What the therapist *is* losing is her role as an attachment figure; the role which may have given her a sense of purpose, meaning and affirmation over decades and which may have been contributing to her own secure base. As with any loss, our way of managing ourselves will reflect our default attachment pattern and residual insecure traits will determine whether we lean towards a more avoidant/dismissing or ambivalent/preoccupied pattern.

Basic principles of attachment theory

Bowlby (1969, 1973, 1980) proposed that, in the interests of survival, an infant develops an *attachment bond* with its primary caregiver. Attachment behaviour includes *seeking proximity* to a safe person who is viewed as 'stronger and/or wiser' (Bowlby, 1977: 203) and *protesting at separation* from this *attachment figure* at times of fear, tiredness, illness and other stress. Ainsworth, Blehar, Waters and Wall (1978) observed that infants develop *patterns of attachment* in response to the caregiving style of their primary carer. These secure, avoidant and ambivalent patterns of relating have been found to be relatively stable through childhood and into adulthood (Fraley and Brumbaugh, 2004), and a further category of disorganised/disoriented was identified by Main and Solomon in 1990. An attachment pattern is the visible reflection of a set of *internal working models* – a set of beliefs about the self and the self in relation to others. These are the mechanisms by which early attachment experiences continue to colour development through the whole lifespan (Bretherton and Munholland, 1999).

When parents are able to be sufficiently accessible, reliable and responsive an infant will develop a *secure attachment pattern* and the capacity to make use of this *secure base* (Bowlby, 1969, 1977). This securely attached child will able to use the parent to regulate distress: once attachment needs have been met and the child feels soothed, she will be able to launch back into playful exploration of the world. Gradually the secure base offered by the attachment figure becomes internalised so that the child can cope with an appropriate degree of separation. Key aspects of security are described by Fonagy and Target (1996): a secure parent can mirror the child's feelings (but not too closely), contain the child's arousal, make sense of her experience, recognise difficulties and deal with them effectively. In a similar way a good-enough therapist is able to field strong emotions without being overwhelmed and can provide the recognition and containment which supports integration of thinking and feeling in the client.

An infant will develop an avoidant strategy (Ainsworth *et al.*, 1978) when their primary caregiver indicates reluctance to engage with their distress. The child internalises a sense of the other as uncaring and a sense of self as undeserving of love. These children achieve a modicum of proximity by apparently deactivating their attachment system and making few demands on parents, hiding their needs first from their parents and eventually from themselves. In contrast, an ambivalent strategy (Ainsworth *et al.*, 1978) develops when a parent is intermittently available. The child finds that hyper-activation of attachment behaviour may elicit parental care but for these children and adults, even when care is forthcoming, it is difficult to take it in and to feel soothed.

The most troubled individuals will have an attachment pattern with *disorganised* qualities (Main and Solomon, 1990), and they lack the coherent strategies of those with avoidant and ambivalent patterns. In infancy these children may have experienced the impossible dilemma of feeling both drawn to and repelled by the same person because their primary caretaker has been a source of fear. For these infants whose parents are themselves very troubled, there is no single strategy which will provide a better outcome. A fallback position for these children may be to attempt to control their caregivers as a way to feel safer, and this might be the position they would adopt with a retiring therapist who is threatening abandonment.

Following this understanding of attachment patterns in children, the 1980s brought the application of this thinking to adults. Main, Kaplan and Cassidy (1985) demonstrated patterns in adult discourse that correspond to the attachment relationships which Ainsworth *et al.* (1978) had identified in children. Main and colleagues identified how in adulthood these patterns reflect particular states of mind in relations to attachment figures, and they named them as *autonomous*, *dismissing* and *preoccupied*. Any one of these three patterns may be overshadowed by *unresolved grief* if an individual has suffered loss or other trauma without the opportunity for working it through. The principal insecure, but organised, patterns are thus described as avoidant/dismissing or ambivalent/preoccupied, though from now on I will generally use a single word rather than the double-barrelled term.

One of the great contributions of attachment theory is its understanding of the tension we all manage between our need for closeness and for separation. The more secure a person is, the more able they are to manage that tension. For people with a disorganised pattern the oscillation between those two needs will be particularly disorderly. It is not that people with a dismissing style have any less need for closeness or that people with a preoccupied style have less need for autonomy. The difference is in how they manage these needs. At times behaviour will clearly reflect the underlying attachment pattern, at other times interactions are less easy to decode. When faced with a retiring therapist, a patient with either of these patterns might suddenly bolt, the difference between a preoccupied or a dismissing style being felt in the countertransference. For example, if a client with a preoccupied pattern left suddenly the manner of their going might convey more sense of 'Come and get me', and the therapist's feelings in relation to this patient would probably contain more guilt or frustration.

The therapist's own attachment experience

Bowlby proposed that attachment needs remain significant 'from the cradle to the grave' (1979: 129). The quality of our own internalised secure base will be important throughout life, but in old age, when our actual attachment figures (parents and partners) are more likely to have died, this internal capacity to sooth ourselves could arguably be even more crucial if we are to keep on exploring and engaging with the world. This kind of security would make it more possible for an older therapist to sustain critical and creative reflection on her own work and perhaps make it easier to resolve the dilemmas around retirement. Although I have presented these attachment patterns as though they were discrete categories, their value is not as a system of labels but, in Slade's terms, to sensitise ourselves 'to observing the functioning of the attachment system and to the internal and interpersonal functions of attachment processes' (2004: 269).

While we hope that practising therapists have achieved a good measure of *earned security* (Main and Goldwyn, 1998), we know anecdotally that we are a profession of wounded healers and there is some evidence that many of us have insecure attachment histories (Sussman, 2007; Adams, 2014). This means that at times of stress our original attachment patterns tend to impact both internally and on the people around us. A therapist who is contemplating retirement is therefore likely to be managing either a tendency to minimise the meaning of the transition, if dismissing is her core pattern, or a pull to hold on longer if she is inclined towards a more preoccupied pattern. Holmes (1997) observes how the fit between attachment patterns in the patient and the therapist can lead to ending a therapy too soon or too late. Perhaps something similar may happen in terms of bringing an end to a whole practice. Where there is residual disorganised attachment, in either client or therapist, there is scope for inversion in the relationship and confusion about who is looking after whom. In the worst cases clients have become carers to ailing therapists.

We may speculate that where there is a residual insecure pattern of avoidance in a retiring therapist, she may find it relatively easy to make a clean break. In this case the risk may be of underestimating and overlooking the impact on clients and minimising her importance in the client's internal world. For preoccupied clients this could result in their distress being uncontained and the ending being insufficiently processed. For dismissing clients the risk would be of replaying an old relational script in which their pain goes unrecognised by themselves as well as by those around them, sometimes surfacing indirectly in the body.

Where the therapist's residual insecurity is preoccupied then the longing and yearning which is normal in grief may persist: ruminative thoughts and regrets may weigh heavily. These retirees may struggle more than their avoidant peers with ambivalence about taking the step to retire. It is possible that this more anxious style of caregiving may communicate itself unconsciously to the clients: there could be an underestimation of patients' resilience and consequently an undermining of it, leading to a messy ending. A strength of therapists with this residual pattern is the ability to identify and empathise deeply with clients' feeling of abandonment; there will be times where this means that the hard-to-reach grief of the dismissing client is affirmed in a way which finally helps them to acknowledge it. Some individuals with strongly ambivalent or disorganised patterns may try to get their attachment needs met through compulsive caregiving. Anecdotal evidence suggests that this type of insecure group, who had an inverted caring relationship with their own parents, may be highly represented among therapists. A possible example of this is given by one of Adams's interviewees, who describes herself as a parenting child:

> my mother needed care, as it were, not my father, but I was definitely a parenting child. It's a sort of way of life really, and I think I just professionalised it.
>
> (Adams, 2014: 74)

For these therapists, the challenge at the point of retirement would be to adequately process their own anxiety about separation, so that they can more effectively tune in to how each client is taking the news. One of the difficulties for the retiring therapist is that her own feelings about ending may interfere with her capacity for containment. Thus at the point when clients may have extra need of responsive attunement, therapists may struggle to supply it. If the therapist is retiring under pressure of illness she will be managing uncertainty about her own future as well as guilt about decamping. At the same time, negative transference from some clients may increase to unfamiliar levels.

Our own internalised secure base, formed from our attachment history as well as our current attachment network, will be a factor in how we come to the decision about retirement and how we carry it through. The context of our current attachment relationships will also impact. At the point of retirement some will be in satisfying long-term relationships, some in less fulfilling ones and some will be happily or unhappily single or bereaved. It may make sense to think of our work, our profession and our circle of colleagues as jointly providing a secure base through their validation and responsiveness. This constitutes a valuable package which may have compensated for disappointments in our own attachment relationships. It is also interesting to think in terms of our theoretical secure base. What is the impact of our chosen theory? The question of why we are drawn to train and work in one style rather than another seems reflective of our own internal worlds. We might justify our choice in intellectual terms but surely we are drawn to that theory which best helps us manage ourselves. The enmity between different schools suggests that we may then cling to that theory as though to a life raft because naturally we want to believe we are in the right lifeboat. Does our specific choice of theory impact on how we handle ourselves through the retirement? I see my own interest in the subject as arising from my own concerns about attachment and loss which, of course, influenced my original attraction to a training based on Bowlby's ideas.

As well as loss of what we value in our work, the threat of ageing and dying carried by retirement may also contribute to a testing of our secure base. The principles of attachment theory might suggest that we would respond to old age as we would to other types of loss. We might thus expect those of us with dismissing traits to tend to deny the losses involved in ageing and those with an ambivalent pattern to be more preoccupied with their losses. Studies on this age group are rare and as yet inconclusive (Magai, 2008). What is clear is that the secure group at this age, as in younger years, are better equipped to face losses. They are both more resilient and more able to accept and use help.

The valuable contribution of older therapists

In a book which supports a timely retirement, it seems important to acknowledge that older therapists may have particularly rich qualities which they bring to the work. Eissler's (1993) paper looks at changes in the older analyst and emphasises the benefits that age can bring. He suggests that in favourable circumstances ambition and illusions are lessened, anxiety about failure is reduced and tolerance is increased. However, he ended by concluding that he 'may have exaggerated the positive contribution of ageing' (1993: 331) and suggested that increased narcissism could manifest in rigidity, or in the analyst eliciting the patient's admiration and awe. Beatrice, retiring at 88, also offered a very balanced outlook:

I think I would agree with people who say that with age we become a bit wiser in the way we can reach patients, but this is offset by the fact that we may tire more easily so that our attention drifts and we may be less vigilant.

One area in which older therapists *might* be well equipped is in helping patients to think about their own ageing and fear of death. Clearly this would only apply if the therapist had been able to reflect on her own approaching end. A chapter by Strauss (1996), still practising at the age of 80, reflects a lively analytic mind. On paper at least she shows that she is able to grapple with the varied transference–countertransference challenges thrown up by being either decades older than some of her patients or, in other cases, being their 'age mate'. Where the therapist can face up to her own demise and has survived many losses in her own life there is a possibility she may have a deepened empathy and patience for the work.

The limitations of older therapists

Being tired by the work: or tired of it

Boyd-Carpenter (2010a) writes bluntly about her reduced energy, yet against this one might argue that older therapists can pace their hours in a way that suits them: 'I excused and rationalised early intimations of failing powers – that I didn't do a good job with late evening clients or working four or five hours consecutively, as I once had' (2010a: 90).

Emma was also outspoken about her tiredness and about the way that analytic work had become harder to sustain:

> Also because I had lost my appetite for the work . . . what with illness and possibly age and the fact that I had been doing it so long, slogging away. I think that's an important thing to put in, though it's not a popular thing to say at all . . . That's why retiring hasn't been a fiasco for me at all. I was glad to leave the work. I have only been able to own that to myself recently. I haven't looked back in regret.

Emma's openness about her process is fascinating. From her remarks about some careful post-therapy contact with patients it was also apparent to me that, alongside her blunt words, she retained a deep compassion. However, we may also wonder whether she has underestimated the 'fiasco' that her sudden departure could have unleashed either for those who had

to end at three months' notice or those whose sessions stopped with just
two weeks' grace:

> Gradually I began to find it too difficult to be constantly putting my
> centre of gravity into somebody else – that exquisite self-control – I
> began to find it boring, I began to get a bit fidgety with it. I began to
> quote lines of poetry to patients when I felt they were relevant.

Emma acknowledged that therapists from different theoretical groups
hold different boundaries in terms of how far they might go in quoting
poetry. Her thoughts link with Beatrice's remark (below) that she felt she
was becoming less vigilant and more likely to act out. Emma was more
explicit about losing commitment to the method. When she spoke about
analytic work as a very demanding kind of relating, I felt this made sense
in terms of the life cycle of a therapist. For the trainee this novel abstinent
way of being with another can feel very strange and it seemed as though
that effort to attune analytically may return at the other end of the working
life. This issue of the older therapist adapting their approach is debatable.
Some older therapists describe similar changes as a positive development
in their clinical style. From Emma's position such a stance might be seen
as self-justifying, and she spelled out what she saw as a regrettable
relaxation of her boundaries:

> *Emma:*   I have quoted poems to patients, which is not only putting
> something there which wasn't there before, but it is also telling
> patients quite a lot about the sort of person you secretly are. And
> if a patient says they were watching a programme on television
> about elephants and did I see it? I began to say, 'yes I did – can
> we talk about it?' Rather than, 'I wonder why you think I might
> have watched a programme about elephants?'
>
> *Interviewer:*   So one of the things which could be described there
> could be an evolution in how you found it most profitable to work?
>
> *Emma:*   Yes it was an evolution . . . but there was also an element of
> treachery: I felt treacherous to the psychoanalytic format which
> had been my guide. But you know friends of my age have also
> found this – we talk about it. 'My boundaries' someone will say,
> 'they seem to have gone all haywire – the baby cried upstairs and
> I was agreeing that it was my granddaughter'.

Emma went on to explain that she saw this behaviour as a possible
slippery slope which could end by putting the analytic frame at risk.

It seems interesting to reflect how two things may be going on. On the one hand there is a change which both Beatrice and Emma see as a failing in themselves, while on the other hand there could be a theoretical development in which the older therapist comes to feel that increased disclosure can be appropriate, provided that what it brings up is worked through. This latter view is advanced by Simon in Chapter 9. It is interesting to consider this tension in the light of Colman's (2006) paper about the analytic superego. He decries the tendency to manage our anxieties about the work, either through adherence to a strict set of rules or, more rarely, by rebellion against the persecutory superego. He argues that, rather than rules, 'it is the maintenance of an analytic attitude of thoughtful reflection in the therapist's mind that constitutes the real boundaries' (2006: 106).

When Patsy described the internal states which had led her towards the decision to retire, I felt she was speaking about a similar experience of weariness with the analytic project:

> I think I can get full up and not want to take any more things in . . . perhaps it is not that I get full up, rather that I feel more anxious than I used to that I will be invaded by someone.

A comment from the literature also describes tiredness: Walcott writes:

> My libido for analysis was at a low ebb. Delving into the unconscious of analysands was a chore, no longer an adventure.
>
> (2011: 214)

He goes on to describe a disengagement in the years leading up to his retirement and is commendably honest in his disclosure of poor memory and drowsiness. In his case the monitoring function of colleagues seems to have worked to some degree because they stopped sending clients, and around the age of 70 he found referrals drying up. His colleagues could recognise before he could, that he was ready for retirement: 'Painfully, I had to face the impression given that the decline of practice reflected a decline of my analytic vitality' (2011: 210). This safeguard might work in cases where referrals come from close colleagues, but it will not offer a comprehensive means of quality control. It will not protect patients who are continuing a long therapy with a fading therapist, nor would it prevent referrals coming from websites or from former colleagues who have not been in touch for a while.

Clementine was one of those who was retiring, not because she was no longer able to function well enough, but because the stress of practising was becoming too great. She mentioned a specific trigger: the counter-transference she was experiencing with one particularly disturbed patient. This made her feel that the work was taking too high a toll and pushed her to begin planning retirement:

> I had been aware that the impact of anger and attack had been affecting my health – there was one patient who was very tough to work with.

A different kind of stress was described by Carol, who spoke of being fed up with bureaucracy. She felt quite oppressed by annual registration procedures and said that part of her wanted to be free of that, and was looking forward to:

> not having to tick the boxes and jump through somebody else's hoops.

Denise did not explicitly mention the 'push' factor of tiredness but I felt it may have been implied when she spoke of her 'thirty years in the caring professions' and her determination not to follow her mother, whose life had been worn out by the time she retired from work in public services:

> Maybe I don't want it to be like that. I'd like to feel that I'm more than a therapist.

Difficulties with a generational divide

Aside from these crucial existential concerns about ability to perform and survive, there are some more nuanced but significant considerations about the impact of age on a therapist and their capacity to work with much younger patients. Questions are sometimes raised about the older therapist's distance in experience from their younger patients. Can the older practitioner who established their clinical understanding and values in a different era attune to the concerns and experience of the young? This question is not just about the degree to which a therapist needs to be a fit in terms of age or gender in order to represent a key figure from the past. There is a question about the actual, as well as perceived, understanding of the old for those who have grown up in very different circumstances. One challenge which is often posed is about Internet awareness: can older therapists understand the experience of 'Internet natives' and do they understand the range of social and intellectual needs which are being met by the Internet? Do they comprehend the risks and necessary safeguards that their clients need to grasp?

Tallmer (1992) looked at therapists and analysts who were becoming old in the 1980s and who had been almost the first wave of practitioners, with some of them qualifying in the pre-war era of brief trainings. She points out that during a therapist's working life patients may change 'in the nature of their symptoms, their attitudes toward those symptoms, and their motivation for seeking analysis' (1992: 385). While these kinds of sea changes are challenging, therapists are accustomed to working with people from varied backgrounds and, if we lacked the capacity to attune to the specific historical and cultural story of each client, we would be unsuitable for the work. We need to listen out for the impact of online bullying on a younger client, just as we would extend ourselves to understand the experience of an older patient whose youth was coloured by a particular war or political upheaval. Most older therapists are able to make this attunement to new experiences without denying that their age may be impacting on the process of therapy. There may be parallels here to children raised by parents much older than the average. When such children reach adolescence the normal tensions between generations can become exaggerated. An 80-year-old analyst, Strauss (1996), writes of a young client's flamboyant sexual acting out: 'The truly judgemental coloration of my countertransference shone through, despite my wish to be perceived as wholly empathic' (1996: 280). However, as Strauss comments, such a countertransference may not be related to age. Younger therapists can also be moralistic, or we might wonder whether this patient needed to produce a judgemental response in her therapist regardless of their age.

Cognitive decline

Fonagy (2009) berates the profession for its silence about the real losses and limitations of ageing. He reminds us that, while there are individual variations, memory and cognitive speed decline throughout adulthood and that this loss of ability accelerates in later old age, with the drop between 70 and 80 being particularly significant. The challenge for the profession is how to develop fair retirement policies which respect both this compelling evidence and the huge individual variations in ageing.

Cozolino's (2008) book about the ageing brain has an optimistic message emphasising the brain's plasticity and the potential for functions to be carried out in different parts of the brain if one part suffers age-related decline. He writes from the perspective of interpersonal neurobiology, stressing the interplay of relationships and environment with our inherited genetic base. There is a broad agreement that those who have stretched their brains in earlier life have better prospects in old age. Explaining this concept of 'cognitive reserve', Cozolino writes: 'you can be born with it or you can build it. Either way, it is better to go into the last third of life with a more robust brain' (2008: 82). Studies in epidemiology provide evidence for this, showing that being engaged in a complex job is protective against cognitive decline (Valenzuela, Brayne, Sachdev, Wilcock and Matthews, 2011).

One particularly interesting piece of longitudinal research which seems to corroborate this is the nun study (Snowdon, 2001), which indicates that linguistic richness and complexity are a strong predictor of cognitive strength in later life. The autobiographical essays written by young nuns were studied decades later, and those nuns whose writing showed a high density of ideas had a greatly reduced likelihood of dementia. I wondered whether this was an encouraging study for therapists who presumably start with a reasonably high level of language skill and whose working life then requires the constant enrichment of the use of ideas.

In addition to identifying the lifestyles which promote growth of neural tissue, Cozolino conveys encouraging news of the brain's capacity to compensate. Yet however much we look to the neuroscientists for evidence of plasticity, most of us can recognise Coltart's warning of the 'arthritic changes' in our thinking and admit that these steal upon us gradually (1991: 101). For most of us this slowing down is initially subtle, but for Celia the symptoms were distinct. With no clear prognosis, but the likelihood of further deterioration, she felt compelled to close her practice. She described the struggle and the exhaustion of working under these conditions:

> I think that I am not completely fluent. I'm having to reach for words that I wouldn't normally reach for – and I'm not anywhere near as articulate as I used to be, and I'm having to think hard about the words that I use and often a word will simply not come to me and I'll have to use another word.

Rosemary was the other contributor who arranged to close her practice because she judged her cognitive power to be reducing. In her case the decline was slight and she was able to continue working for many years with her remaining patients until each came to a natural ending. Colleagues queried her need to retire, but Rosemary held a very principled position that she would take on no new patients:

I would think, 'Was this his nephew?' and when a patient said, 'I've been thinking about what you said on Tuesday' – and it wouldn't come back to me . . . It doesn't matter when it happens once – you just don't say anything. But I quite rightly saw it as the beginning of the end and I knew then I shouldn't take any more patients.

It was clear that the step had been taken at a deep cost to herself. When I asked her about the dilemmas which arouse for her around retirement she was forthright:

I didn't have a dilemma I just didn't want to do it, but I also knew that there was really no choice. You can't take the risk of thinking 'What the hell is she talking about, who is this Philip?'

Fonagy (2009) provides a focused description of what cognitive decline could mean in a session:

Thus, we might expect that older analysts will experience no difficulty retrieving familiar or readily accessible past experience, but will experience difficulty making links between things they heard in the past from a patient and what they are listening to at the moment, or between yesterday's session and today's, or even the first half of the session to the second half.

(2009: 216)

In her dissertation on the experience of therapists working in old age, Jaffe (2011) analyses interviews with six older therapists. She challenges the views of both Guy, Stark, Poelstra and Souder (1987) and Fonagy (2009) that a system is needed to monitor the competency of older therapists. Though her exploration of the subject was exceptionally interesting, she is more optimistic than I would be about the core dilemma: if a person begins, through age, to lose some of their cognitive acuity and memory, then the very faculties which would enable them to monitor their decline are being undermined. As Quinodoz (2010: 177) writes in her comments on working as an older analyst, 'Knowledge is like equilibrium or love: when we think we possess it, we have already lost it.'

There must be a danger of therapists having a grandiose defence along the lines, 'I'm well-adjusted and undefended about my limitations so I will be alert to diminishment if it should happen to me'. The loss of capacity to make links which Fonagy describes would be extraordinarily difficult for a therapist to self-assess. By definition, if we are not making a link between today's dream and that from last week, we will not be able to notice that failure. Josephine Klein's (2006) rare account of her process is valuable for its frankness:

> I realised I was not remembering as well as I used to. Sometimes there seemed a wall between me and an association just the other side of consciousness.
>
> (2006: 65)

Friends and doctors told her they could find nothing wrong but she could observe the change in her ability to recall the previous session as the patient referred to it.

In her assessment of her own ageing, Beatrice describes quite a subtle loss of function. Her case illustrates how partial the decline can be: there may be a reduction in memory alongside a very sharp mind. I think her comments on how her analytic capacity was changing seem to reflect her continuing capacity for nuanced observation. She reflects on one very specific way that she feels she is less able to do analytic work:

> I can become too complicated when I talk; I am less sharp. And another thing I've noticed is that I've tended, in the last two or three months, to not be quite so sharp in ending the session on time. I think there is something in the [particular] transference/countertransference which has to be analysed but I also felt it is as though I was being less vigilant and therefore in more danger of acting out . . . it is simply that my mind was so engrossed in her state of mind that I was . . . not driving my car properly.

The patient in question, whose session had run over, had arrived late and in a particularly distressed state. Beatrice explained that she did not see this as a question of strictness about time; her concern was that she had lost track of time and given in to an unconscious pressure to act rather than to think.

Duty of care: in view of anticipated cognitive or physical decline

The risk of death in service

A therapist's working life will conclude either with a planned closure of their practice or with some kind of unplanned ending, usually illness or death. While poor health can occur at any age, it becomes more frequent and likely in older people, hence the dilemma for individual therapists and for the profession about how to choose the time for retirement. On the one hand, precautionary retirement could lead to the unnecessary loss of therapists when they are at the height of their experience and possibly 'wisdom', but on the other hand the harm to patients who lose their therapist suddenly can be very severe. Beatrice articulated this dilemma:

> My personal problem is that I feel extremely young and I am very healthy, but I do not forget that I am over eighty, that my memory is not what it was ... But even if your mind is still very sharp, the realisation that death is no longer a far-off event has to be taken into account.

In my first year of training our attention was drawn to Winnicott's dictum: 'In doing psychoanalysis I aim at: Keeping alive, Keeping well, Keeping awake' (1962a/1990: 166); and the story of Masud Khan was told to us as a moral tale. Khan had lost his first two analysts to death. The story is worth looking at because it is one which is relatively well documented and reflects how the loss of an analyst may be exacerbated by contextual factors. It appears that the losses were deeply harmful for Khan and prevented him from achieving the internal connections and the integrity which are essential for the work. It seems important to remember that Khan's two curtailed analyses took place when he had only just arrived in Europe and his homeland (India) was in the midst of the terrible turmoil of partition. Reading Hopkins's (2008) biography of Khan, I imagine a patient whose denial of vulnerability made him very hard to help. This defence appears to have been buttressed by his natural endowments of being tall, handsome and clever. He had the added real power of being very wealthy, together with the arrogance of one born to power and privilege. That someone with this profile should then be abandoned by two successive analysts made it unlikely that subsequent work could repair so much emotional damage.

Whether consciously or unconsciously, all patients will ask themselves, 'Will my therapist stay alive and is she capable of understanding me?' If the therapist is visibly ageing then the client will have real as well as fantasised reasons for these fears. The risk to the patient through sudden illness or death is explored by Gervais (1994), who suffered a serious illness which resulted in the sudden closure of his practice for two months. Gervais recovered fully and could work through the anxieties which his patients had suffered. Clearly when the therapist is not able to return to work, the repair will be even harder, whether or not the patient can face working with another therapist. The extent of regression and the type of transference in play at the time of the therapist's collapse will crucially influence how disturbed a patient will be. One common fantasy is the fear of having caused the therapist's collapse, another is the belief that parts of the self being contained by the therapist are now lost with her.

Still working just before she turned 80, Strauss (1996) described the 'sometimes laughable reactions of patients if I so much as cough or clear my throat' (1996: 294). But how laughable are such responses and is an ageing therapist well placed to help the patient explore their fears about her vulnerability? Looking back on her own years as a patient, she comments that the question of ageing can easily be avoided in analysis. By the time of her second analysis she was very concerned about ageing, but sensed it was anxiety provoking to her analyst and they colluded in not mentioning it.

Eissler (1993) writes in a broadly positive tone about the effects of the analyst growing older, though he suggests that those over 60 should tell patients to whom they could go if the analyst should die. This honesty about mortality is impressive, but I wondered whether a therapist with a significantly heightened risk of dying should be working with vulnerable patients. Work with more robust patients might be considered more ethical, and Clementine's experience supports Eissler's suggestion that the therapist speak openly to patients about her possible death. She had had an analysis in midlife with a senior analyst and then when she trained had returned to him many years later when he was 80. She described him as one of the old guard who tended not to retire and she was still seeing him when he died some years later. In this extract Clementine is responding to a question. I had wondered if, given her own care over her retirement, she felt her analyst should really have retired:

> No . . . he was clearly going to go on to the end. No, that's interesting, I hadn't thought there was a contrast there. I remember a teacher saying that it could be a terrible thing for clients if their therapist died and I think for some it must be, but I had already had a lot of therapy with him and we talked about it in fact. When I first went back to him, having not seen him for seventeen, eighteen years and I asked him if he would take me on and he said, 'There is the question of my age' 'What do you mean, you think you might die?' and he said 'well it's a distinct statistical possibility'. He was eighty then. So it was something we could talk about though we didn't often. I had about four years.

In Clementine's case the stage she had reached in her own process meant that the impact does not appear to have been destructive. She also much appreciated the sensitive way in which he himself handled his mortality and later the arrangements his widow, acting on his wishes, made for patients to make a last visit to his consulting room.

Clementine and Mary were two contributors who spoke clearly of retirement in terms of duty of care; they were taking this step as an anticipatory measure while they were still in good health. Here Clementine lists several factors which contributed to her decision:

> If you suddenly die you are doing something avoidable – usually – and it seemed to me wrong. I suppose a sort of professionalism. I'd been a social worker and done jobs where you have to think and plan and consider colleagues and people on the receiving end. And I didn't want to leave it too late. The clients that I tended to work with had very long therapies so I wasn't likely to say I want to see people who would finish in a year or two. It would be very wrong with these long term patients to start and then say in a couple of years, 'I'm retiring'. Part of the decision then was, 'I'm not taking on new people so I need to plan retirement' – it was pragmatic.

Mary expressed very similar considerations to Clementine. In her case there was some pressure on her from a partner to retire, but on reflection she did not feel this had swayed her:

> No, it was an age thing really. I just thought it was right, once you got near seventy, to start thinking about finishing. I think it's about this idea of dying 'in the saddle'; I'm really opposed to people going on until they are past it.

Like some others who had reluctantly made the responsible decision to give up work, she added a rueful comment on the fact that some colleagues were not of the same mind:

> Well, age – I don't believe in going on and on, as some people seem to manage to do.

For Emma the risk of dying while still seeing patients became very real when her cancer recurred. She had made a hurried ending with the majority of patients three months after her first operation; here she is speaking about her decision to make an emergency ending with the remaining five patients whom she had kept on for a further year. She was facing a second operation for cancer and decided it would be best to end abruptly at that point:

> Then I thought I'm going to stop working with these people because I don't want them to be subjected to so much uncertainty.

Alan was in reasonable health when he decided, in his late 80s, that the risk of dying had become too high. He was clear that he owed his patients a proper ending rather than the experience of sitting with a dying therapist:

> I was much older than most of my colleagues at retirement. I had been thinking about it because I didn't want the patient to be coming to check my pulse to see whether I'm alive. I didn't want to be a lame duck and I had a duty to give these people as long a notice of retirement as I possibly could. And it worked out very well. I left a healthy man.

A worrying number of therapists in my small sample had direct experience of a therapeutic or supervisory relationship being brought to a sudden end through the foreseeable illness or death of the clinician. Others had indirect experience of this, citing the 'mess' often left when a therapist dies in harness and the difficult work they had done with patients who had come to them following such bereavements. Celia was one of those who had been deeply attached to an ageing analyst who collapsed suddenly.

> I had a terrible experience in this respect – my analyst disappeared suddenly – she was taken to hospital and she didn't really recover. That was a terrible experience for me and I think that it has precipitated me into thinking I would rather retire sooner rather than later. I could have seen if I wanted to see that my analyst was getting older and more unable to function – but I didn't want to see it. I turned up one day and she wasn't there. There was no answer to the doorbell.

I was very struck by how Celia articulated the power of the transference: 'I could have seen if I wanted to see . . . but I didn't want to see it'. She clearly illustrates why we cannot rely on patients to let us know when we need to retire. Celia's analyst had had a therapeutic will in place and arrangements for an emergency but she collapsed before she could alert her executor. As she lived alone there was a delay before the necessary support for patients was set in motion.

Most therapists have worked with clients whose previous therapy had to end under crisis of illness or death; the challenging task which faces a bereaved client and their subsequent therapist is documented by Traesdal (2005). She emphasises how isolated these patients are in their grief, whereas deaths in other circumstances usually provide an opportunity for co-mourners to validate each other's experience. Robutti (2010) has also written movingly about the experience of bereaved patients:

> If the analysis works, the patient experiences a very special relationship of great intimacy, trust and safety. However, should the analyst become ill suddenly, or even die, this privilege is transformed into solitude like no other solitude.
>
> (2010: 131)

This isolation is described by Freeth (2001), who wrote about suddenly losing her therapist. Her rage and despair in the first two weeks meant she was unable to work in her role as senior house officer in psychiatry:

> One of the most difficult aspects of my grieving process has been the loneliness of it and the constant feared misunderstanding from others that Elizabeth was 'only' my therapist and not, after all, my parent. Except that after a year of seeing her I was finally receiving things that I felt I had never received from my parents.
>
> (2001: 19)

I think that Doka's (1989) concept of disenfranchised grief may be appropriate for this experience; he adopted the term to describe losses which are not publically mourned or socially supported. Some patients who live through this kind of bereavement receive almost no acknowledgement from those around them. Even trainees, who work alongside others who could understand, often report a lack of support.

Emma was another contributor who felt that her personal experience served as a cautionary tale:

> My therapist broke down and I was enormously attached to her and all her boundaries slipped. It gave me an enormous amount of Oedipal victory because I was invited into her life. It was bliss, but for such a naughty part of me. I was very aware latterly in my own practice 'I mustn't get like that whatever happens'.

A study by Sorensen (2009) looks at the therapist's illness and death from an existential viewpoint; her data provide evidence that Emma is not the only patient who has transitioned into becoming carer to her therapist. Such reversal of roles and exploitation of clients is a severe breach of professional ethics. Sorensen's paper charts very disturbing experiences, including multiple losses for patients and profound ethical challenges for therapists and supervisors who are struggling to contain their own life-threatening illness. Carlisle (2013) has written first-hand about this reversal of roles and describes performing caring tasks for her analyst in the final months before the abrupt end of the work. It was only after this that she learned of his progressive dementia. Through the years of his decline her own need to maintain him as a good object had constrained her conscious awareness of his illness and when she had managed to share concerns with a senior colleague, these had been trivialised. She charts his painful disintegration, his visible loss of self-care and her own tortured feelings on the couch: 'I felt shame for him' (2013: 80). These stories which have come to light presumably represent a greater number that remain untold. The risk of the therapy relationship becoming abusive, with the dependant client held hostage in this way, is one of the most pressing reasons for the profession to learn to manage retirement.

Of my three interviewees who had lost their therapist, one of them, Clementine, felt she had not been adversely affected. She had been coming towards the end of her therapy and perhaps the critical factor here was the state of the transference at the time of the death. This and the length of the therapy seem to be the key factors in determining how a patient will cope when their therapist dies (Garcia-Lawson, Lane and Koetting, 2000). Probably it is also significant that Clementine's therapist had been commendably open about the risks of his dying, as Eissler (1993) exhorts us to be.

When Lord, Ritvo and Solnit (1978) researched patients' responses to their therapists' death they gathered information both from patients who had lost a therapist, as well as from therapists who had taken on a patient after the death of the previous therapist. Their key finding was that patients with complicated and prolonged mourning for their analyst were those who had experienced early loss or abandonment. Interestingly they speculate that patients might cope better with the therapist dying than with their making a choice to close their practice. This suggestion seemed unlikely to me because, even if envy of the therapist's other life is very strong, a planned ending does allow the opportunity to work through this. Their suggestion does, however, highlight the very different meanings that each patient will attribute to the ending; if the therapist is closing their practice to move to another city or to have a baby this will invite different fantasies from a retirement. In Haynes's (2009) account of the death of her analyst we have an opportunity to hear directly and in detail about the experience of one bereaved client. She conveys that the loss was terrible but she was able to make developmental use of her grief: 'Your death has provoked me, in a way that nothing else could, to live more bravely in this arbitrary world' (2009: 83). Many factors will influence the degree to which loss can become opportunity. The difference between an ending with potential for growth and one which is destructive is indicated by Pedder (1988). He critiques our use of the word 'termination' and feels the term, with its negative associations, is apt if the therapist dies or otherwise becomes unavailable but is not appropriate when an ending is part of a healthy developmental process.

Pull factors

Boyd-Carpenter (2010a), who retired at 61, describes some of these positive reasons for wanting to take the step, as she became 'increasingly aware of a new set of claims on my time, my energy, my creativity and my thinking'(2010a: 90). For most contributors the desire to end work in order to enjoy the next life stage was impacting alongside a duty of care. For the younger group this was the key factor, while those in the classic group described a mix of push and pull factors. Clementine spoke of two pull factors which were mentioned by many interviewees:

> I also felt that the longer you put it off the less likely you are to develop other interests and friendships. You have less energy and as you get older and so work could become your main source of interest and emotional satisfaction . . . That was a major part and I didn't always want to live in a big house. I needed to downsize and I thought finding a place where I could see patients didn't seem sensible as it would mean a much bigger home. There were a lot of things coming together.

Mary was another classic retiree who was poised between regret about the need to make a dutiful retirement and anticipation of time to pursue cultural and family interests. She added that 'free' time can feel disturbing, noting that for many of us this desire for time to ourselves is countered by the fear of how we will cope with such freedom:

> And I think that partly applies to me, though there are loads of things I do do, but there's a scary thing about stopping and knowing who you are.

Also part of the classic group, Annette's retirement was particularly
gradual as she had let her patient numbers reduce a few years earlier when
she was being treated for cancer. She found she enjoyed having time to
herself:

> So once I was back on my feet again I didn't go looking for patients.

It was interesting that the younger group expressed the most direct
anxiety about their own deaths. Some of them specifically mention this
below. Others speak in terms of wanting to have time with partners. Hannah
had not planned to retire young but she wanted to have time to do things
with her new partner who was already retired. It seemed to me that this
aspiration had extra poignancy for her because her first husband had died
at a young age. Nicola was also influenced by her husband's retirement,
though she felt more ambivalence about this:

> That [my husband's retirement] has been quite a significant piece of
> the jigsaw. So it's been a rollercoaster of emotions this past year
> of 'Shall I? Shan't I? – Shall I? Shan't I?' I want to give myself a
> bit of a break to see how it feels and to sort of ease myself into what-
> ever retirement means.

Like Hannah, Patsy's thinking about retirement had also had also been
coloured by a premature death. Some years earlier she had lost a sibling
at a young age. This had made her intensely aware of the uncertainty, which
is there for all of us, about the age at which we will die. She recounts:

> I found myself thinking 'How many years have I got left?' If I only
> have a short time left it's important to do more than work, but if I have
> years and years of time left then I want to go on working longer.

Denise spoke most directly about her existential anxiety:

> I didn't want to be someone who worked until I died. I wanted to retire
> feeling there was still life after retirement and not just the sort of life
> which is the acceptance of the ageing process. I wanted to feel that I
> was healthy and vibrant enough to get on with living.

Carol also linked her decision to the awareness of her own mortality:

> I think another really deep reason about my decision is that I've had
> a few friends die recently and it's made me reflect . . .

Mechanisms for knowing when to retire

Anxiety and ambivalence among therapists over how to know if it's time to go

I have been struck by how difficult this question feels to some people in the peri-retirement age group. There is uncertainty as to where to look for guidance about when to retire – how will a therapist know they are no longer up to the task? In workshops this is often raised as an anxiety and some therapists have a longing for an external authority (such as the therapist's supervisor or the accrediting body) which would take this responsibility away. There is also a recognition that a system for a compulsory retirement age will feel too prescriptive and an equitable assessment process for ageing will be very difficult to achieve.

One colleague spoke of 'senior moments' of memory loss and her anxiety about how bad things would need to be before she felt she must stop working. When, at a conference, she happened to meet a therapist who was retiring, she was keen to understand how this colleague had reached the decision. She hoped the woman would say something very tangible, such as tiredness which had made her fall asleep in sessions. This longing for a *deus ex machina* who would guide us reflects how hard therapists find it to make the decision. An anonymous correspondent to *Therapy Today* writes in an urgent and anxious tone: 'So, who is going to tell me I am past it; that my concentration, memory and energy are not up to the work?' (Anonymous, 2011: 18). In the same issue a letter from another correspondent, Sugg, echoes this question: 'So, how to be sure we do not keep on working past our sell-by date?' (Sugg, 2011: 19). She proposes some helpful questions which therapists might put to themselves. Adapting her questions, we might ask: What feedback would I imagine a respected colleague would give if she were a fly on the wall in my therapy room? If I think about my current motivation for doing the work, how does this differ from my original motivation?

In their study of eight retired counsellors and therapists from different trainings, Russell and Simanowitz (2013) look at how these practitioners had come to their decision. They noticed that some of their sample were explicit about using concepts from their therapeutic models to inform their decision. Where a humanistic practitioner spoke of relying on the 'felt sense' (Gendlin, 1996), a psychoanalytic one looked to her unconscious. Another, who was a Buddhist, made the decision while holding in mind the natural cycle of life and death. There is a striking correspondence between these experiences, although each is described in the language of a particular tribe.

Comments from contributors, particularly from the younger group, confirm how difficult the decision to retire can be. Nicola summed up the dilemma:

> Retirement is the moment when being pulled two ways comes right up in your face – and I think that's where I have been wobbling in my loyalties.

Carol expressed how uncertain the younger retirees could feel when their motivation for retirement was based largely on pull factors rather than pressure of ageing:

> I think that's what I've been living for the last year – the existential dilemma of choice and choosing to lose something is very different from something being taken away.

Mary from the classic group also conveys the ambivalence she felt about the decision:

> I found that very difficult because I didn't want to face an end, so I muffed it for a while . . . two years away, three years away and that seemed alright but an actual end point, I probably only faced up to it eighteen months ago and even then it was a bit muffed. It was in that 'after Christmas some time . . . next summer' way of thinking.

She described her struggle with the word 'retirement' and had initially told her patients that she would be 'stopping work'. She had worked through her allergy to the word and was acutely aware of difficult feelings in both the patients and herself. She wryly commented:

> It's very hard to work out which you are trying to protect.

Carol's retirement had evolved in stages. When her husband's redundancy triggered a house move she had to close her practice for a few weeks. This meant that she had arrived almost at the point of retirement while still doubting whether she would carry it through:

> I'm still at the stage of finding it difficult to say it out loud, to say . . . and you can hear I'm still finding it difficult to say out loud. And I said it yesterday to a friend that 'I'm retiring' and it's taken a huge long process for me to get to this point where I can actually say,

'Yes I've decided to retire'. I thought, 'Well I'll have a sabbatical', I didn't start out thinking . . . Well I did think possibly I would retire.

For Patsy the uncertainty over her decision to retire resulted in her making an initial aborted retirement and then, a few years later, coming to a sustained decision to go through with it. Patsy had informed her patients and was working towards endings when she decided to go back into therapy to explore this more deeply. She explains why she did this:

Because I was so undecided. I really did not know if I was doing the right thing.

Her new therapist was very challenging about Patsy's decision and he was direct:

That really quite shocked me when he said, 'You will find it very difficult if you don't know why you are doing it'.

She chuckled as she recalled this and said he had been right: she had needed more time as a therapist to clarify what the work meant to her and why leaving it was so hard. She had come to realise that her uncertainty was about her ambivalence towards her depressed mother. She described having always lived with the feeling that she ought to have done more for her mother and that giving up the work was increasing this sense of having abandoned her mother.

A number of my interviewees told how the real crunch had come quite early in the process of retirement at the point when they made the decision not to take on new clients. This decision had been hard to hold to and one spoke of the phone almost 'burning her fingers' as she explained to a would-be client that she was not available.

Can peers tell us when our time is up?

If it is difficult to recognise a decline in our own performance, can we do better for supervisees and colleagues? The weakness in this safeguard seems to be that colleagues are reluctant to deliver bad news. It is reasonable to expect supervisors to be able to give bad news, but we need to bear in mind that they can only 'speak as they find' and if they are only allowed to see the supervisee appearing at her best for 50 minutes, they may not have the evidence they need – even if they have doubts.

Guy and colleagues (1987) asked members of the American Psychological Association 'how they would determine whether they had become incompetent to practice psychotherapy due to either physical or emotional disability' (1987: 818). Fifty-six per cent said that their own self-assessment would be the main source of information and 17.6 per cent said that feedback from clients would be their main way of deciding. The most striking findings for me were that 13.5 per cent of respondents planned to practice until their death and that the older therapists were more likely to postpone retirement. The results of this study indicate the risk to patients when therapists take too optimistic a view of their health, or to be more blunt, when therapists are in denial about the impact of their ageing and ultimate death.

I have heard a number of older therapists say that they have asked trusted colleagues to let them know when they are 'past it'. Although a formal supervisory relationship does occasionally provide a successful prompt for a supervisee to retire, this seems rare and in peer supervision it would be even harder to suggest this move. In my opinion, a simple colleague relationship, outside the frame and containment of a peer group, would be the least reliable safeguard. I have never heard a retired therapist say that they had been counselled by a colleague to move on and I have never spoken to one of the trusted colleagues who had been the bearer of such bad news. This makes me doubtful about how well this informal system of feedback from colleagues is working, and Galatzer-Levy (2004) lists the kinds of factors which might inhibit therapists from confronting a colleague whose capacity is waning: 'Decades-long friendships, compassion for suffering colleagues, and the awareness that "there but for the grace of God go I"' (2004: 1015). Similarly Mander (2010) notes that the problem with feedback from peers is that this 'could feel like an envious attack from one's colleagues' (2010: 22). The power of envy does seem to be what scuppers informal feedback as a safeguard. The fear of being seen as an envious attacker could make peers reluctant to speak up. The conviction that the advice is inspired by envy could make the elderly therapist reluctant to believe the news, and it is also possible that an envious attack *could* be made in this form.

Reliance on patients to indicate the need to retire

Now and again sad anecdotes circulate of therapists who are unable to recognise their diminishing capacity and who have to be pushed by means of difficult patient or supervisee interventions. Weiss, Kaplan and Flanagan (1997) write about the analyst turning the patient 'into a caretaker-hostage' who dare not leave because of the wound this would inflict on the therapist who is clinging to life through her work (1997: 475). In a subsequent paper, Weiss and Kaplan (2000) state the problem even more clearly: 'We believe that leaving the decision up to the patient poses an impossible dilemma: leave and feel guilt over abandonment; stay and express the guilty motives in doing so' (2000: 458). A case such as this is indicated by Mander (2010), who recalls the painful closing stages of Paula Heimann's life and the distress of her final patient whom she had insisted needed to stay for more work.

Noak (2011) gives a first-hand account of attempting to raise the issue. After her elderly analyst had a serious heart attack she voiced anxiety about his health, but he responded with an interpretation:

> I experienced his retort as sharp and accusative, and it made me feel as if I had been accused of wanting to kill him. It made me feel guilty and unable to raise the issue again with him.
>
> (2011: 3)

He died a few months later while still seeing her. Fonagy also tells a story which illustrates how inappropriate it is to rely on patients to monitor performance and to initiate ending. He recounts a session where an elderly analyst fell asleep but describes the unlikelihood of this being properly worked through, 'given how deeply it touched the narcissistic vulnerabilities of both participants' (2009: 211).

Three of the 15 therapists I interviewed had experienced the sudden loss of a therapist through illness or death and one had lost a supervisor to unexpected death; while such a small sample is not representative, it reminds us of how common this occurrence is. Their stories illustrate how difficult it is for most patients to allow themselves to know that their therapist is waning and needs to step down. If a youngish therapist makes a lapse, the joint reflection on what has happened is often challenging but extremely fruitful; if an ageing therapist makes a lapse, the fear that this is part of decline rather than 'normal' carelessness will make it much harder for the therapeutic dyad to explore what has happened.

Training organisations and policy

Retirement has proved a very challenging issue for training organisations to address, though some have tried. Some of the dilemmas about fitness to practice and a duty of self-care are addressed by the regular ethical codes, but institutions have found it very difficult to achieve specific policies on retirement. If a policy sets a simple age bar to practising it would address the concern that sudden illness and death become more likely with age, but with the downside that some careers would be ended unnecessarily early. However if the policy recognises that we all age at different rates and is built around an assessment of the elderly therapist's capacity, it will be very challenging to implement.

There is a spectrum of practice among therapy organisations, and Quinodoz (2010) reports that some analytical institutes do have a peer review system. Some training organisations now offer support and training days for members who are in peri-retirement. Unfortunately other institutions are still in such denial that they remain distressingly unsupportive; one contributor reported that she did not receive any acknowledgement when she informed her organisation of her retirement. Some organisations have made a small start in acknowledging the issue by introducing a retirement category of membership. This allows retirees to pay a reduced annual fee and to continue to attend conferences, special interest groups and to subscribe to journals at a discounted rate.

Awareness of and pressure for transparency and policy are growing but experience shows that even when policies are agreed, their implementation is a challenge. Where no system exists, we remain reliant on informal safeguards. One factor which helps to protect patients is the drying up of referrals, because if an older therapist is fading most colleagues will cease to send people to her. However, there may be some former patients and supervisees whose loyalty blinds them to reality and even if referrals dry up completely the existing patients may sense this and find it even harder to leave.

In the past, certain professions have had particularly strict age limits, but anti-discrimination legislation is making it more difficult to sustain mandatory retirement age. Airline pilots are one group who have always had a rigid retirement date, but in recent years this has been raised in several countries, with most now holding 65 as the age limit. Judges are another group whose age has been closely debated. Prior to 1959, judges could continue to sit until any age; legislation in 1959 and 1993 fixed the age limit at 70 or 75 depending on the type of court. Although it runs the risk of seeming self-important, a comparison with judges seems relevant. There is *some* overlap in skill set in the requirement to grasp, remember and analyse an unfolding story and crucially to link up parts that others may have overlooked. In both professions, individuals' performance may mature and deepen with age but ultimately will be useless if memory fails or stamina becomes too depleted. If it seems important that judges retire before they become incompetent, how could this not apply to therapists?

A report by a House of Lords committee comments on the issue of mandatory retirement age in a paragraph which might have close relevance to our profession:

> A set retirement age is undoubtedly a blunt tool by which to assess whether someone is no longer fully capable of performing their job. In the light of new laws preventing age discrimination in other sectors, there is a case to be made for having no set retirement age at all. However, the principle of judicial independence necessarily makes it very difficult to force a judge to retire on the grounds of declining capacity to act: who should assess when the time is right for a judge to step down from his or her post? The weight of the evidence we received was in favour of a retirement age of around 70 or 75.
>
> (House of Lords, 2012, para. 191)

Why denial is so entrenched

The loss is so multifaceted

We might like to think that therapists would have insight into their avoidance of an issue. Perhaps the denial about retirement is not surprising as this transition involves such a mixture of losses as well as possible guilt, envy, loneliness and increased awareness of our own deaths. Barratt and colleagues (2012) were atypical and impressive in the degree of attention they gave to preparing for retirement. They anticipated how they might deal defensively with the loss, imagining 'either withdrawing into depression as time goes by or a manic attempt to fill the emptiness' (2012: 111–12). Kelly and Barratt (2007) write of the reparative meaning that we find in our work – whether we are seeking unconsciously to heal a family member or to make reparation for societal trauma. This experience is voiced (above) by Patsy, who describes her retirement process as being muddied by her guilt about her depressed mother.

We know that any taboo maintains itself through the element of shame, which prohibits constructive thought, and Fonagy (2009) offers some convincing reasons for why the taboo is so great. He stresses that the shame is not about ageing, which we can (jokingly) accept, but the analyst's cognitive decline. This is vividly conveyed by Carlisle (2013) (above), who felt vicarious shame for her dementing analyst.

It is understood that burnout is more common if we have over-invested in our work and this is also likely to make retirement harder. If our sense of meaning were derived exclusively from our work we would find it exceptionally hard to give up. This fear of losing our sense of purpose seems to be a critical part of resistance, and one supervisor spoke of a supervisee who had faced down cancer with much grace but was buckling under the prospect of retirement. In this case the prospect of living without the role of a therapist seemed to stir up something more alarming than dying. Eissler (1993) makes the point that if the therapist becomes emotionally dependent on the work with her patients, this is unlikely to produce good clinical outcomes.

Could it make sense to think of this dependence as an attachment insecurity and a failure to internalise the benefits we have taken from our work? It is no secret among therapists that we chose this career out of our own needs. The fact that our dedication to our own growth can bring relief to clients creates a win-win situation. For some of us there is a history of being a parentified child. For others the history is the simple narcissistic deficit of the child who did not feel she mattered and being an effective therapist is a way to matter very much to people. A key point here is the degree to which the work of being a therapist can build our lasting sense of worth, rather than just provide a daily fix. We would hope that our original therapy will have enabled us to metabolise the affirming aspects of the work, but supervision may also have a part in supporting that. For this to happen we need a model of supervision which allows space for some personal reflection. This could even be one of the ways that supervision achieves its central aim of supporting effective work with clients, since when the therapist feels fed by the work they may function better.

Perhaps financial concerns are the most concrete factor which can make retirement difficult; our taboo around wealth makes it even harder to address its profound ethical challenges. Sometimes therapists say, half-jokingly, 'I won't be able to retire, I haven't got a pension'. I think the same people would readily accept that if a therapist were unfit to practice, for whatever reason, it would not be appropriate for them to continue, regardless of their financial position. Perhaps if we could think more openly about retirement then questions of pensions and income would also be addressed. If a career as a therapist is not paying enough to support provision for old age, what can be done? For some therapists, working part of the week in a salaried post provides a solution. The situation we would all want to avoid is one where financial pressure impacts on clinical judgement.

Another very tangible thing we forfeit on retirement is contact with colleagues. Sanville (2002), a therapist still working at 80, writes, 'one of the rewards of continuing to work is . . . meaningful relationships with those who share my interests and concerns' (2002: 637). This aspect of loss was mentioned by several contributors as significant to them, and some had coped by structuring ongoing social and intellectual relationships with colleagues.

Collective denial in the profession

The challenges of ageing and the harm done when no action is taken are explored in Junkers's collection of essays (2013). Several of her writers cite instances of organisational and individual denial as well as charting sincere attempts to address the problem. On the one hand, clinicians with psychodynamic understanding may be well equipped to monitor their motives and behaviour through their interest in unconscious process; on the other hand, this group have a poor record and some poor role models for facing up to ageing. Cohen (1983) offers an interesting hypothesis about this: he suggests that in our formation as therapists we become more aware of the existential aloneness of each individual and this may make death even more terrifying. He argues that this loneliness combines with a sense of timelessness, which long-term therapy creates, to foster denial in the profession. Fonagy (2009) identifies another way that psychoanalytic thinking may be perverted to protect us from the unwelcome knowledge of ageing. He speculates that there is an organisation defence based on the Oedipus complex which gives analysts an ideal excuse when challenged by younger colleagues: 'youthful' feedback can be written off as a wish to replace the parent.

Writing of analysts in general, Weiss *et al.* observe: 'They do not regard retirement as a given, as a developmental phase of professional life' (1997: 469). Dewald and Schwartz (1993) point out that this denial of illness and death was unfortunately modelled for us by Freud.

> Freud's failure, at least in print, to share his own struggle with his illness may have deprived the field of a supervisor with whom to identify who otherwise could have reduced the seductiveness of professionalized denial and grandiosity.
>
> (1993: 191)

Our unconscious does not know about time. Freud claimed as much, and we experience this when we 'lose' ourselves in creative endeavour. We also observe it in the freedom from time enjoyed by little children and then the rebellion against time by the adolescent. Where one of the strengths of short-term work is the discipline around time, in long-term therapy the task around time is more paradoxical: there is benefit both from the sense of the analytic couple having all the time in the world, but also from the knowledge that this will end, both when 50 minutes is up and when we finally say goodbye. Keeping hold of both the 'as if' and the reality is the constant challenge of the work. In her immensely thoughtful account of ageing, I felt there was a telling moment where Quinodoz (2010) leant too far from external reality. Writing about deafness, she observes how important listening and hearing is to the therapist and suggests that when a therapist's hearing is impaired, 'the intensity of their inner listening may be able to compensate for their objective loss of hearing' (2010: 175). I recounted Quinodoz's comment to a colleague who uses a hearing aid and she retorted, 'Listening with the *third* ear does not mean you don't use one and two!'

The lack of open conversation about retirement means that unless a middle-aged therapist has been close to an older colleague, she may have no role model for retirement. This lack of contact across the generations is enhanced by a practical concern: if a therapist begins to think aloud with colleagues about her retirement, there is a risk that rumours of a possible ending could reach patients before the therapist has fully decided or committed to a date. Where patients are themselves part of the therapy world this is a real concern. Perhaps as we begin to break down the taboo and become more accustomed to helping each other think through the issues of retirement, we may feel more able to trust each other to provide the careful boundaries and containment that are needed.

The therapists in my sample who were already retired seemed to have achieved a constructive experience of retirement. The transition had been challenging, but 'arrival' at the other side had been positive, and this optimistic view is spelled out by Boyd-Carpenter (2010b):

> Generally I don't think many people find much excitement or interest in the subject of retirement but I have found it to contain all the great issues of any life stage – in some ways enhanced by a reduced agenda and an inevitable awareness of the shortness of time.

Chapter 2

How to begin?

> It felt quite brutal in a way – cutting off something unfinished and really important . . . it goes against the grain of what a therapist is.
>
> (Mary)

> I do think that if people are phobic about retiring then they are not so good at it . . . what is it that makes them think I have to retire on Thursday 10th of whatever?
>
> (Rosemary)

One patient responded with incredulity when his analyst broke the news of an imposed ending: 'I can't believe it . . . it makes no sense. Could you be telling me this for some special purpose, as a joke, a cruel one, to test my reactions?' (Weiss, 1972: 507).

Attachment implications

Unlike Weiss's patient, most will be able to take in the news of an imposed ending but the consequences beneath the polite and grown-up acceptance may be considerable. The impact will depend above all on the person's early losses and their subsequent attachment pattern, as well as on the depth of engagement in the relationship and the age at which the patient is working in the transference. There will be a type of bereavement for both parties. For long-term patients it makes sense to think of the therapist as an attachment figure (Bowlby, 1988: 140) who responds empathically to their experience, who helps them to regulate their states, who provides some measure of secure base and to whom proximity is sought (if only internally) in times of distress.

Farber, Lippert and Nevas (1995) suggest that the patient's relationship with the therapist is significantly different from a childhood attachment relationship but that 'viewing the therapist as an attachment figure can offer new perspectives on therapeutic work' (1995: 204). In most long-term therapy relationships the threat of separation which retirement poses is likely to trigger some degree of attachment behaviour. In attachment terms the patient may then seek for proximity and this seeking of help may be exaggerated, inhibited or distorted according to early relational experience. In the working through of this increased vulnerability lies the opportunity that retirement brings.

Patients at earlier stages of the work may not as yet have given themselves as deeply to the process or have allowed the therapist to become as important in their internal landscape, and they may be less troubled by the news of retirement. On the other hand, anecdotes indicate that some new patients feel particularly betrayed when a therapist 'decides' to retire soon after taking them on. At the other end of the process we would expect that patients in the final stages of therapy would have more insight into their responses and more awareness of the 'as if' quality of the exchanges with their therapist. Thus it is likely that patients in the middle stages of the work will be most affected. These are the clients who are dismayed at how important the relationship has become to them, but are not yet able to make sense of the way they are using their therapist. Patients in these middle phases of therapy, or any who struggle with normal breaks, will find the imposed ending difficult. In an ideal world a therapist will have anticipated the closure of her practice and will not be working with such fragile individuals when the news is broken.

We are familiar with the connotations of sadness implied by bereavement, so it is shocking but illuminating to discover the violence implied in the word: *Webster's Collegiate Dictionary* of 1936 defines 'to reave' as 'To rob or plunder; despoil; also to seize; to tear away', and this puts us in touch with the traumatic assault which bereavement can involve. The fact that this 'tearing away' has been deliberately chosen by the therapist is quite logical to our conscious self but might feel vicious and confusing to the unconscious of both client and the therapist herself. The violence of bereavement is also suggested by C.S. Lewis in his account of mourning for his wife: 'No one ever told me that grief felt so like fear' (Lewis, 1961: 5). Bowlby (1980) also puts it starkly: 'Loss of a loved person is one of the most intensely painful experiences any human being can suffer' (1980: 7). Murray Parkes's (1972) description is particularly eloquent – he speaks of grief as the cost of commitment and the price we pay for love.

Patients who feel bewildered and wounded by the news will fall back on their customary defensive patterns. If there has been good progress in therapy there will, by this stage, be a measure of earned security but at moments of extreme stress we are prone to default to earlier insecure strategies. The patient with a broadly dismissing pattern will respond to the news in ways which minimise the relationship and contributors give varied examples of this compulsive self-reliance. Individuals with more preoccupied traits tend to be more obviously dysregulated by threats to their attachment security than the dismissing patients who are skilled at hiding their distress. Preoccupied patients will be vigilant for signs of abandonment and, when these occur in the shape of retirement, their response is likely to be to try to impact on the therapist by explicit or implicit communications. As the retiring therapist may be a magnet for guilt at this point, the patient who takes up a blaming stance could be knocking at an open door. For clients with a disorganised/unresolved pattern, the anxiety about abandonment might be communicated in particularly challenging, aggressive and incoherent ways: these are the clients who may ricochet between conflicting states, putting the therapist under tremendous pressure to hear the pain behind the raging attack.

The therapist's own attachment pattern will also influence dynamics around separation. As mentioned in Chapter 1, most of us have residual traits of attachment insecurity which will impact at times of stress. These insecure patterns may be roused by the decision-making process around retirement and may be further evoked by the task of announcing our departure and by the responses from patients. Ambivalent traits will enhance the therapist's sense of guilt and possibly pull us towards compensating for our perceived failing. Avoidant traits may pull us towards collusive denial with dismissing patients, with part of us only too pleased to believe that our retirement is not having a significant impact on a patient's process and grateful to be spared signs of grief which could connect us to our own denied ambivalence about ending. The therapist's own degree of insecurity and their own secure base will influence how well they can attune to each patient. Countertransference coloured by our own attachment insecurity may mean we do a better job at providing an appropriate secure base for some patients than for others; the hope would be that in the difficult cases we can use supervision effectively to help us identify and address that imbalance.

Bowlby (1969) observed the inverse relationship between attachment behaviour and our exploratory mode: when attachment needs are taken care of we are free to be curious and engage with the world. This oscillation between adventuring, returning to an attachment figure for soothing and then re-venturing out is particularly visible in the older baby and toddler. Stranger anxiety is one of the factors operating here alongside stranger curiosity (Fraiberg, 1969). Szajnberg and Crittenden (1997) offer a creative analogy between the experience of an infant who meets a stranger in the presence of her mother and the patient who meets new material/new parts of the self in the presence of the therapist. They describe an eight-month old held by its mother as a stranger enters the room; the most important factors in the child's experience of the stranger are the infant's attachment pattern and the mother's own reception of the stranger. The way in which the therapist 'greets' new material in the therapy room will influence how much curiosity/anxiety the patient brings to the meeting. I think we can extend this analogy to the news of the therapist's retirement, which is likely to be experienced as 'a very strange stranger': the way the therapist introduces this newcomer will be important, the patient will be watching how she relates to the intruder. One of the fantasies which patients may develop about their therapist's retirement is the idea of the other people that the therapist is going to spend time with; these people, whether lovers, children or friends, are being chosen over and above the patient. This hurts.

How much notice to give for an imposed ending?

Before arriving at the point of giving notice to their patients, contributors had been preparing for an ending. Some of them had not taken on any new clients for a few years; others were seeing new clients but only for time limited work. The classic and older groups had been particularly careful about this. The question of how much notice to give is one for which contributors had found very little guidance.

Boyd-Carpenter (2010a) took one year from making her decision to having her last session. She writes that in practice this meant giving most clients about nine months' notice: 'doubtless unconsciously reflecting the space nature has allotted for the development of a new life' (2010a: 91). Writing about voluntary endings, Coltart (1996) also mentions nine months' gestation being a suitable length of time. Most contributors had chosen a period closer to twice this, judging that patients needed more time to work through the experience of rejection. Several contributors felt that too much notice of ending can make it harder to get to grips with the meaning of it and they pondered whether the 18 months they had given had been a little long. In one case the therapist, Nicola, had had a long-term plan to retire at a certain date and she let patients know this when they started. This meant the news came in two stages – a piece of initial background information and the specific setting of an end date. One retiring therapist described an alternative model which she was using. Anticipating her retirement by a few years, she deliberately let clients know and encouraged them to end well before the closing date so that there would be a buffer period in which clients could return for a little more work.

As well as the decision about the length of warning given to patients, there are decisions about where to place the final end date. Do we want to spread the endings out to avoid creating more intensity than we can manage? Would it make more sense to fix the ending at the time of a regular break or would it be of benefit to patients to face the ending at a more unusual time of year and thus not be lulled into feeling this was a normal summer break? It may also be appropriate and possible to keep in mind factors particular to each patient, as we would when choosing an ending date with an individual who was making a voluntary ending. For example, we would want to avoid imposing an ending which coincided with the anniversary of a painful bereavement.

Schwarz (1974) was closing a full practice in order to relocate but, in common with many retirees, he reduced his practice 'organically' by not replacing patients who came to an end in their own time. He stopped taking patients as soon as he began considering relocating; by the time he was sure he would move he was only seeing five people and most of these were in the closing stages of the work (1974: 283). Murdin (2000) also writes of closing a practice in order to relocate and finding that 'For most people one year's notice gave time to move through variations of love and hate to arrive at some sort of readiness to end' (2000: 82).

Rosemary was the contributor who took longest over her retirement and Denise the one who allowed least time for a planned ending. Rosemary's comment at the start of this chapter fits with her aim of achieving a seamless organic retirement, with each patient ending 'naturally' in their own time. Denise's contrasting choice, of setting a six-month cut-off, was based on her wish to make the ending very real and thus to facilitate mourning which had not happened sufficiently at the end of her own therapy. Some therapists will have practical constraints which preclude a very gradual retirement process. Others take the view that too much delicacy could be infantalising and that clients need to cope with the realities of life. When therapists work with relatively high-functioning patients over briefer time frames, then the shorter period of notice could work well. The overall number of patients in the practice is also significant, as working through many endings in a short time frame would be much more stressful than closing a small part time practice.

Clementine had asked an older retired colleague how long to allow for the process and was given a blunt answer:

She said, 'Oh you'd better get cracking, it took me ten years', so I thought 'Goodness', but actually what emerged was that two years was absolute maximum. And I don't think anybody had the full two years because what I realised when I thought about telling each individual person, was that two years is an impossible time to hold in your head.

Clementine told people over the course of a few weeks and she also paced the ending so that she phased the impact on herself and was able to work in an optimum way with each patient:

Each one required a great deal of thought and dealing with feelings and they all did things in their own ways.

Beatrice told all her patients that she would be retiring in 18 months and then with each person a specific ending was settled on, usually coinciding with a natural break and according to the personal plans of each individual – with none of them leaving in less than a year. I commented on how carefully the ending was being adapted to each patient and Beatrice's response was succinct:

I am privileged. I am not pushed by illness.

Finance is the other practical factor which might prevent some therapists from providing this tailor-made retirement planning: payment for therapy rooms, insurance and organisational subscriptions can become onerous if client numbers are reduced one by one. Annette's process around planning the ending illustrates the mixture of practical and intuitive factors which may contribute to the decision.

And I'm not really sure when I came to the conclusion that eighteen months would be the time. I decided Easter was the best time because that's when you pay all your subs for the financial year, and it doesn't make sense to go on to July.

Another comment from Annette illustrates how much patients may read between the lines at such a critical point. Big existential questions tend to arise, though they may not be voiced – 'Is my therapist retiring because she is dying?' and 'Will she be moving away?'

It wasn't as though I was going to die and he knew where I was, I wasn't moving house again, there was nothing like that and I think that helped quite a bit.

Annette conveys that the point at which a therapist takes her last new client may be as significant a threshold as the moment of telling patients. She describes how it felt to turn clients away.

> When the phone rang and somebody asked for therapy it was so tempting. I'd think 'I've got all this time and wouldn't it be interesting'. I really had to struggle with that. Or in the peer group someone would say 'I've got someone I'd like to refer, would one of you like to take them?' and I'd think 'Yes I would!' It was so difficult, having made the decision to really stick to it.

Denise's retirement date had been chosen as the earliest she could retire without negatively impacting a training patient. Having privately set her target date about a year in advance, which allowed this trainee to complete her registration, she then decided on six months as the most helpful period of notice for all her patients. She recalled the ending of her own therapy and said that the date had been set a year in advance but they had not worked on the meaning of this until the last six months, and for this reason she had opted for this tighter schedule with her own patients.

Rosemary's retirement was a very reluctant one – she stopped taking on new patients because she judged her memory to be deteriorating. Even though this was a 'forced' retirement Rosemary's process was the most gradual, with her patients leaving one by one over a period of about eight years. I wondered whether she had been concerned about her memory being good enough for the existing patients and she explained that it was not *that* bad but not good enough to allow her to begin new long-term work. She stressed that she had been busy with supervising and leadership roles in therapy organisations and had not been keeping her remaining patients on because she was bored but because they were not ready to leave. I wondered whether these select few patients had guessed at their privileged position:

> Well if they guessed they never mentioned . . . they had time, you see, to do it when it suited them.

Therapists who are relocating face the same question as retirees as to how much notice is clinically optimal; however, they have additional time pressures arising from the practical issues of their move. Aarons's early paper on relocation judges 'not less than four months' to be ample time for working through reactions (Aarons, 1975: 304). Aarons was seeing patients several times a week for psychoanalysis, and there may be a paradox here that patients in less intensive treatment need at least as much time to work on what the ending means. For more typical once-a-week clients, four months would allow a mere 16 sessions, perhaps fewer with bank holidays, illness and clients travelling for work. During that time a client could also face emergencies in their own life which could mean that the issue of abandonment gets put to the side. For long-term clients who are used to being given the dates of holiday breaks many months in advance, four months' notice could feel disrespectful. The imposed ending can be equally challenging for patients who have been recently taken on, and Alice's comments here describe this. Because the need to move house can arise relatively suddenly compared with the more predictable need to retire, therapists who are relocating are more likely to be faced with the situation which Alice describes:

> I had one client who I had recently taken on when I made the decision to move. When I took her on I didn't know I was going to move and if I had known I wouldn't have taken her on. She was a very troubled client. After a while I realised she was quite borderline; she had a lot of issues; she became very attached to me very quickly and was very angry when I said I would be going. So there was a lot to work through with her and had I known I wouldn't have taken her on. She did work right through to the end. She found another therapist before I left but she was going to have a break. She was very young in her process.

The process of relocating presented Alice with some additional logistical problems arising from the sale of her house. As she had part-time salaried work as well as her private practice, she was not economically reliant on keeping patients with her, but for some therapists the transition will be more financially fraught. Having told her clients she was selling her house and they would have to end in six months, the house sale did not happen:

> I had said to them we would end in December, but when it came to it I had to tell them I wasn't moving and to ask them what they wanted to do. I said, 'We can still finish – what do you want to do?' They said they'd like to carry on seeing me until I definitely moved.

When the period of notice is dictated by illness

Emma's retirement process was dictated and shaped by the progress of her cancer and its treatment. Her diagnosis came during her break and she made a delayed return to work after radiotherapy. By that point she had decided that she would end with the majority of her patients three months later when the next break was due. I was interested in how Emma had selected which patients she would keep on, and she explained that this was partly based on her sense of who was closer to being ready to end and partly about the intensity of the work. Her reduced health meant she could no longer see people three or four times a week and she finished her work with these high-frequency patients. When the cancer recurred a year later, Emma was faced with a major operation and decided to conclude her work with her remaining patients. Again she was obliged to condense the ending into the time available – this time she had just a fortnight:

> I must have said something like 'You do remember don't you that I've got cancer and I know it's something we've talked about in various ways. I'm sorry to say there has been a recurrence and I'm going to have to go into hospital for an operation.' I said 'I'm going to stop working now. You must feel free to be in touch with me but I'm stopping working now.'

Emma undertook to let each of these final patients know that she had survived the operation and was still alive. In fact in the months after her operation she had a certain amount of contact with these patients. They were in touch by email partly to discuss referral ideas but also because they wanted to let Emma know of significant events in their lives.

The impact on the therapist of the pace of ending

Our own histories naturally inform our idea of the optimal period of working through a forced ending. Hannah and Denise, who chose a shorter period of notice of six months, both felt that the ending of their own therapy had been too protracted. In Hannah's case this happened because her training client left prematurely. She had been intending to end her own therapy at the earliest opportunity but was then obliged to continue for two more years as she worked with a new training client. Denise explained that when she had felt ready to finish her own therapy, she and her therapist had agreed to work towards an ending in a year's time but she felt this had been too long.

It seems important for a therapist to pace the ending in a way which supports her. On the one hand there is the gradual strategy employed by Rosemary which allowed patients to end in their own time. The provision of the indefinite span of time is very generous to patients, protecting them from the intrusion of the therapist's own needs, but this gradual letting go would not work well for all therapists. Some of us might find it hard to produce our best work when we are going through the final protracted endings with the last one or two patients. It might also be difficult to avoid making a self-interested interpretation if that final patient announced that she would, after all, do another year. On the other end of the scale, to close a full practice in 'one go' could mean several final sessions in the last week. The emotional weight of so much ending would make it difficult for a therapist to be wholly available to each client as they end. I was struck by a comment from a therapist working regularly with a time-limited model, and therefore accustomed to multiple endings. She said, 'I can't finish more than two people in a day' (Vowles, 2011). This need for space to process both the endings and the announcement is echoed by a number of contributors. Hannah explained why she chose to spread out the announcement:

> I told them over a few weeks. It needed careful picking it up in the material.

This comment about pacing the announcement was echoed by Alice, who was closing her practice for relocation and recounted spacing out the announcement of the news:

> I certainly wouldn't tell more than one a week, because I needed to be with that process with each one, with their response to me – it was huge for both of us.

Special patients

A number of writers mention one patient who was hard to tell. Schwarz (1974) describes delaying the announcement to a patient who was making good progress in the work but definitely needed more time for working through. He noticed that the work became bogged down with long silences until finally the patient spoke of feeling pushed to achieve more. Schwarz acknowledges that 'In essence I felt bad about the forthcoming interruption of the analysis and was indeed pushing him beyond his present capacity in order to "give him" as much as possible before we terminated' (1974: 286–7). When Schwarz did break the news, this hard-working patient believed it was a gimmick to get him to work even harder. Martinez (1989) says, unsurprisingly, that patients who were in the process of ending were easier to tell. She adds that she also found it was easier with those who had just started. Alice's comments above indicate that this is not always so.

It seemed that for almost all my interviewees some patients were particularly hard to tell. These were often those whose bleak internal worlds had made the establishment of a productive relationship very hard work for both therapist and patient. Where these patients came more than once a week, had almost no other social contact in their lives and had been attending on a low fee, the difficulty was greatest. Beatrice outlined the ethical dilemma that could arise around a particularly fragile patient who has done very well in a long therapy and who had been banking on coming to therapy until they died. She had one such patient and had thought carefully about whether she might continue to work with just this one person, but in the end she felt it would be omnipotent to see herself as indispensable.

Denise and Clementine both described one patient slipping through the net when they made their announcements. Clementine recalled a very fragile older patient whom she saw for a low fee:

> The person I was most worried about – I really dreaded telling her because I thought it would be very hard to find another therapist.

This predicament was resolved in a very dramatic way when the patient was diagnosed unexpectedly with terminal cancer:

> So that dreaded decision was in this very strange way taken right out of my hands. She left me.

One of Denise's patients was also diagnosed with cancer; because Denise had allowed a shorter period of notice, this created a significant difficulty. Denise delayed the announcement of her retirement as the patient was waiting for major surgery, but this meant that the news had to be given the week that the patient returned from treatment and they then had much less than the intended six months to work towards ending. Patsy spoke of giving most of her patients around 18 months' notice, but with one very challenging patient she found herself delaying the announcement:

> And I was never quite sure why except for some reason I thought that a year would be a better way for her to handle it, than that bit longer. And actually I'm not sure that people don't tell patients too soon.

She added the following view:

> With 'P . . .' there wasn't a single session where she wasn't talking
> about the ending. So something gets really focused into it rather than
> things being more open and fluid.

In my own experience of taking a planned medical break (Power, 2003)
I found it useful to keep a log of my clients' responses to the unexpected
news. This was important first because I needed to be sure that all of them
had been told and none told too close to a break or at a time when their
own issues made it particularly inappropriate to intrude with my business.
In addition, noting down my observations and comparing the various ways
that clients managed the news deepened my curiosity and reflection on what
was going on. I felt it made sense to understand my patients' experience
through thinking of this in terms of the separation and reunion which is
engineered and observed in the strange situation research (Ainsworth,
Blehar, Waters, and Wall, 1978).

A number of participants spoke in some detail about training patients
and also took particular care to stress that material about these patients
should not be published. Clementine described the final stages of her work
with a training patient and how they kept postponing the ending to give
this trainee more time to write her final paper. Annette mentioned that she
had always been mindful that a regular patient might decide to train and
would then need an extra-long therapy. As a training supervisor, Denise
also had in mind the needs of a particular trainee supervisee who was
working towards registration with her training patient. I wondered about
this particular concern which the training patients were often evoking, and
speculated that this might be partly a sense of identification with the young
therapist and a sense that one was nurturing a son or daughter to carry
on the work. I wondered whether performance anxiety was also operating:
there may have been a sense of the training organisation watching and
therefore a desire to stay in good repute with the parental body. (Countertransference to training organisations is looked at in Chapter 5.)

In a paper looking at ending, Craige (2002) makes the point that in some
ways trainees are better equipped to make the difficult transition which all
patients face in even the best-planned ending of a long therapy. She points
to studies by Schlessinger and Robbins (1974, 1975 and 1983) which
suggest that the self-analytic function which the patient develops during
analysis will be critical to their ability to tolerate and manage the impact
of losing the therapist. She writes, 'Candidates may have greater intellectual
preparation for their self-analytic work and so may be better prepared than

other patients to sort through transference residues after ending' (2002: 537). There is one respect in which trainees might be more vulnerable in the process of retirement, and this is because they are more at risk of hearing rumours about their therapist. If news of a therapist's likely retirement became spoken of before her patients knew of it, there would be a risk of training patients hearing about this on the grapevine rather than in the containment of a session. Another thought on this is suggested by a comment from Milner (1950), who writes with great compassion about the patient's loss at the point of ending. She suggests that this separation is something that we therapists avoid by becoming therapists themselves:

> for by the mere fact of becoming analysts we have succeeded in bypassing an experience which our patients have to go through.
>
> (1950: 191)

If Milner is right and this dynamic has been operating in our internal world, then retirement will pose a profound loss as the therapist eventually faces the separation which unconsciously they had been hoping to avoid.

The announcement: how much to say?

Like most of the contributors, Boyd-Carpenter did not disclose reasons for retirement beyond saying that she felt it was 'the right time' (2010a: 91). Dewald (1982) addresses the question of how much to tell when returning to work after a sudden and serious illness. He suggests that too much detailed reality may interfere with unconscious fantasies and feelings, but to withhold information could overburden the patient's capacity. He points out that 'What the patient hears and retains from the information provided is significantly influenced by transference factors' (1982: 350). This would seem to support the idea of tailoring the information slightly differently with different patients.

Kaplan, Weiss, Harris and Dick (1994), writing about an imposed ending for relocation, also weigh up the real and the fantasy implications of the news. They consider how to direct a communication about the real event to the patient's functioning ego, while also allowing the patient's younger self to respond through the transference to the unconscious meaning of the news. They suggest that if the real hurt to the patient is not acknowledged in a non-defensive and empathic way then transference reactions might become unmanageable. In an earlier paper, Weiss (1972) had reported uncertainty about how much to tell his patients. His reflections are interesting because he shares his doubts and his striving to find the optimum stance. He initially withheld any detail; then he shared a little more, but finally regretted this and felt it had been a loss of nerve (1972: 507). Galatzer-Levy (2004) makes a strong case for sufficient appropriate information being shared. He worked with 10 patients whose therapists had died and reports several cases where the loss was made worse by the lack of information. He noted that analysts who would normally scorn the use of reassurance had offered unrealistic assurance about their health. Some patients had therefore discovered information about their therapist's illness from other sources, which had confirmed what they had guessed about its seriousness but which had been denied to them by their therapist.

Martinez (1989) argues very strongly in favour of disclosure, suggesting that giving information need not restrict fantasies. She disclosed considerable detail about her relocation to some patients according to her sense of their need and she observed that, 'having the facts seemed to increase patients' capacity to fantasise and to reveal their fantasies' (1989: 102). Subsequently Martinez had feedback from the therapist to whom she had referred one of the patients with whom she had disclosed less. This therapist believed the patient had had more trouble resolving the rejection in the transference because she hadn't had enough detail about the real reasons for relocation.

Writing from a strictly classical position, Abend (1982) takes issue with this balanced approach. When he made a planned suspension of his practice for two months of medical treatment and convalescence he decided not to disclose any information. He asked:

> What is the beneficial effect of revealing anything more informative than the fact of interruption and the scheduling of the resumption of sessions? What is the basis for deciding that specific information relieves unbearable anxiety?
>
> (1982: 371)

He held to this very pure position with his analytic patients when he took his medical break, though he relented slightly with his psychotherapy patients whom he judged to be too ill for interpretation. If this fundamentalist approach were taken by a retiring therapist, they would perhaps simply announce the date on which sessions would end. Also writing from a classical position, Aarons (1975) discusses the question of disclosure for the relocating therapist. He suggests it is not helpful for most patients to be told where and why the analyst is moving as he sees it undermining the transference. Interestingly he would make an exception for a patient who was raised to be 'seen and not heard' and who therefore feels he has no right to know. He had a contrasting approach with a patient who had a more entitled style. When she became enraged by him withholding the information, he paraphrased Anna Freud, saying:

> she had a choice of whether to have her question answered or analysed and, as she knew, if she adhered to our analytic rule (far from arbitrary) she would gain by it.
>
> (Aarons, 1975: 306)

I felt that the success of this approach would hinge on the degree of collaboration which the dyad had already established. This naming of the dilemma as a shared one could be very engaging, but I also felt it ran the risk of sounding like a threat. On this issue of disclosure, contributors seemed to be of one mind: they all revealed that the imposed ending was caused by their retirement and in cases of illness they made minimal but clear disclosure. The only further details which were given related to relocation, and these were sparing and mostly given on a case-by-case basis. Most interviewees recalled that their announcement had been something along the lines, 'I need to tell you that I am going to retire in eighteen months and we need to think about that'. Or, as Beatrice put it:

> I am an elderly lady as you are aware and I am thinking of retiring; I am telling you very early so we have plenty of time to think about it.

Working to a tighter time frame, Denise had told almost all her patients in the first week back after the break as she wanted to give them all six months' notice. As Nicola's retirement plan was less definite than other contributors, the announcement that she made to patients was that she would be closing her practice in a year's time when she would be moving and possibly retiring. As she worked through endings with patients, she was also working through her decision as to whether to open a new practice once she had moved. She had considered but rejected the option of transferring her practice from her home into a rented room to which she might commute back each week.

Hannah conveyed the kind of logistical considerations which many participants recalled around the making of the announcement.

> I was taking September off so I thought I wouldn't tell them in October as I would just have come back and I didn't want to tell them too near Christmas, so I told them in November.

A further issue concerning the announcement is the question of how colleagues will be informed. The uncertainty and rumours which surround retirement are perhaps exacerbated by the fact that therapists have often been quite shy about sharing news of their retirement. Once patients have been told, this secrecy seems unnecessary and perhaps contributes to the sense of taboo about retirement. This lack of open conversation on the subject means that decisions over retirement may be more isolated and less supported by collegial exchange than other clinical choices.

Patients' responses at the moment of the announcement

A few patients respond to the announcement with open reproach. Weiss and Kaplan (2000) report a tirade from one patient who upbraided Weiss for thinking of such a thing, mocked him for choosing golf and drinking over analysis, and concluded that Weiss's wife was surely against the plan (2000: 452). This echoes the incredulity of Weiss's patient at the beginning of this chapter and of the patient whom Schwarz had delayed telling. It also tallies with Alan's comment (Chapter 3) that patients did not at first believe he really would retire and Mary's report of a patient who complained that she was retiring when other therapists manage to keep going.

Martinez (1989) is one of a few writers who describe some patients already seeming to sense that abandonment was on the cards. Prior to Martinez's announcement of her relocation, one of her patients dreamed that his parents had sold their house and were leaving his home town. After sharing his dream he scanned her face and questioned her closely about her plans. She decided to share the truth with him but later questioned her timing, writing, 'My guilt at abandoning him and my anxiety over his profound dependence on me pushed me to answer directly when an interpretation was more appropriate' (1989: 99). However, she believed that ultimately her direct acknowledgement achieved a distinction between the real and the transference image of her and that this was essential for insightful work.

Patients who already planned to end

There are different views on whether to inform those clients who would be making a natural ending before the therapist retires. Schwarz (1974) writes about informing one of his patients, who was already working towards an agreed ending, and finding that the news of his departure was still very significant for her. They recognised that she had been managing the approaching ending by believing, 'I could continue if I wanted to but I don't want to'. One retiree summed up the dilemma as a choice between two risks. On the one hand, if we share the 'unnecessary' information about retirement we risk both intruding on their lives and also conveying the message that we doubt they can manage without us. On the other hand, if we do not tell, we risk some clients discovering the news at a later stage and feeling deceived that they ended without realising we were on the point of retirement and that they would not be able to re-contact us for any follow up sessions.

Hannah was one of a few contributors who had chosen to share the news with patients who were ending anyway. She decided to give them her mobile number as she knew she would be closing down the landline for her practice. She had also decided to inform some patients who ended in the period between her making her decision and the point where she informed the bulk of her patients. Anticipating that they might assume they could come back for more therapy, she let them know they could contact her and she would be able to refer them on. Hannah criticised herself for this. Her dilemma highlights the challenge of providing continuity as an independent practitioner:

> So perhaps that's my difficulty in letting go. I think that must be very distressing to find that your therapist has disappeared.

Groups

Two of the contributors worked with groups as well as individuals, but to support anonymity I have not identified them. Both of these therapists described the ending dilemma which is specific to group work: whether to close down the group or to hand it on. The gentler option of letting patients end in their own time can work for an individual therapist but not in a group setting.

> With a group it's not possible to fold down gradually – it's either handed on or you cut it off –so the option which you had with individuals doesn't exist. So you've got to face the music of either handing on or ending.

Handing on involved the very practical challenge of finding the right person who could do the specific time. If the group was handed on there would also be a question as to whether the same setting could be used.

As with the referral on of individuals, there was recognition of how the therapist's own needs and defences might play into these choices. The challenge of facing a group with the news of ending is understandably very daunting, and the sense of unfinished business and transference left unexplored is multiplied across several group members. One of the contributors was going to close her groups and she speculated about the likelihood of the group members meeting up with each other with the aim of running a self-help group. She reflected that in her experience this was a very difficult thing to achieve as it was so hard for the group to deal with transferences.

One contributor described the contrast between two groups she was running. The one with more neurotic patients was more able to work with the pain of ending and grieving, while another group with more troubled psychotic patients found that too hard:

> Two people have just walked – a couple of people have decided that they can't bear it. There are various reasons that they give, but I feel they can't bear it.

Stock Whitaker (1985), writing about less disturbed groups, points out the positive opportunity which ending brings for some risk-averse members: 'the wish to make use of the group for personal help while the group is still available can begin to outweigh the fears or worries that may be attached to confronting painful feelings or issues' (1985: 363). In contrast, she also acknowledges that the sense of threat in the group can escalate at this stage. Like the individual therapist, the conductor of a group is aiming to contain anxiety enough to allow exploration, but still hoping that the prospect of separation can be productive.

One contributor described an oscillating defensive process in the group:

> On the one hand they can be very defensively sort of upbeat and saying 'we are all going to set up a group of our own together' and then the next week they are having to . . . to feel the abandonment. The other thing is that for some people it's a kind of 'kick up the pants'. I don't mean that quite, but for some people there is no way out.

She went on to describe her sense that something was shifting in one group member who had been particularly stuck, that the kick appeared to have come at a stage when he could make use of it. In letting go of his group therapist he was finding he could let go of an unhelpful relationship in which he had been embedded for years. She spoke of another group member for whom the abandonment was not turning into a rich opportunity. This patient said bravely that it might do him good to be booted out, but his therapist feared that this was an avoidant defence:

> I think he will experience a loss but he will not experience the sadness, the anger – the whole process is going to go by the board for him. I will try to facilitate it but I don't think it's going to happen.

Her comments convey an acceptance of the imperfect outcomes which are inevitable in any ending.

Imposing an ending on couples

Much work with couples is to a shorter time frame than individual work, and it will often be possible to let the work end organically rather than being cut short by an imposed ending. However, for those couples who have wanted and needed to be in therapy for years, the impact of an imposed ending could be considerable. In such cases the losses for a couple will be slightly different from those experienced by individuals but the fear of not coping without therapy can be at least as severe. As well as the loss of the therapist as a container for the struggles of the two individuals, there will the loss of the therapist as a good object to the relationship. Siegel writes of the therapy becoming 'a valued object to each spouse and to the couple as a system' (1992: 185). At a certain stage in the transference this could feel as though the couple have lost the godmother who blesses their union. As well as feeding fears of the relationship breaking down, the ending may also underline the loss of the idealised relationship (Scharff and Scharff, 2004).

The couples who are likely to suffer most from this loss of a container are those who have strong mutual negative projections, yet have been committed to the relationship and through therapy have come to recognise the need to reintegrate the disowned parts of the self. Such a couple may rely on the weekly meeting and may have some reason to fear that their conflict will re-escalate without the witness and the affirmation for their joint struggle. The news of retirement signals loss of a place which both have come to trust, a safe space to unpack the destructive use they make of each other. One possible meaning to such a couple is that this parent, like earlier ones, is saying 'I wash my hands of your sibling rivalry'. As with individual clients, there may be a fantasy that the therapist is keeping on more favoured, less troublesome clients.

When ending is premature the couple may have achieved repair in some areas but not others. Often there can be a split between sexual and other functioning. If the couple came because they were not having sex, their sexual relationship might have been restored but a deeper fault line in the relationship might now be in full view. Contrastingly a couple may have improved their everyday relating but found that sex has tapered off. Assessment of where the couple have got to will naturally guide discussion about referral on, and for some couples this could be an opportunity to move to more focused work with a psychosexual therapist.

As the ending approaches, couples, like individuals, sometimes seem to lose the gains they have made. The transference message reaching the therapist might be 'You shouldn't leave us, we can't manage'. Boyd-Carpenter (2010a) writes of a heterosexual couple who had made considerable progress in withdrawing projection. She reports how the news of the imposed ending re-evoked their pattern of splitting, with the female partner being numb and the man manic and excited about possible new avenues. She recalls her countertransference and the pull to be caught up in the man's flight into adventure which matched her own hopefulness and interest in projects for her retirement. Recognising her countertransference for what it was enabled her to notice how their defence of splitting had re-emerged, and to support the couple in holding both the loss and the opportunity.

Retirement from organisations

Retirement from an organisation will vary in many ways from the closure of a private practice which is the focus of this book. When a therapist retires from an organisation (whether the NHS or a voluntary agency), continuity for clients is less problematic as there will be the possibility of referral on within the team and the organisation itself usually has a containing function. The therapist's sense of loss will depend in part on the state of the organisation. Where a clinician has come to a timely retirement and has a sense that the organisation is in good health, there may be satisfaction from having contributed to a going concern, though there could also be envy of colleagues who remain in post. Where the organisation is itself in crisis or decline, there may be a relief about getting out but also a deep sadness that the project as a whole is fading. One contributor who had been working for decades as a group analyst in an outpatient setting commented with great sadness:

> The service I'll be leaving is a very different kind of service from the one I came into.

When an institution closes there can be an impact on former as well as current patients. This was poignantly illustrated to me when a local children's hospital was being relocated and the old building was about to be converted into private housing. Parents of children who had died there over the preceding years were invited to a memorial event before the building closed, and they described how consoling they found this.

Sometimes organisations will be obliged to make staff redundant and to impose endings which are clearly detrimental to clinical needs. Withdrawal of funding is one very painful instance which may necessitate premature endings of treatment because a service is being cut. At a time when therapists may be invested in personal and organisational protest about the changes, the challenge will be to think carefully about the impact on patients. One imposed ending which should be anticipated and planned for is the ending of a trainee therapist's placement. Hopefully this would have been anticipated from the start of the contract so that the work was known to be time limited, and consequently in this sense it is not a breach of contract in the same way that retirement often is.

How ethical is it to take short-term clients during the period of notice?

I spoke to therapists who had worked with new patients on a time-limited basis while they worked their period of notice. These contracts were based on the therapist disclosing at the start of the work that they would be retiring at a specific time. While this worked well in some cases, with the anticipated ending enabling a good working through, it appeared that for more troubled clients this was not a good model and it seems critical for short-term clients to be very thoroughly assessed for suitability. Informing the clients about the time constraint does not itself provide any safeguard, as a novice patient has no way of knowing how much time she will need in therapy. Patients with a history of abandonment but little insight into their patterns might even grab at the chance to work with a therapist who will leave them. The title of a song comes to mind: 'If you won't leave me I'll find somebody who will' (Zevon, 1993).

Chapter 3

How do patients respond to being left?

The most difficult part was intruding into their narrative to bring it up . . . because with most of them it was almost as though I hadn't said it.

(Clementine)

'The analysand is asked to love and hate with abandon, an abandon that would be extremely reckless in any other context' (Mitchell, 2000: 133). In this vivid warning, Mitchell names the risk that patients are invited to take; he also reminds us that this is made possible because the therapist too is emotionally invested in the relationship. In focusing this chapter on the patient's response to the forced ending, I risk imposing an artificial separation on the feelings which flow in two directions between the analytic partners. I think this is justified as a way of narrating the experience of retirement, but it is important to keep the two parts of the whole in mind.

Attachment implications

In this chapter I refer to the range of psychoanalytic opinion about how much weight to give to the real relationship. This question has been debated over the decades since Bowlby's theory originally made him unpopular with mainstream psychoanalysis, but few now argue with the contention that attachment patterns evolve as an adaptation to the caregiver's style (Bowlby, 1969; Ainsworth *et al.*, 1978). Holmes has indicated the contribution that attachment theory has to offer to more classical schools: 'Psychoanalysis struggles to theorize the real relationship – while this is home base for attachment theory' (2010: 64). The therapist's capacity to bridge the two states of relating is always critical, but is particularly relevant for patients who are about to leave and lose the protected relationship of therapy, and will be having to conduct themselves purely in the wider world of real relationships. With the announcement of retirement, the real person of the therapist has crashed into the analytic space of therapy and therapists need to find a way to keep their balance when the frame which contained the dyad has taken a knock. Emma theorises this in her comments below: she describes owning what had happened but then drawing a fresh boundary in the new place where the therapist judges it needs to be held.

The reliability of the therapist is a key ingredient in the talking cure. If she becomes unexpectedly unavailable the patient is bound to experience attachment insecurity, even though this may be manifested in very different ways – including that of no apparent response. The threat to an attachment bond is described by Bowlby:

> Since the goal of attachment behaviour is to maintain an affectional bond, any situation that seems to be endangering the bond elicits action designed to preserve it; and the greater the danger of loss appears to be the more intense and varied are the actions elicited to prevent it.
>
> (1980: 42)

The unexpected news of ending will be easier to digest if the therapeutic couple have already been able to establish some degree of secure base. In this case the patient will have internalised some of the capacity for regulation which the therapist has offered and consequently will have increased their reflective function. The repeated experience of having recovered, with the therapist's help, from dysregulated states enhances the possibility of managing alone at times of intense stress.

The announcement of a unilateral move by the therapist is bound to undermine whatever level of secure base has been achieved, and the critical issue will be whether the pair can recover enough safety to explore the experience as they go through it. Ideally the therapy is the safe place in which the patient explores the challenges she faces 'outside' in the world as well as 'inside' in herself. Now that her proto-attachment figure has let her down, will the space be safe enough for the pair to explore this disappointment? For our most disturbed patients with disorganised patterns, the imposed ending may echo early attachment trauma when the person to whom the frightened child would have turned to for comfort was the very person who had hurt them. Understanding our patients' attachment patterns will help make sense of their explicit and implicit responses to the ending, and a comment by Clementine neatly sums up the dismissing and the preoccupied strategies. She describes clients as being:

either overwhelmed with things they want to tell you, or ... quite avoidant of the subject and don't want to face it.

To make sense of these responses from patients, we need to keep in mind how a client's attachment pattern may be interfacing with the stage at which they are working in the transference. Together these two factors would indicate how ready they are to 'leave home' and how deeply they may be protesting at an unconscious level. Attachment theory describes how some of our fiercest anger is mobilised in the hope of reconnecting with an attachment figure, and the anger is thus in the service of attachment (Bowlby, 1973). Kleinian theory offers an alternative way to understand the rage which abandonment might invoke. This perspective provides more sense of the wish to punish and destroy and reminds us how terrifying it is to be in that murderous state (Likierman, 2001). Kohut (1971) gives us another perspective on how pain becomes converted into aggression. He describes the intense dependency on a self-object which is being used as a substitute for missing parts of the patient's own psyche:

> They [self-objects] are not longed for but are needed in order to replace the functions of a segment of the mental apparatus which had not been established in childhood.
>
> (1971: 46)

In these theories where the therapist is seen variously as an attachment figure, a container or a self-object, there is a joint understanding that alongside, or behind, the anger lies fear. For a long-term client who has allowed their therapist to have this important psychic function, the news of the rupture will be alarming, for some it will bring terror.

We might anticipate that following the news of retirement, clients' experience may approximate to stages of grief (Kubler-Ross, 1970; Murray Parkes, 1972). First there may be a 'pre-protest' (Bembry and Ericson, 1999: 186), which would correspond to the initial numbness of mourning. Second, as the sense of abandonment registers the patient's customary attachment, insecurity may become visible (either the dismissing deactivation or the preoccupied hyper-activation of their attachment system) and we hear this in contributors' comments below. Thus there could be denial and withdrawal, or on the other hand, strategies aimed at demanding care and proximity, possibly through eliciting guilt. For a patient with a traumatic past there is likely to be a combination of these as the disorganised individual lacks a coherent strategy. For such patients who are not yet at a developmental stage where grieving is possible, communication may be through projection of unbearable states into the therapist. Somatic responses are also likely from clients who cannot symbolise their grief.

If things go well and distress is sufficiently contained, a third stage may see a period of deepening understanding. For some patients this exploration will be very rich and the forced ending can open up opportunities for growth, along with real sadness for what is being lost. However, in some other cases it appears that the therapy gets stuck in the protest or pre-protest stage. An example of this was described to me by someone whose therapist had imposed an ending for relocation. This former patient said that in their mind the therapy had ended at the moment their therapist shared the news. Perhaps one way of understanding this might be that the patient's distress was enacted by rendering the therapist impotent and irrelevant from that point. Where mourning is able to proceed there will be anger, guilt and sadness and acceptance of the real loss of the therapist. A further aspect may come into play as the patient begins to relish their sense of independence; there may be competitiveness as well as the satisfaction of maturity. Of course these 'stages' do not unfold sequentially and there is likely to be a fluctuation between these elements of the process. Although this chapter focuses on the patient's responses to the ending, we know that it is the conscious and unconscious interaction between therapist and client which determines outcome.

A case which illustrates this kind of grieving sequence is described by Holmes (1997). The therapist who was imposing an ending had one patient for whom the loss represented a particular challenge; this patient made a range of responses which we might think of as elements of mourning. Initially she denied the loss, and then she expressed aspects of mourning (insomnia and anxiety about not coping, including a terrible dream in which both her hands were cut off). Next she spoke of a possible replacement for the therapist – she had visited a doctor she had not seen for years. After that she listed the benefits of the therapy but then swung into denigrating it. Finally, as in terminal illness, there was even an element of bargaining where the patient weighed up the possibility of being allowed to visit the therapist in his new post.

When retirement is carefully planned, the announcement will probably involve a shock for the patient but there will then be time to process and prepare for the final parting. For some patients the moment when the news is first shared may be the point at which the abandonment feels most threatening; for this reason the therapist's management of that initial impact will be critical in order to avoid premature withdrawal regardless of whether this is an actual physical withdrawal or a psychic one.

A patient with a residual dismissing pattern knows unconsciously that they can protect themselves from vulnerability by minimising their feelings or diverting their attention. Patients who successfully deny their feelings about the imposed ending may be using defensive exclusion, which leads to dissociation of the painful feelings about loss, making them very hard to work through. Bowlby anticipated that individuals who avoid grieving *may* be at risk of distress being triggered by an association in the future, and of this being experienced psychically or physically. This view is supported in the writing on grief by Worden (1983: 94), who describes a 'masked grief reaction' which often leaks out through physical symptoms or acting out. In such cases a therapist needs to be alert to the possible emotional meaning in illness or chance accidents. Some critics of attachment theory feel that Bowlby gives too negative a view of denial as a functional defence, and Fraley and Shaver agree that he 'probably overestimated the extent to which suppression of grief is harmful' (1999: 754). Bowlby (1980) himself recognised that some very avoidant people have so little investment in relationships that they are able to let them go without suffering. Various examples of avoidant defences are mentioned below by contributors: simple denial of distress; deciding that it was time to leave anyway; developing a sudden interest in cognitive-behavioural therapy (CBT); and making an immediate request for the name of a new therapist.

For a patient with an ambivalent profile, the news that the attachment figure is departing will present a significant threat. There are likely to be explicit or implicit demands which convey blame; these could be particularly hard for the therapist to unpick as she would probably be also managing a 'real' sense of guilt. Clients in this group might use passive–aggressive strategies. One contributor spoke of a patient who was very reluctant to take details of a possible new therapist, but did so grudgingly on the very last day. Other indirect communications might be made through psychosomatic symptoms or regression. Another channel for transmitting feelings is the patient's speech pattern: discourse style can be a valuable indicator of attachment pattern. In one example below, it seems as though Denise's patient, who felt the need to go back each session to the subject of retirement, was manifesting a repetitious preoccupied/unresolved pattern.

Patients with a disorganised pattern of attachment are not so clearly represented in contributors' stories, and I wondered whether this might be because interviewees were very careful not to speak about distinctive cases. The pattern seemed occasionally to be visible in the aggressive response of clients who felt most threatened by the abandonment, such as that described by Patsy (below). Similar aggression was reported by Emma (Chapter 5), whose patient menaced her with the spectre of dire outcomes to the surgery she was about to undergo, and by Flora, who recalled one client who had attacked her mercilessly after she announced her pregnancy (Chapter 9).

The literature offers us some cases of this very troubled response. Dewald (1965) gave his patients five months' notice of his move to another city and his paper provides vignettes of his most disturbed patients. In one case, a patient with early attachment losses communicated her distress through threatening not to leave the office at the end of the hour. This patient sometimes clung physically to Dewald, and on one occasion fainted as she left the room. Dewald relates that together they were able to make sense of these desperate feelings and that, in this case, his departure became a catalyst for increased insight and ego strength. Weiss (1972) was also closing his practice to relocate, and he writes about a very troubled patient whose depression was so severe that Weiss briefly considered advising him to move to Denver with him in order to continue the treatment. It seems to me that concern for one particularly vulnerable patient is a pattern both in the literature and among my contributors. Clearly patients with a history of early parental loss could be re-traumatised by the imposed ending, but I wondered whether this identification of one patient as outstandingly vulnerable also served as a way for the therapist to manage her grief and regret in relation to her whole practice.

The narcissistic wound to the patient when a therapist 'calls time'

Schwarz (1974) sums up the break in the frame which a forced ending brings: 'In essence the guide who had contracted for this journey had resigned' (1974: 284). This is echoed by Glick (1987), who argues that an imposed termination intensifies the dynamics which occur in regular endings and will always be experienced as a narcissistic injury. Regardless of the reasons or circumstances of a forced termination, at some level the patient will struggle with the sense that the therapist has 'kicked him out' (1987: 450).

In a more formal tone, Limentani describes the injury as being to the frame but is clear about how serious the impingement is, referring to 'the inevitable scarring left by the attack on the setting and the very essence of the analytic process caused by the broken trust and promise' (1982: 420).

Craige (2002) surveyed former patients whose therapy had ended in a regular, unforced manner. Her respondents convey how significant the loss can be even when the ending has been voluntary. 'What I lost . . . it's immeasurable really, a relationship with someone who knew more about me than anyone else in my life, who was completely committed to understanding me' (2002: 507). Respondents in my study were not able to share details of cases for reasons of confidentiality, but they described their patients experiencing the following:

- abandonment and loss ('I am being left to cope alone'), leading to rage and sadness;
- rejection ('my therapist prefers to be with her own family'), leading to sadness;
- omnipotent guilt ('I've worn her out'), leading to triumph and unconscious despair at my destructiveness;
- protective feelings ('I'm worried about my therapist's fragility'), leading to despair about how alone this leaves me with my pain;
- liberation ('I'm going to reclaim my time, money and effort'), leading to relief and excitement.

One of the factors feeding into a patient's response will be the perceived age of the therapist: there might be a different set of fantasies when a healthy-looking 60-year-old announces her retirement than when a frail 80-year-old stops working. In the first case there might be more sense of being rejected, whereas in the second case there could be more sense of guilt. The length of notice given can also contribute to these fantasies. As Annette had suffered an earlier cancer she was particularly careful to give a long warning of the ending in order to signal an unhurried departure and avoid feeding the fantasy that she was about to die.

The patient's first-hand account of this narcissistic wound is given in an anonymous article written by a trainee, after the relocation of his analyst (Anonymous, 2001). In this case there were additional factors which enhanced the level of distress, but the paper is an important statement of how disturbing relocation can be. The writer points out that a patient does not relate to the analyst as one competent adult to another. 'In this regressed, dependent, and longing state, how is the analysand to experience the forced ending other than as a recapitulation of the ways he was abandoned earlier in life?' (2001: 51).

Denial and other avoidant/dismissing defences

Almost all my interviewees spoke about the importance of listening for protest at the imposed ending and for the need to watch out for patients 'letting them off' from their disappointment. This brought to mind Langs's (1994) warning that breaches in the frame will be marked by encoded messages in the patient's narrative even though she may be all the while *consciously* signifying acceptance of the situation.

We may think of denial as the opposite of mourning: mourning is about letting go and internalising the lost object, denial is about seeking substitutions. Leowald (1962) points out the contrasting forms that denial can take. Some people may leave very quickly in order to minimise the pain of separation while others may drag out the leave-taking in an effort to hold onto the person they are about to lose. The former group, whom we may think of as dismissing, are trying to deny the meaning and value of the person being lost: they are denying the past. The latter group, possibly with a preoccupied strategy, are trying to deny that the separation has to happen: they are denying the future. Clementine described how tricky it can be to confront denial and how the therapist's new agenda can distort the formerly unstructured process. She recalled challenging a client to recognise that their time together was passing away, only to recognise towards the end of the session that she had been missing a new, very real health concern that the client was wanting to bring that day:

> You have to be very aware of where people are at. I was missing the signals in my own concern to get it said.

Chapter 2 has already looked at the phenomenon of incredulity at the point of the announcement; reflections in this chapter are about denial as a sustained defence. Even though Alan was 86 when he gave his patients two years' notice, he recalled that:

> They all had the idea that I would change my mind: I belonged in that room, sitting there, and they would be coming there as long they wanted to.

Aarons (1975: 303) writes of 'a delusion of permanence' and Mary also reported her patients' fantasy that she would not age or die:

> The longing that the therapist would go on for ever and see them out and still be there.

Boyd-Carpenter (2010a) describes in detail a patient who believed the news but denied its meaning. After a violent and very deprived childhood, this patient had emerged with a tendency to attach himself to unattainable mother figures who repeated the uncaring exploitation of his own mother. He and Boyd-Carpenter had worked together for two years and the pattern had softened, but he responded to the news of his counsellor's retirement by denying that there was anything much to lose – he had been thinking of ending anyway. His attendance became very unreliable and in the countertransference Boyd-Carpenter felt she was a nuisance to him, she sensed she had become 'the demanding mother who had trapped him into coming when he didn't really have the time and that it would be a relief to get away from me' (2010a: 92).

Clementine suggests a distinction between avoidance of the ending and avoidance of the therapist who was imposing that ending:

> What I didn't find, and thought I might have found, was that people didn't develop avoidant ways of dealing with me ... This didn't happen and I think that in many cases this was because their defences against knowing that the ending was coming were pretty effective.

She went on to recall some of the strategies employed to achieve this defence:

> 'I hope you have a very happy retirement' and 'of course you need more time for yourself' – they defended against experiencing their own feelings by thinking about others.

Clementine was aware that at times patients had a genuine wish to convey warm wishes to her in an adult-to-adult way, while at other times she felt the goodwill could be a sign of the compulsive caregiving which Bowlby identified in insecure attachment.

Ambivalent/preoccupied responses

The resurgence of symptoms is reported as quite common in the ending phase and it makes sense to see this as a protest by the patient. As this is the kind of communication designed unconsciously to convey neediness and to elicit care, it may be understood as a form of ambivalent defence. Coltart (1996) suggests that this return of symptoms is part fear of launching out alone and part punishment of the therapist. She also movingly describes a reluctance to say goodbye to these parts of the self:

these demonstrations are a kind of leave-taking ceremony, in the presence of the only person who is likely to tolerate them, let alone understand them.

(1996: 153)

They also of course offer an opportunity for working through what had not been so accessible before the bombshell of the news. In contrast to these indirect care-seeking strategies, Denise told of a patient asking to come more frequently in the final months. This patient spoke of the impending retirement at every session, she feared being left abandoned and empty and so she hoped that extra sessions would fill her up. At the time when I met her, Denise was not sure whether to accede to this or just to explore this request.

One contributor spoke of a patient who reverted to a strongly passive–aggressive style, communicating largely through angry silences. Eventually she could agree that her anger must be connected to the ending though she could not feel the connection. She was very reluctant to accept a referral, but her therapist checked the availability of a colleague whom she hoped would be a good fit; on the very last day the patient said she would like the details. The patient's comment that the journey to the new therapist's home would not be 'too bad' seemed to be her way of acknowledging that she needed and wanted to continue the work.

Patsy spoke of a patient who had always had a challenging hostile transference. When this woman learned that Patsy was to retire, her anger intensified and Patsy recalled thinking after a session that she had just spent the worst hour of her life.

I just couldn't say anything to her, without it being ignored, or chewed up. And I think I was quite frightened; I ended up being a bit timid in those sessions, but she did respond well when I stopped being timid. But I was surprised how sad she was to end – and how sad I was to end too, in the end. So something shifted.

Mary also named anger as a key feature of this phase and pondered the very different ways that people managed it. She felt that while the anger was a challenge, it was balanced by the opportunities that were thrown up: the work was deeper and more urgent and she noted a keenness in herself to grasp opportunities and not let them escape. She also noted a complicated sequence of vulnerability, attack and defence in which patients experienced loss and rage and then a consequent need to deny these in order to protect both her and themselves:

I suppose [there was] the need to be hurtful back and protecting me from that and protecting themselves from knowing about it.

Patients making their own exit

Almost all patients were able to stay the course and work through to an ending, but several contributors recalled one client who had responded to the announcement with their own plans for leaving, often rationalised by finance or other practicalities. This kind of quick exit is what Glick (1987) calls a pre-emptive departure, and it may be an actual departure or an emotional withdrawal from the work. In Glick's words, 'The emotional bags are packed' (1987: 455). It may be particularly useful for supervisors to have this in mind when supporting therapists through retirement, because the supervisee's complicated feelings about leaving may inhibit full exploration of a client's disengagement.

Coltart (1996) writes with passion about patients who try to snatch away control by leaving suddenly:

> I believe that no effort should be spared to get a patient back who has done a runner at this point; forget your dignity and analytic persona.
>
> (1996: 154)

Hannah recalled a patient who had ended quite soon after her announcement and she offered an interesting reflection on how she had handled his 'flight'. His overt reason for ending was financial, but Hannah felt it was clear that he had felt abandoned and had not been able to acknowledge the meaning of the relationship. She described her response:

> I suppose that I wasn't as rigorous in pointing out why he was going as I would have been if I hadn't been retiring. If I had been continuing with the work I might have pressed harder for us to look at the issues.

In a case with some parallels, Mary recalled a patient who developed the idea of ending during the period when she had decided she would retire, but had not yet made the announcement. She was tempted to let him go and avoid imposing the ending on him, but she was clear that this patient was not ready to end:

> I do remember thinking when he first thought of ending, 'It would be so easy to go with it now and accept it' but I knew that it would have

been a defensive ending. I know that feeling of thinking 'this would be really handy – I could help him to leave now'.

Clementine spoke of a truncated ending with a patient who cancelled his very last session. She wrote to ask whether he would like to arrange another session, and when there was no response she felt very sad as this echoed his life story of abandonment. She took some comfort from her belief that he had made huge progress after nine years of hard work between them, and then later there was a heartening follow up to the story. Clementine was having lunch with an ex-colleague when she glimpsed this former patient entering the café; she looked away, not wanting to confront him, but he purposefully came over to greet her and say how well she looked and to share a little of his news.

Denise spoke of one patient who did not physically leave early but signalled that she had packed her bags and thus achieved the emotional withdrawal which Glick (1987) mentions. This had been a very long therapy, which Denise felt had reached a standstill. She had often challenged the patient that it might be time to leave but had not been able to engage the patient in working towards an ending. Denise describes this same bleakness between them when she announced her retirement:

> She responded 'Oh', with a big smile, and didn't address it at all. And then she came up with the idea that when we finish she'd like CBT.

It is possible that for some patients, making a proactive early ending might be the best that can be managed. Nicola felt this was the case for one particularly vulnerable long-term patient, 'M', who had been coming for some years. At assessment, M's very bleak attachment history had been apparent. Because of this and because Nicola expected to retire in five years, she had offered to refer 'M' on for more intensive analytic treatment. 'M' had chosen to stay but four years later, when Nicola confirmed that they would end in a year's time, the news was no less painful. Nicola and 'M' worked on it together for some months until unexpectedly an email arrived from 'M'. She wrote that it was too painful for her to carry on but asked whether she could have a photograph of Nicola's garden. Often in sessions 'M' had avoided eye contact but had gazed into the garden. Nicola responded with a photograph but felt regretful that they had not been able to keep working through the distress of the ending. She took some comfort from her supervisor's comment that it had been valuable for 'M' to have a good enough ending, under her own control, in contrast to the many unhappy endings which had scarred her childhood.

One of Alice's cases also reflects this possibility that, for some clients, the best way to handle an imposed ending might be to take back some control. Alice felt it was particularly important for vulnerable clients to have some autonomy through the choice of the actual ending date. She let them know that she would be moving out of London, that the house would be on the market and they could decide together on a date to end. The patient whom she had seen the longest was the one who wanted to go first:

> That was important because of his history of adoption. So we worked on what would be best for him and he chose the date. So I was able to co-create the endings for people.

Comments from Beatrice indicate the range of factors which surfaced when she announced her retirement. As well as the concerns for her health and the fear of having been too much, there was anxiety that siblings had been preferred and also a desperate hope to manage the abandoning parent by being 'good':

> Others were very anxious that I could be displeased with them and if they tried harder would I would still see them – and many were concerned whether I was stopping altogether. 'Do you want to get rid just of me?'

How ready is each patient to 'leave home'?

In her paper on relocation, Martinez (1989) considers the developmental stage of each patient and the potential harm if they are forced to distinguish prematurely between the real and the transference object. Gervais (1994) also recognises how the impact of ending will depend on the stage of the work. He is writing after a serious illness resulted in a *sudden* break in his work (and thus a different circumstance from retirement), but his concern is also relevant to patients who are being 'retired':

> The analysands, however, may be at different phases or stages of their analyses in terms of time, and they may be in a variety of transferential moods . . . There is uncertainty: Have I maimed or killed my analyst? Will my analyst take with him parts of me that I can never recover?
>
> (1994: 200)

This last point would seem to be profoundly important and therefore might need naming by the therapist. If important parts of the self are at that point being projected into the therapist, there may be an unconscious panic as to how it can be possible to live separately from this other being who carries my hatred, my despair and whatever loving parts of the self may also have been split off. Gervais's other point, the fear of having harmed the therapist, is mentioned by Beatrice. One of her patients responded with relief to the news of her retirement and it became clear that he had been unconsciously carrying great anxiety about her ageing. Apparently in this case, news of retirement had not caused the fantasy but had enabled it to be spoken:

> I think he struggled with a deep fear that I would die on him and it would be his fault. The news of my decision to retire brought all this into the open.

If ending represents a kind of 'test' of the work that has been achieved in the therapy, then when the ending is an imposed one, the test is a particularly harsh one and may be set too high for some patients. When an individual is not ready to mourn, has not internalised enough, cannot let go of the idealisation and accept the disappointments of reality, then an imposed ending will represent intrusion and impingement. Craige (2002) counsels that in normal circumstances, before setting a date to end, the therapist needs to consider how well equipped the patient is to cope with ending. In particular she needs to assess whether his capacity for both self-analysis and holding onto the positive image of the therapist are strong enough to withstand the disruption of ending.

Because an imposed ending creates a narcissistic injury it threatens the illusion of omnipotent control and forces the recognition of separateness, whether or not the patient is ready for this. Winnicott's thoughts on gradual disillusionment are relevant here: 'The mere ending of breastfeeding is not a weaning' (1953: 13). In his terms, the intrusion of the therapist's needs will represent an impingement (1962b/1990) or a premature challenge to omnipotence (1969/1989). Weiss (1972) uses a metaphor from a later stage of development to convey the value of taking time over separation. He comments that 'The healthy adolescent wishes to leave home . . . but he also wishes to know that the parents are around for support or help if this should be necessary' (1972: 510).

These many references to developmental stages are helpful, but Schwarz (1974) uses a travelling metaphor to particularly good effect. He suggests that regression is the passport by which the client revisits the troubling past and when an ending is imposed then this passport is being revoked 'before the analysand and the analyst have reached their agreed upon destination' (1974: 284).

What happens to the transference? Holding the real and the symbolic

Firestein's (1974) review of the literature on ending suggests that the assessment of the transference is the most contentious area. Some therapists consider that transference should be resolved before ending is agreed, while others see the experience of ending as being essential to the continued working through of transference. Others, including myself, would contend that a residue of transference will remain. I find a comment by Norman, Blacker, Oremland and Barrett (1976) very helpful. They suggest that the transference is not exhausted but 'Rather, the patient experiences, understands, and senses varying degrees of control of it' (1976: 491). This sense of a progressive understanding is in line with Murdin's (2000) writing about endings. She says it is important that the dissolving of the idealising transference be a continuous process throughout the therapy, and not a sudden change which is visited on the patient at the end. She suggests that a sudden disillusionment brings into question the sincerity of what has gone before and in effect says, 'OK, now we are finishing, you are grown up enough to know that there is no Father Christmas, although I thought it was good for you to believe in him for a while' (2000: 142).

There is a difficult assessment to be made about timing the ending: how long does each patient need to work through the transference so that they can leave without a part of themselves forever yearning for a lost home? With limited time remaining, therapists will prioritise that aspect of the work which they believe most crucial to the patient and those working in a classical style will tend to have most concern for the transference. Kaplan, Weiss, Harris and Dick (1994) describe what they see as the risk.

> In an attempt to adapt to the sudden loss of the as-if quality of the analytic process and situation the patient may focus defensively on [the] analyst as real object in order to avoid the transferential component.
>
> (1994: 255)

Weiss (1972) makes a very surprising comment which appears to minimise the importance of the rupture. He writes that 'The analyst is primarily a transference figure, and a transference figure can be replaced, not without pain, but without harm to the patient' (1972: 512). For psychoanalytic therapists working in a less classical style, this comment seems to deny that the therapist has an important role as an attachment figure and that there is a real relationship running in tandem with the transference.

Beatrice indicated how important it is to separate out the real from the symbolic.

> Giving plenty of time to the ending allows us an opportunity to clarify what is fantasy (for example the fear that they are killing me) and what is reality (that I'm old).

Her comments suggest a patient unpicking of fantasy, and this was particularly evident around the very real issue of her age, which was being highlighted by her retirement. She emphasised the opportunity thrown up by patients' anxiety about her age, provided that the meaning of their concerns was explored rather than closed down with answers or reassurance:

> My aim is to understand the patient's great concern about me, and I and the patient try to find out a bit more about this.

> Because the patients of course feel very let down and also feel unloved, and they also of course don't believe what you say. So some were very anxious – 'What is wrong with you? Why now?' And so on.

When illness in the therapist perturbs the connection between transference and reality

For Emma and Celia, whose ending was overshadowed by illness, there were times when the reality of their experience overshadowed the symbolic meaning. Emma was forthright about the challenge she had faced as she began the closure of her practice under threat of terminal illness. She was having to impose an ending on patients at the same time as she was dealing with the physical and emotional repercussions of cancer and its treatment:

> Now that was a nightmare; it was a very difficult term's work that autumn.

She recounts that all of her patients came to the assumption that she had cancer and describes how she managed this change in the frame:

> One could have explored what the fantasy was about cancer, but then again it was true. So I decided to say, 'Yes, I'm afraid it is cancer'. Because my theory has always been that when the frame is broken by the therapist, rather than by the patient, one should come clean about the situation in the real world. So that is what happened there.

Having disclosed her cancer, she then had to deal with questions about what sort of cancer. She saw these detailed questions as distinct and followed them up as fantasies:

> I said 'I'm not trying to be difficult by not telling you but I've told you what I need to tell you and what you need to know, and that's going to be enough'. That's where I decided to make a fresh boundary.

Emma added that it had been rewarding work because there was so much to do:

> There was something about it that was rather refreshing because ... we did have life and death issues, it wasn't at all boring and the fact of their loss of me, my loss of them, the possibility of my death.

The challenge brought opportunities:

> In a way it demystified cancer – that I was sitting here with cancer and going on being the same person. One of them said to me that what one fears with getting ill and dying is becoming a different person – 'and that hasn't happened to you'.

Celia's retirement was also taking place under pressure of illness and I was mindful that I was inviting her to make very painful disclosures, but she was clear that she wished to share this story. It was striking how she deployed her capacity for therapeutic reflection to explore the experience of losing that capacity. She framed the challenge in terms of learning:

> I feel that increasingly I want to withdraw from life ... Well I feel as if I am withdrawing ... But also I think ... I don't know really what the withdrawal consists of but maybe it is partly a sort of shame I feel because I am not any longer the person that I used to be; already I can see that now compared to how I used to be ... I feel that after a certain amount of time I can't do that any longer and I have to go into retreat in order to recuperate in order to be there for the next time. That's what I've learnt about myself ... I think it is effective to withdraw a bit. I've always been more active than it is probably good for me to be.

Celia specifically applied this last comment to her style as a therapist, explaining that she is tending to intervene less and the impact seems positive. Her observation made a lot of sense to me because I can recognise a more trivial version of that in myself: when I feel under the weather I tend to say less and the outcome often seems better.

Envy of the retiring therapist

A number of contributors voiced a sense of envious resentment from patients which they said was mostly conveyed in tone of voice. One of Annette's patients had evolved a fantasy of Annette as a gardener, which sounded to me like a creative way of managing envy and achieving comfort: she pictured Annette transferring her caring attention to plants:

> There was an idea that I would be spending a lot of time gardening – the idea that I could nurture other things.

When the therapist is relocating rather than retiring, there may be even more scope for envy about the desirable new life she is stepping into. As Alice's decision to move had arisen out of her partner's terminal illness, the resentment may have been hard to bear.

> A lot of them were envious – they had these fantasies of what one does living in the country . . . I told them I'd be moving out and not keeping a practice in London – because some of them asked me to.

These brief allusions to envy provide scant evidence, so it is all the more valuable to have a first-hand account from Carol of the resentment she felt about the retirement of her own therapist:

> I think part of me was jealous that she could be so clear about leaving the profession, so I was a bit jealous. It was not just a personal abandonment, it was the professional thing as well, it was bigger than just me. It was 'How could she just leave the profession?' I felt quite resentful that she was leaving so happily – she might not have been for all I knew, but she seemed really clear and unambivalent.

In the following reminiscence, Carol's voice tailed off as she recalled the painful feeling that her therapist had had better things to do than sit and listen to her:

> And here is this person waltzing off quite happily. I remember her saying 'I'm going to be doing other things' and I didn't ask her what but I thought . . .

Demographic issues affecting clients' experience of loss

In a study looking at patients' reactions to the death of their analyst, Lord, Ritvo and Solnit (1978) identified factors which influence the outcome of this loss. The sudden death of their therapist is a more shocking threat to patients than a planned retirement, but their research is still interesting. Unsurprisingly they found that early attachment losses were a clear cause of vulnerability, as were narcissistic qualities which may make the helplessness unbearable. An interesting finding was that older patients were most badly affected. 'One could speculate that their anguish was heightened in part from a realistic fear that an opportunity to resolve their difficulties had been irrevocably lost' (1978: 196). It seems likely that the patient's age may similarly impact on their experience of the therapist's retirement: for the older patient who was not ready to end therapy and who needs referral on, this could be a more daunting loss. The retirement of the ageing therapist presents all patients with the spectre of their own ageing and death, but this may be more easily denied by the younger patients.

As well as those patients whose early broken attachments make them clearly vulnerable to subsequent rejection, we might consider whether patients from minority groups might also be at a disadvantage. When a patient is less privileged than their therapist, in terms of social class or ethnicity or any of the other markers of power and status, there will potentially be additional dynamics in play. In the case of a working-class patient, the possible sense of the therapist as an authority figure may make it particularly hard for that patient to 'mind' about being abandoned; the implicit belief may be that middle-class people get to do as they please. If the resentment and pain about that lifelong experience can be allowed into awareness and processed, this would be the kind of 'bonus' that an imposed ending sometimes brings. A patient from a black or minority ethnic group working with a white therapist is seeking help from a member of an oppressor group, and such a dyad will have had to work through the meaning of the therapist's knowledge and power. An implicit fear of exploitation may become very real in the face of the therapist's 'high-handed' action of announcing a unilateral ending. As in any clinical work where an 'outside' power differential is operating, it is incumbent on the therapist to tentatively name this rather than relying on the client to take responsibility for exploring an oppressive dynamic.

Chapter 4

How to manage the ending?

Even if I retire and the treatment is cut short, if we can achieve a good ending with a patient then there is more chance that the experience we have shared over the years will stay with them.

(Beatrice)

I know I'm not finished, but I've got my tool kit now.

(Mary's patient)

Picture a client who has been 'retired' and leaves his therapist's office with the name of a possible new therapist carefully selected by her. Now imagine different potential narratives diverging from this moment, as in the film *Sliding Doors* (Howitt, 1998). In one, the client keeps the piece of paper with the referral details, and in another these contact details are lost. In the first story the client starts working with a new therapist and in time makes a powerful connection, is able to see good and bad in the old therapy and to continue to mature and grow. In the other story, where he does not get help from a second therapist, he might become quite depressed and withdraw from friends. Of course, another possibility is that this particular client loses the note because part of him feels ready to be free of therapy and is secretly excited to be rid of it. This new kind of energy is picked up by a colleague at work and a romance is born – his first, long-postponed, adult relationship.

Attachment implications

What can attachment theory tell us about the patient's readiness to end? In unforced endings we hope that patients who presented with anxious ambivalent traits have gained confidence in their ability to self-regulate and have become less dependent on the therapist. For those patients who presented with high attachment avoidance we hope for increased capacity for intimacy and trust. In a paper on regular endings, Holmes (1997) considers the tendency for therapists to end too soon with dismissing patients and to go on too long with preoccupied ones. This imbalance is especially likely if the therapist's own pattern matches that of the patient, overemphasising either structure or empathy. Holmes (1997) sums up the aim of therapy in attachment terms as the task of setting up a secure base, both in the reality of the therapy and in the internal world of the patient. 'A secure base arises partly out of the responsiveness and attunement provided by the therapist, partly from her capacity to accept and metabolize protest and anger' (1997: 167). Another sign of readiness to end might be reflective function (Fonagy and Target 1997). This capacity is a very telling measure of security because unlike introspection or self-awareness, which are more deliberate processes, 'reflective function is to do with the way affects are pre-reflectively processed' (1997: 680).

By noticing and exploring how our patients manage ordinary holiday breaks and the endings of each 50-minute encounter, we gain a sense of how each of them copes with separation. Typically the return to therapy after a regular break may cause patients with a dismissing pattern to question whether they want to continue, while those with preoccupied traits would be more likely to emphasise their need for sessions and possibly evoke guilt in the therapist. We could expect that by the time of retirement, therapist and client will have a joint sense of how an imposed ending will impact.

As the patient's capacity to manage breaks increases, we may see this as a signal of readiness to end but we also know that patients can learn to manage the *expected* breaks. It is the unexpected which can cause dismay. Many of us have had the experience of needing to make a very modest change in session times and then being taken off-guard by the strength of protest. Such striking responses remind us that for this patient the frame is still serving a profound holding purpose. Clearly for patients who are troubled by minor changes in the frame, the news of an imposed ending will have a considerable impact.

For any client and therapist, the very last session is usually a poignant time, as they move towards the final transition back into the real world. For the retiring therapist these final partings are likely to carry intense feeling, and perhaps in the therapist's very last session it will feel strange to keep on doing the work up to the last minute. The therapist's understanding of the frame will guide how she manages the final goodbyes and the message she implicitly, and perhaps explicitly, gives the clients about the future frame. In regular endings, clients may have fantasies about the possibility of becoming friends once sessions are over and this hope may seem even more tantalising when the therapist is known to be retiring. We may imagine a client earnestly reasoning: 'Since you won't be a therapist any more, why shouldn't we meet for coffee?' At least by this stage the client will be familiar with the experience of her therapist holding a boundary with empathy and respect so that the client's longing can be thought about without the feared humiliation raining down on her.

In her research into post-termination experience, Conway (1999) found that the build-up towards the ending carried a special meaning in patients' long-term experience. This was particularly true on the issue of boundaries. Conway reports how one former patient recalled her struggle to believe that the relationship really was ending, and the anecdote speaks poignantly of the challenge which faces all patients who have had a deep attachment to their therapist. This patient had plied her therapist with various fantasies and requests, eventually saying,

> What if we were in adjoining beds in an old people's home, you know, when we're about 90. Still no conversation? I mean, how far are you going to take this no interaction with me?
>
> (Conway, 1999: 569)

Mindfulness of attachment dynamics can usefully inform the many decisions involved in referral on. As the literature explored in this chapter indicates, therapists have quite different policies on referral, which would suggest that decisions are based as much on the theoretical perspective of the therapist as on the individual needs of the patient. The first question is whether the patient has done enough work for them to make a full ending at this point. The key indicators will be the degree of self-regulation, reflective function and internalised secure base. If therapist and patient initially have different hunches about this, the working through of this difference might itself be very fruitful. If the decision is to go for more therapy, the second question is: how soon? This is an issue for which some writers and contributors had fixed policies. Where contributors explored with each individual the meaning to them of either moving swiftly on or taking a break first, this seems to have contributed to a good outcome. In a comment below, Beatrice describes making different arrangements for one young patient. She felt this young woman's story made it particularly critical that she would not be exposed to illness or collapse in her therapist and they therefore negotiated a relatively early ending and referral on. Most patients prefer the referral to come from their therapist, but some want to feel that they have found their own person and perhaps to have the benefit of a different kind of therapy. Understanding what this means in each case will be interesting.

A therapist who takes on a patient who has been forced to end will have their own views on how long a gap is appropriate, or whether it may be helpful for the patient to come to see them prior to ending with their retiring therapist. They will expect signs of grief and protest from the new patient, however well hidden these may be. Theorists and researchers are conflicted about the concept of anticipatory grieving, but however much mourning can be done in advance, there will be a critical transition. Any bereaved person fears that they have lost not just the single person who has died or gone, but also the internalised form of that person. When those internalised forms have never felt sufficiently secure then the threat of internal loss is greater and so is the risk of complicated and chronic grief.

Referral on

As the retiring therapist thinks with the client about the usefulness of referral on, they are weighing up how far they have got together and how much remains to be done. We long for perfect endings even though we know that psychic and emotional work is never completed. 'Good enough' is perhaps when patients leave with enough reflective function and ego strength to continue a reparative trajectory. There will always be an element of uncertainty or ambivalence about ending, and it would be a mistake to idealise 'natural' endings which are not imposed. The considerable overlap between imposed and voluntary endings is indicated by Coltart, who says of the latter 'there is a phase when it feels as though it is the therapist's doing' (1996: 152). The idea of a 'completed' analysis comes to us from an era where analytic work was measured in months rather than years (Mitchell, 1993). Speaking from that period, Ferenczi (1927/1955: 86) informs us that the concept was always of limited use: 'If I am asked whether I can point to many such complete analysis, my answer must be no.'

In the literature and among contributors I found a range of ideas about referral on. Dewald (1965) and Weiss (1972) referred on only a small minority of their patients whereas Martinez (1989) referred all those who were not ready to terminate and suggested that the choice not to refer might reflect defensiveness in the therapist. I felt that if defensiveness were operating perhaps this could work either for or against referring on. If guilt feelings are heavy the therapist may counter these with a speedy referral on, or there might be a reluctance to make a referral as the act of doing so makes the abandonment seem more real. Another resistance to referring on might be an unwillingness to have one's work 'inspected' by a colleague, especially as there has been a failure to complete the contract.

As well as this difference of opinion on the overall desirability of referring on, there was difference in terms of how to manage it. Several interviewees and writers report that it worked well for patients to meet the new therapist before having to let go of the old one. It was usually felt that the benefit of achieving a good placement outweighed the risk of splitting between the two analysts. Martinez (1989) found that her patients were helped by having one or two sessions with the new therapist while still seeing her. She asserts that this assisted their mourning for what they were losing. It also provided an opportunity for patients to articulate their disappointment in the new therapist. Martinez says that the transference in their remarks was obvious, and 'This reaction yielded easily to interpretation, as most patients were pre-consciously aware of its defensive character' (1989: 106). She reports one patient as returning from such an initial visit adamant that the proposed new therapy would not work out and, on reflection, Martinez had felt that the suggestion she had made had not been appropriate. She could recognise that frustration in her countertransference had coloured her initial choice.

A contrasting view suggests that focusing too early on the idea of a new therapist may spare the dyad from acknowledging the difficult feelings which they need to be sitting with. Denise mentioned the risk of the referral serving as a way of avoiding the ending with the retiring therapist:

> I don't want to confuse the ending with me and the referral on – making it a seamless thing where they just change from one to the other.

The predominant view among participants was that the process of fixing an ending date and possible referral on was unique to each patient. Contributors were attentive to the degree of anxiety in each patient and most were flexible about whether there was a gap. A few clients wanted to look for a different kind of therapy. In some cases the therapist believed this to be more of a protest or defence, as happened with Denise's patient who said she wanted to do CBT next. In other cases the client's desire for change appeared to be a constructive move, an example being a patient of Hannah's who felt that she wanted to move on to group therapy.

Clementine conveyed the effort involved in the many stages of referring a client, including the thought and research to find therapists for those patients who needed an experienced therapist but at a low fee.

The other whole issue was discussing with them whether they wanted to try and finish therapy, or whether they wanted to be introduced to someone else – and the process of getting there and finding that person if they wanted it, which most of them did.

In one case the task of helping with a referral had been exceptionally time consuming. Clementine had provided six introductions to possible therapists. Eventually one was accepted, and there was then a false start before finally a new relationship that settled.

When Emma made the emergency closure of her practice, the majority of patients had not wanted a referral on. She let them know that if they changed their minds she would try to help them subsequently and she had given them her email and mobile details. She felt that in doing this she was making an adaption to the psychoanalytic frame, but she conveyed that in this dilemma she had felt that contact beyond the frame was the right course. Annette also indicated that referral on may happen after the moment of retirement. She felt that a gap would be appropriate for her very long-term patient, but she felt that the most important thing was to signal her permission for him to go on and gain benefit with another therapist. Emma also addressed this issue of loyalty to the old therapist, and she noted the particular danger of this when the therapist is retiring suddenly through illness, as she was:

> There was a degree of 'Oh, no I don't want to go and see someone else' which had to be worked with. To what degree it was a sort of cry of loyalty to a sinking ship and to what degree it was that really we had done the work and maybe we should have ended before. And in some cases, we worked out, this was a moment when they could end, when they couldn't have ended otherwise. This drew a line under it for them without either of us having to say 'Yes we will end', as a decision.

Emma indicates here, what the literature maintains, that the imposed ending had sometimes provided a valuable opportunity for bringing the work to a close.

The final session

Perhaps it would be fair to say that the patient has a need for a good enough ending but the therapist often secretly hopes for a perfect one. If we work long term we do not make a high number of endings and our skills may not be that well honed, yet both therapist and patient expect a lot of the final encounter. In our conscious mind this last meeting is a key factor in how the work will be rated. Viorst's (1982) research confirms this emphasis on achieving a good ending. One of her interviewees provided a poignant anecdote from the last session of a woman who had made huge progress in the therapy but had always denied her transferential longing for her therapist. At the last minute the patient announced, 'I always had the idea that I was going to marry you, but it's not going to be' (1982: 415). This perhaps stands as a warning that when there are significant unworked areas these cannot be dealt with at the last minute. Such reminders of our fallibility may have extra weight when we are at the end of our career and there is no opportunity to 'try again'.

Writing about endings in general, Murdin (2000) indicates the heavy longing and expectation which the final parting carries. 'It is a very private moment and we do not know much about what happens, although it is likely that there is often a wish on both sides to express the inexpressible at the last moment' (2000: 147).

Just as a first session may present all the elements which will be worked on over the years and the opening of each session sets the theme for that hour, so the way a client ends each session may give us clues to how the eventual ending will be managed. It is interesting to consider a corresponding pattern in the therapist. Some therapists may diffuse the intensity of sessions towards the end of each 50 minutes and may correspondingly feel it is appropriate to dilute the intensity in the closing months of the work. Others feel they serve the patient better by offering a rigorous analysis to the last moment. Murdin (2000) points out how the pressure of the ending may lure us away from our normal understanding of what helps a patient: 'When we are in the endgame, we may be tempted to try to give something extra' (2000: 147). Perhaps the best we can aim for is to offer what that particular patient can best use at that point.

If former patients continue to draw support from the idea that their therapist is still practising and still working in that same familiar room, how do they feel walking away from their last session knowing that the therapist is shutting up shop? None of the contributors had much that they wanted to say about the final sessions with patients, and this seems in tune with Murdin's comment about 'the inexpressible'. One unsurprising theme was that several therapists indicated that they had adjusted the frame to receive gifts or other appreciative communications. Annette described the last session and the last communication from her very last patient – a man she had seen for many years:

> I gave him a hug – or he gave me a hug. I think it was acknowledge-ment on both our parts that we had meant something to each other.

He was very clear that he wouldn't forget me and he didn't expect me to forget him either.

Patients' and therapists' anxiety over discontinuity

When a patient ends treatment in a therapy organisation they have the comfort of knowing that the location and provider of their therapy is likely to continue in existence indefinitely, and this was briefly discussed in Chapter 2. Clients may draw an implicit strength from knowing that this aspect of the frame still endures, and there may also be a comfort from knowing that they could return one day for more help. There may be illusion in this comfort, but it is a tangible source of continuity which may help to support the internalised therapeutic figure which we hope they also have.

Patients who have been seeing their therapists in private practice will not have the background presence of an institution to help support their internalised good object. When the therapist works in a rented office there may be less investment in the surroundings. If patients are seen in a room in the therapist's own home, this tends to evoke more fantasies which mean that the setting becomes woven into the patient's internalisation of the therapist. When the therapist is retiring and possibly moving house as well, then the whole of the former frame is being dismantled. Therapists are mindful of the impact of changes to the setting and Clementine, for example, had pondered the impact on former patients of seeing a 'for sale' board outside her house.

Galatzer-Levy (2004) contends that the most common post-termination fantasy is that the analyst is always there and available if needed. This seems to be confirmed by comments by several contributors who report enquiries by patients about their future health and location. Mary identified the existential issues which can prompt former patients to contact their therapist: she suggested that they might want to see whether the therapist is still alive, or to share news of a new baby. She mused that patients would have the possibility of contacting her through registers and then realised that she would not be on a register. One of Denise's patients voiced this kind of anxiety about what would become of her:

> I had one client who said to me, 'I always thought I would know if you died, but if you retire, can I still know?'

Denise had said this would not be possible and made the point to me that her family could not be responsible for letting past patients know of her death. She linked the patient's concern to attachment needs:

You can interpret all the murderous feelings but there is something very powerful in terms of the attachment and dependency.

Another colleague, Anna, told of this 'need to know' taking another form. Anna had worked for over 10 years in a successful therapy with a patient, 'P', who was diagnosed with cancer at the very end of the therapy. P had been able to cope with the illness and they went ahead with the ending. Many months later Anna had a call from the patient's sister who said she did not know who she was speaking to, but P had specifically left instructions that Anna should be informed of her death. Anna knew that the sister on the other end of the line would want to know who she was, but she just thanked her for contacting her and for carrying out P's wishes. She thus maintained confidentiality for her former patient.

In her endings over previous years, Clementine had anticipated her retirement and the possible dilemma this could pose regarding patients who hoped to come back for more work. She had taken care not to imply she would be there for ever:

> I had always said to people when they left, 'You may want to have some more therapy in the future and I don't know if I'll still be working'. Remember I was obviously not a young person.

Clementine recalled managing the final stages of client contact after sessions were over:

> I talked to people about whether they would like to know if I moved and I know I had two or three Christmas cards soon after the endings and I replied with my new address and a card. People were so different – I didn't do the same with every single person, I very much judged it on the person.

Nicola also spoke of making decisions according to each patient's situation. She was moving house at the point of retirement but was not intending to give out her change of address in a general way. She said she would consider with each patient what this would mean and spoke of one long-term patient who asked whether she could send a Christmas card:

> I think that they want to know where you are so they can place you. And it's hard for them if they don't know where I'll be.

Through a related anecdote, Nicola highlighted the universality of this existential concern about time and place. She associated this need to know with the attachment behaviour of her four-year-old grandson to whom she was very close: when he chatted to her on the phone he always liked to ask, 'Where are you Nana?' Beatrice had a patient who had guessed that she would move house after the ending and was desperate to know where she would be. They worked on analysing the meaning of this and finally Beatrice agreed to let the patient know when she moved. When she did this the patient wrote a brief and touching 'thank you', while Beatrice felt the exchange of notes had helped she added her reservations:

> There was something unfinished in our therapeutic work. This patient did not feel able to turn to her inner representation of me and feel held and nurtured. She still needed outside reference points to feel safe.

Beatrice's comment reflects those from the literature which emphasise the dual nature of the loss. Alice, who was relocating, also faced this task of keeping real and symbolic needs in mind as she made logistical decisions. She chose not to inform clients of her new address and found the best way for her to manage ongoing contact was through her website, from which she can write back a few lines. She described the agreement she had come to with one former student:

> She doesn't know where I live now, but she sends an email – a Christmas update. We talked about that, that she could hold me in mind – and she holds the boundaries . . .

Alice also addressed the issue of clients who had ended long before her relocation:

> Obviously I'd had former clients who used to send me a Christmas card, so I took to supervision what to do about them, when I was moving. Eventually I wouldn't have re-directed mail. So what I did was send them a brief note to say I'd moved and they could contact me through the website – and I didn't hear from them again.

In contrast to the minimal comments about final sessions, participants spoke in some detail about questions of post-termination contact. I am aware that this focus may have been partly guided by their sense of my interest as I was particularly curious about this boundary. Most interviewees mentioned patients who have in the past returned for further work, and they recognised that this opportunity could not be offered to their final cohort of patients. The issue is not a small one. Hartlaub, Martin and Rhine

(1986) studied the frequency with which patients contacted their analysts post-termination and found that as many as two-thirds of those considered to have had a successful analysis made some kind of contact. Craige (2002) suggests that when access is denied to recently ended patients this may be harmful, and Pedder (1988) put this in the context of the young person leaving home: in the course of separating they may want to come and go more than once.

Frommer (2009) recounts a poignant case which illustrates how complex the ethical dilemmas can become once the frame is removed. The patient had lost his mother at a young age without the chance to say goodbye and later in life he had bolted from treatment to avoid the anger he felt towards his therapist. A year later, when this former therapist was dying, she realised that he would be likely to hear of her death on the grapevine. She decided to contact him, saying that she 'did not want to leave without saying goodbye and offering him a session in which they could try to resolve their relationship in a better way' (2009: 123). Although this former patient had not wanted to see the therapist, her intervention had been reparative for him both in terms of the distant as well as the recent past. Frommer acknowledges that, in making the approach, the dying therapist was meeting a need of her own as well as the possible need she intuited in her former client.

Imposed ending as opportunity: can we learn from time-limited models?

If the therapist and patient can manage both to acknowledge and hold the real loss and to work through the disappointment, a forced ending can be a rich opportunity. Most writers on relocation report that some patients were able to use the abandonment to work through earlier losses, and some of them are upbeat about the potential for the forced ending becoming a useful catalyst. Sherby reports positively on her own forced ending for relocation:

> Patients stayed engaged with me to the very end, often increasing the frequency of their sessions and, in most instances, doing an incredible amount of productive work through the last day.
>
> (2004: 79)

Weiss and Kaplan (2000) also give a positive spin: 'Despite its imposition by the analyst, the termination phase not only compared favourably with those mutually agreed on but may have been a richer, more rewarding experience' (2000: 458). Mary described a case in line with this view. One patient's anxiety symptoms were at first exacerbated by the announcement, but this amplification had made the anxiety more accessible so that it was more available to be worked with. She felt the therapy had deepened as a result.

It is interesting to wonder whether an imposed ending date can reap some of the benefits of focus and urgency which contribute to the effectiveness of time-limited therapy (Mann, 1973; Malan, 1975). Perhaps therapists who have been used to doing some time-limited work will be better equipped to use the imposed ending and to work with a focus. Brief models exploit the energy which a time constraint can generate, enabling the client to confront their failed hopes and unfulfilled expectations. However, they all insist that the ending be kept in view from the very start of the work and for this reason we cannot assume that a truncated long therapy will yield the same benefits as short-term work.

For some patients whose therapy has lost momentum, the setting of a date to end could serve to breathe life into the work. This tactic of imposing a date has sometimes been used by therapists, and was most famously exemplified in Freud's treatment of the Wolf Man (1918). When Freud opted to impose an ending with one year's notice, this patient was initially disbelieving, but once he recognized that his time was almost up he applied himself so earnestly that when they parted Freud believed a lasting cure had been achieved. As the years passed, this proved not to be the case: the Wolf Man's lifelong investment in being Freud's patient would imply that his transference was far from resolved. Freud himself later concluded that the value of 'this blackmailing device' was limited, 'while part of the material will become accessible under the pressure of the threat, another part will become buried, as it were, and lost to our therapeutic efforts' (1937: 218).

It is important to acknowledge that for some clients the forced ending really might offer the opportunity they had been seeking to leave the relationship. When patients say they do not mind about the imposed ending, or see it as a chance to work with a different kind of therapist, this could sometimes be true. Clementine felt this was the case with one of her patients who had had an unsatisfactory end to an earlier therapy and professed to be cheerful about the news:

> One client made a most unexpected response: 'Now I'll be able to make a proper ending to therapy'.

Where there is relief about the ending this would ideally be named and explored, just as we would explore protest or grief. Beneath the relief there may be additional feelings, and these may include a long-standing disappointment in the retiring therapist which has never been voiced. One former patient I spoke to explained that he had been wanting to change his therapist because he had needed more challenge, but had not quite plucked up the courage to say he would end. This patient told me he was genuinely pleased to have a way out but that his therapist had not been convinced. It sounded as though there had been a stand-off which sadly prevented a productive exploration.

Former patients who return during the therapist's last year

Sometimes when patients arrange to return for just a few sessions, part of their reason for coming may be the need to check that the therapist has survived and to show that they have too. Whether the motivation to return was a fear of their therapist's fragility, or myriad other psychic pressures, when the therapist has retired, extra resolution of the transference will not be possible.

The question of informing former patients about retirement is directly addressed in a paper aimed at psychologists in private practice (McGee, 2003). Though McGee is addressing a slightly different professional group, his suggestions are interesting. He recommends that a retiring psychologist in private practice make contact with patients who ended less than five years earlier, and with those who had had very long-term therapies or strong transference feelings.

A few contributors spoke of dilemmas arising over patients who reappeared during the period when they were closing their practice. Typically these former patients declared that they wanted a short refuelling but sometimes became heavily reinvested in the work. Celia had made a clear decision to close her practice and not to take new patients, but admitted that one or two people had 'got in' because they were returning clients. Carol described a former patient who had needed to break off therapy with her for practical reasons but had done so with the clear intention of returning one day. He had contacted her to resume sessions at the point where she was thinking about retirement, but was unsure about the decision. She recommended work with him, explaining that she could not commit to long-term work, but then experienced considerable guilt about telling him there would have to be an ending. She then mused about the risk of more 'returners' appearing:

> And it might happen more, it might happen again, because I used to sometimes say to people 'you can come back'.

It is clear that therapists feel commitment to former patients and can feel particularly reluctant to turn them away. Carol speculated that this dilemma would be acute in relation to the most vulnerable patients: the therapist might be very tempted to make space for them but these clients, more than others, could be hurt by interrupted treatment. Hannah felt anguish about one of her returning clients. This young woman had made a positive ending at the point when she was about to have her first child, but had returned with severe postnatal depression just before Hannah made the decision to retire. Although they made good progress in this further year of work, there was regret that Hannah would not be available in future times of need.

Carol provided a first-hand account of being the patient who seeks to return to a former therapist but finds out that it is too late:

> I left before she retired, it was a natural ending but then I wanted to go back to do a short piece of work maybe a year later. Though I knew she was retiring I didn't know when and I rang her and I wanted to go to her because she knew me, but she couldn't see me because she had retired and I felt really rejected and . . . I didn't get another therapist, it wasn't the same . . . So it really had a big impact on me . . . I just didn't want to go to somebody else . . . she was no longer there for me. And she was very clear. She had probably told me when she was going to retire but I hadn't taken it in and I suppose when I rang her back I was hoping that she would see me!

Carol paused several times as she recounted this disappointment, and she conveyed how difficult it can be for former patients to process grief about former therapists. As in all major bereavements, the person whose help is wanted with the pain is the person whose departure has caused it.

Post-termination: the tasks of this phase

When a patient makes a planned ending, the more classical view would expect a cleaner psychic break and a relational one would see the therapist remaining an important intrapsychic presence and not just because residues of the transference remain uninterpreted. Holmes (2010) and other attachment theorists have seen a connection between ending therapy and leaving home. The analogy conveys the bond that young adults often retain to the parental home. From a different perspective, Sabbadini (2007) describes this in terms of function rather than relationship: 'the analytic sessions end, but the analytic process continues' (2007: 706).

The post-termination phase of analysis was first identified as a discrete stage by Rangell (1966, 1982), and he saw a parallel with the postoperative phase in which surgical patients have to recover from the trauma of the surgery before they can achieve the fuller resolution of symptoms. He describes the early part of an analysis as a process of uncovering and the second part, crucially, is about 'absorption and the necessary steps to effect the use of what has evolved' (Rangell, 1982: 371). If that is so, we might wonder whether an imposed ending would threaten this ability to use what has been learned. Put another way, how much does a foreshortened therapy interfere with the long-term survival of the therapist as a good enough object in the mind of the patient? Kohut (1971) is one who addressed this, observing that when the loss of the analyst is experienced as a repetition of a traumatic loss, or in his terms, as the rupture of a self-object transference, then there is a risk of the patient losing the earlier gains of the therapy. A phenomenological study of post-termination experience by Conway (1999) supports this view that the manner of the ending can be critical to the patient's capacity to use the internalised therapist. Another study by Craige (2002) also points to the risk of the work miscarrying at this point. She found that after the work ends, the internal image of the therapist may change from good enough to bad and that 'Because some latent transferences emerge only after ending, even a skilled analyst may not be able to predict how an analysand will experience loss in the post-termination phase' (2002: 539).

I did not specifically ask interviewees for information about how their patients fared after the ending, but they often volunteered what they knew of their clients' progress, sometimes via a Christmas card and sometimes via indirect information. It seems likely this last cohort of clients will stay on in our thoughts. Boyd-Carpenter's reflection three years into her retirement includes a tender picture of the way the clients retain some corner of the therapist's mind:

> But yes I have, from time to time, missed the counselling, the clients and being a counsellor ... Quite unexpectedly I wonder what has become of this or that client and think of them with affection and nostalgia.
>
> (Boyd-Carpenter, 2010b)

Annette conveyed the anxiety of not knowing how patients were doing after the ending; this had left her with feelings of uncertainty and perhaps doubt. Here she is reflecting on a patient she had seen three times a week over many years:

> We worked very hard on the ending; I hope it was alright. You are never sure about endings really. [And later in the interview] He'll be alright, he'll be fine. We also talked about whether he might go on and have a second therapy; he is adamant not, but we'll see.

This unknowing about the fate of former patients could be uncomfortable and there may be a temptation to project certainty. We could idealise the impact of our work, or be fearful that we have made no difference. Sometimes the unknowing may be pierced by an unexpected piece of news. One retired therapist told me of receiving a book in the post from a former client. He had started this first novel during their work and had greatly valued how the therapy had helped him break through writer's block. The therapist was moved to find her name included in the acknowledgements and on reading the book was even more heartened to discover what a profound novel he had written.

Chapter 5

Guilt in the countertransference?

I tailored it slightly differently and felt really apprehensive; it felt quite brutal in a way – cutting off something unfinished and really important . . . it goes against the grain of what a therapist is.

(Mary)

It was very difficult. I found the whole process of dealing with my retirement very hard because you are intruding something about your own life into theirs and that's so much against your training.

(Clementine)

Picture an intermittent stream coursing down a steep gully. For a leaf caught in the current there is noise, speed, sudden whirling and bruising against the rocks. This aggressive watercourse is an 'arroyo', the image given to us by Szajnberg and Crittenden (1997) to describe the collision of attachment dynamics between client and therapist. They write about the 'arroyo of feelings', the transference/countertransference currents which can pick us up and carry us along. We may be most susceptible to tangle if we ourselves have enmeshed traits and we encounter a client with a similar preoccupied pattern (1997: 435). In contrast, a therapist with dismissing traits might cope by withdrawing and stepping well back from the deep, rocky gully, avoiding the fear but also the opportunity to accompany the client. The word seems so apt because uniquely among topographical terms, arroyo denotes *both* the dry ravine and the stream which surges down in certain seasons.

Attachment implications

Coming to the end of a long therapy is a challenging task for the patient and therapist even in regular circumstances, and it brings into focus the artificiality of the process. Important relationships may sometimes be cut off by relocation and of course by death, but there are very few other circumstances where two people who have been very close choose to separate. When this does happen we regard it as the stuff of tragedy. We might think of the enduring power of *Brief Encounter* (Lean, 1945), where two people have fallen in love but decide ultimately that their own situations make a long-term relationship impossible. Coltart reflects on the strangeness of ending a therapeutic relationship and writes that 'we create an arbitrary situation that has much in common with a death' (1996: 151). When a patient ends therapy in their own good time, there will have been a chance to retrieve the parts of the self which had been projected into the therapist. We would hope that in a planned retirement this disinvestment would usually be achieved in a way that builds strength, but if an ending is imposed suddenly the process of disengagement is likely to be traumatic.

An ending is an attachment crisis in its own right and protest responses are inevitable, indeed their absence would be noteworthy. Faced with a patient's protest against abandonment, each therapist's response will be coloured by their own internal world and so transference/countertransference experience can usefully be thought about in terms of the attachment fit within each dyad. The therapist as well as the client is contributing to the speed and direction of the arroyo. With this kind of turbulence in the relationship, the relevance of good supervision is self-evident.

On the one hand there is the client's transference to his therapist and the subtle stage directions he may be giving her. On the other hand there are the therapist's unconscious responses to this client – how does his story impact on her and how are her unspoken communications guiding the relationship?

The discomfort that the retiring therapist feels about closing down the work may stir up her own residual insecure attachment pattern. If she has some avoidant traits herself then when a patient has a similar pattern there might be a pull towards a collusive denial. Both patient and therapist will be feeling anxious about the impending attachment loss and may defend themselves by minimising the meaning of the connection which is coming to an end. This could take the form of the therapist initially buying in to the patient's avoidance of vulnerability and their claim to be 'fine' with the imposed ending. As the therapist recognises her own defence she can become more aware of the patient's hidden distress.

When an avoidant therapist is working with a preoccupied patient she may be tested by the patient's readiness to protest against the impending abandonment: the patient's angry sense of entitlement may touch her own disallowed unconscious grief. Once this distress can be thought about and the patient's hyper-arousal is understood in terms of inconsistent early care, this fit may feel easier to work with than a blank transference/counter-transference. Denise describes (below) this kind of numbness which might indicate an extremely avoidant or possibly disorganised pattern.

Bowlby (1988) suggested that a non-complementary response from the therapist is generally helpful to patients, meaning that a dismissing patient benefits from the most welcoming stance and a preoccupied patient needs particularly clearly held boundaries. Bernier and Dozier (2002) review studies which seem to confirm this. They suggest unsurprisingly that therapists with secure attachment are best placed to work with a range of patients, being able to tailor the way they relate to the vulnerabilities of either preoccupied or dismissing individuals. Where therapists are less secure it appears that dyads with dissimilar insecure patterns have the most productive relationships.

Dolan, Arnkoff and Glass (1993) suggest that the optimal level of complementarity varies over the lifespan of the therapy relationship. This point of view is supported in a study by Daly and Mallinckrodt (2009). These writers propose a model for therapeutic distance which indicates how a therapist enables a dismissing patient to move towards intimacy and a preoccupied one to achieve more autonomy. They illustrate this with an interesting diagram showing the relative positions of the two parties over the life of the therapy. The result for the preoccupied patient and her therapist is the outline of a Christmas tree. Initially the therapist matches the patient's need for closeness, at the apex of the tree where the two lines meet. Over time they are able to increase therapeutic distance so that their positions begin to match the base of the tree. For the dismissing patient the diagram looks like a vase with a wide mouth and a narrow base, the dyad starting far apart but moving closer together as tolerance of closeness increases. Where an ending is being imposed this would mean that patient and therapist are working against the clock to achieve an optimal distance by the time they must part.

The tangible circumstances of the therapist's retirement are likely to impact on her sense of security and thus on her capacity to contain difficult countertransference. Martinez's (1989) paper about relocation deals with this directly: she writes about the challenge of helping patients with loss while simultaneously managing her own difficult feelings about her move. Celia's comments (below) indicate the emotional cost for therapists whose retirement is forced on them by illness and who face the loss of a practice without the pleasant anticipation of a fulfilling retirement. When a therapist makes a free choice to retire, the feelings can be uncomfortable in a different way. If she has chosen to retire in order to protect her patients from the possibility of her capacity declining in the future, she may feel resentful about being compelled into this good behaviour by her superego. If patients then complain bitterly about her ending the work, this may feel doubly unfair and very provoking. Comments by some of the younger contributors show that when the decision to retire is made purely on the basis of pull factors, there may be heightened anxiety as to whether this is the right thing to be doing. The therapist's own capacity to self-soothe, to draw on an internalised secure base, will be critical to managing herself through these kinds of countertransference. Supervision can provide the opportunity to share and explore these uncomfortable feelings provided a good enough supervisory alliance has already been established.

The countertransference of guilt

I use the term countertransference in its broader sense to include the therapist's own affects as well as her empathic experiencing of the client's feelings. Sandler, Dare and Holder (1992) make the point that early definitions of countertransference were too narrow and often polarised around seeing it as either an obstacle to analytic work or a valuable tool. They consider that later definitions sometimes became so broad as to be meaningless and therefore propose:

> a useful view of countertransference might be to take it as referring to the specific emotionally based responses aroused in the analyst by the specific qualities of his patient.
>
> (1973: 96)

I regard this definition as an aspiration but admit that my own usage strays into the embracive meaning of the term. In this chapter, for example, I have stretched the term to include possible feelings towards one's training organisation.

If countertransference of guilt is to provide information about our clients, we may need to distinguish between different types of guilt. Aarons (1975) distinguishes between two kinds of guilty feelings about failing our patients. On the one hand our narcissistic omnipotence is offended by failure. Aarons sees this as arising from our need for gratification – our exhibitionist drive. On the other hand there may be a more mature guilt arising out of the superego, because in letting the patient down we have betrayed an ego ideal. He sees this anxiety as more helpful and rewarding, and this constructive form of guilt is perhaps what Clementine conveyed when I had asked her about the main dilemma which she had faced in retirement:

a sense of responsibility for people – that you were leaving them not at a time of their choosing.

She conveyed the heaviness she felt around having cut off the relationship she had been offering her patients, and her words tailed off into an unfinished sentence as she recalled the experience of telling her clients she would be ending the work:

> I found it hard finding the time to tell people and also knowing that for some people this was going to be very difficult news and especially as . . .

As Clementine was able to speak directly about feelings of guilt, it seemed all the more poignant when she made a slip of the tongue referring to one of her patients who 'retired when I did'. Perhaps the image of a patient who retires rather than being forced out helps to soften the guilt.

My decision to have a separate chapter on countertransference is in part because I was tempted to reference Winnicott's (1949) paper on 'Hate in the countertransference'. The parallel seems strong: just as Winnicott contended that some patients may need us to hate them, the retiring therapist who imposes an ending on her patients usually feels some guilt and her patients may need her to feel this. Winnicott gave us permission to know about our hatred and he made the case for its usefulness in some therapeutic relationships. In instances of forced ending there is perhaps a corresponding necessity for guilt and for this to be worked through.

A countertransference of relief also corresponds to Winnicott's case. When there is relief at ending, this suggests that the therapist may have been feeling resentment for some time. Such resentment may be the visible tip of a deeper countertransference hatred towards an 'impossible' patient. Being glad to get away from clients gives us feelings which are counter to our idealised sense of our self as a therapist, and some contributors mention this (below). When relief is present, it is likely that the therapist will also feel guilty for having positive emotions about something which is a cause of distress to her patient.

When I transcribed these interviews I was surprised by an apparent inconsistency. On the one hand was my sense that most of the contributors had conveyed discomfort or guilt at foreclosing the work with their patients. On the other hand were their actual words, which revealed minimal direct evidence of self-reproach. It appears that much of the guilt I thought I was hearing was being conveyed implicitly and might be regarded as my countertransference. In pondering the difference I guessed that those expressions of guilt I had heard had impacted on me disproportionately. This may be partly that I was permeable to this affect, because I anticipated that I might feel this when I retire, and perhaps also because where guilt had been expressed it had been very deeply felt by the contributor. It seems likely that the disparity is a function both of a hyper-receptivity on my part and the fact that guilt was largely conveyed in implicit ways.

At the end of her interview, Denise disclosed a distinct physical symptom which might perhaps be thought of as body countertransference. She explained that the stressful months of closing down her practice had produced back pain, to which she had never been prone in her long career as a therapist and supervisor. It seemed to speak for the burden of many tangled feelings which the retiring therapist faces and perhaps reflected the reality that we communicate sadness and loss through a sagging of the body. Other contributors described various symptoms of ill health improving once they were retired, even though they had not at the time seen these health problems as being caused by their work.

If we consider the profound link between loss and guilt it would be astonishing if clients did not feel resentment and retirees did not feel a corresponding guilt. Greenberg and Mitchell (1983) provide a very apt rendering of Klein's insight into our unconscious experience of grief: 'All loss is experienced as a result of one's own destructiveness and as retaliation for past hatefulness and injuries' (1983: 127). At times contributors conveyed anguish about a fear of doing harm. Nicola's voice also trailed off as she described the process of ending with patients:

> I've done all that I can, all that I can really. It's about trusting that isn't it? It's like having your own children and you get them so far and then it's . . .

Carol implicitly acknowledges that organising a retirement which was largely organic, with only one imposed ending, has spared her from dealing with more guilt than she could face:

> I haven't had to tell people really, except this one client who I'm having this guilt about. And I'd love to carry on working with him in a way, because we work really well together, so that's quite sad but a good note to end on.

She went on to speak of her procrastination in setting an ending date with this one client:

We haven't clipped it yet but, um ... And I think that's about me feeling a bit guilty about abandoning ... that's my countertransference.

Carol described another potential source of guilt, or possibly a fear of envy.

I think I have some guilt about that [retiring relatively young at 61] because all my friends and colleagues have to work, they can't afford to retire for a long time. So I do have guilt which I'm trying to come to terms with – I've got to get over that.

The way we each handle our guilt will depend on the kind of energy that drives our particular superego, and this may be augmented by what Colman calls our 'analytic super-ego'. He suggests that this operates 'as a critical, threatening persecutor long after the formal training process has come to an end' (2006: 99). He observes that in dealing with this inner policeman we tend to move between anxious compliance, rebellious denial and omnipotent identification. It seems likely therefore that these are some of the internal dynamics that retirees are managing. Benjamin (2004) also encourages us to become more generous in our expectations of ourselves and 'to find a different way to regulate ourselves, one in which we accept loss, failure, mistakes, [and] our own vulnerability' (2004: 32).

Some contributors felt a particularly profound reluctance to make the step, and there was a sense that for them guilt was interwoven with the loss of a part of the self. Patsy was able to voice her ambivalence about retiring in terms of her internal world. Her words may resonate with many therapists, who see their motivation for the work as linked to their need to repair their own object world:

Somehow it has felt like [I'm] abandoning my mother.

It made sense to me that guilt might be more conscious in some therapists than others. Some retirees might have fewer misgivings than others and, in addition, some might have a different tolerance for knowing about their guilt. A few of the contributors who did not convey self-reproach were more open about anger towards the profession for failing to manage retirement more effectively, and this made me curious about a possible trade-off between guilt and anger.

I wondered whether there was a difference in guilt between therapists whose decision to retire was influenced by push or pull factors. Where a therapist feels they are retiring out of duty of care, does this reduce her guilt and possibly also the strength of her patients' protest? Where the choice is made on the basis of opting for leisure and rest, does this potentially increase the feelings of guilt, and possibly also the clients' resentment? Perhaps this dynamic could apply at the conscious level, but in our unconscious the therapist's real-life reasons for departing would make less difference. A few contributors spoke of clients deftly implying indulgence when they referred to the therapist's retirement. These contributors felt that the remarks conveyed a picture of the therapist sunning herself by a pool while the client continued the slog of everyday life with their neuroses.

It would be interesting to ask how therapists' countertransference was impacting on their work, but the data do not answer that question well. I have included here quotations where feelings of regret and guilt are directly expressed, but other indirect evidence of possible countertransference enactments may be found in other chapters. An interesting example is from Chapter 3, where Hannah comments on the premature ending with one of her clients. She reflects that if she had not been retiring she might have pressed harder for the client to look at what this early ending was really about. It may be that feelings of guilt were impacting on Hannah at this point, and her client's premature departure may then have punished her and given more cause for guilt. Other examples seemed apparent in stories about 'the patient who was hard to tell', as several contributors spoke of delaying the announcement to one particular person. I understood that the client's fragility was a factor in all these cases, but it would be interesting to also identify what may have been projected by the therapist in each case. Dewald (1965) speculates about how unacknowledged guilt might influence our decisions about referral on. He wonders whether such guilt might lead a therapist to refer on an unnecessarily high proportion of her patients. He suggests that if we find that our clients can interrupt their treatment and be no worse off, we might question the value of our work: 'In other words, the therapist may need to assure himself that the treatment is absolutely necessary for his patients and that they cannot get along without it' (1965: 123).

Comments from therapists who relocated reflect a range of attitudes towards their own guilt. Aarons (1975) writes firmly that the feelings of guilt about abandoning 'children' need to 'be immediately recognised and surmounted by self-analysis' (1975: 304). A critique of this approach is offered by a training patient who experienced an imposed ending when his analyst relocated (Anonymous, 2001). He indicates that therapists may be denying their guilt in cases such as his:

Is it possible that the voluntary interruption of an analysis for the analyst's own personal considerations evokes so much guilt in us as a profession that it has been largely avoided for defensive reasons?

(*2001*: 42)

In contrast to Aarons's account, papers by Martinez (1989) and Sherby (2004) describe working in a more relational analytic style. They give more attention to the strong feelings that arose in them in response to their patients' sense of abandonment. Similarly, my contributor Alice, who suffered bereavement at the point when she was relocating, was very conscious of her own painful feelings:

The thing I found incredibly hard was leaving them before the work was finished. We talked about that a lot and about my regret.

At this point I posed a question about guilt and Alice clarified the quality of the feeling she had carried:

Yes . . . and I was also managing loss in my private life . . . Was it guilt? I'm not sure that's the word I would choose; it didn't feel like guilt it felt like . . . I never thought to put it into words . . . Sadness I think – that I couldn't be on that journey with them. It was a loss for me.

How therapists worked with their countertransference

In their paper about ending for relocation, Kaplan *et al.* (1994) suggest that therapists risk being swallowed in a deep whirlpool of guilt or distracted by their efforts to escape it: 'the analyst must pay careful attention to countertransference vulnerability, avoiding the Scylla of defensive self-justification and the Charybdis of unwarranted guilt' (1994: 263). Several commentators mention the importance of the therapist containing the significant personal feelings which are very likely to arise in the process of closing a practice. Boyd-Carpenter (2010a) saw a particular risk of acting out where her own defensive strategy dovetailed with that of the client, and she was mindful of the need to sift through the layers of her countertransference if they were to become useful in the work:

It has been my responsibility to try to understand myself sufficiently to not allow my material to unduly influence, contaminate or high-jack the clients' own experience.

(2010a: 94)

Weiss and Kaplan (2000) make a similar point and suggest that the therapist work through her feelings about ending before informing patients. I believe this is overly optimistic and that the working through must necessarily happen as the process of retiring proceeds. Weiss and Kaplan highlight the risk that countertransference distortion will impact on the work and they mention that a return to therapy, whether brief or longer term, is appropriate if supervision and discussions with colleagues are not enough to process the personal issues. Carol's experience illustrates their concern about countertransference affecting the work. She described how she felt her guilt might be filtering into the relationship:

> He said to me that he felt I'd got him by the jugular the previous session ... and I thought, 'what's that about my countertransference?' – because I was being quite crisp ... and usually I work quite slowly and organically with him.

Emma described the grim challenge from a patient who was deeply threatened and attacked by her illness and retirement. This woman managed her own distress by inducing painful feelings in Emma by means of a well-aimed counter-attack:

> Of course I was a hardened psychotherapist who didn't take things personally, but with her, she would say things like, 'You are sure to die in the operation. If you don't die you will be a cabbage ever after because of the anaesthetic.' You know it did get to me a bit and in the short notice I did have a bit of trouble wondering how to interpret.

Viorst (1982) writes about the analyst's experience of loss in regular endings and she reports a fantasy which arose towards the end of one long analysis. In this daydream the patient is given a concert ticket by his analyst and when he attends the performance he chats to the young woman sitting beside him. This delightful young woman turns out to be the analyst's daughter, who had also been given a ticket by her father. The two fall in love and marry. Far from being a typical patient daydream, this was the *analyst's* fantasy and neatly incorporates both the therapist's loss and the patient's need to hold on. This fantasy was from an analyst who was ending with just one patient. The retiring therapist faces greater losses, with several clients being let go and no new ones to replace them.

Sherby (2004) closed her practice in order to relocate, and her experience was strongly coloured by the fact that she was reluctant to make the move. She had agreed to go because her retired husband had incapacitating arthritis which could be helped by a warmer climate. This meant that she was facing a forced relocation, which matches the forced retirement of Emma, Rosemary and Celia. Sherby points out that this creates a 'confluence of experience' between therapist and patient, with both parties facing the feelings that go with being obliged to take an unwelcome path (2004: 70). She writes that this shared identification affected the therapeutic process and was both a burden and an opportunity. In a paper written nine years after the event, she is able to contrast that experience with the more routine endings in her new practice where her own feelings are less involved. Her conclusion is that the affinity with her patients at the time of their joint loss had deepened the work and helped patients to grow through it.

Sherby (2004) and Boyd-Carpenter (2010a) both used writing as a way to process the experience of closing their practice. Sherby kept a journal as a way to support herself, and she later used these process notes to write her interesting paper. Similarly Boyd-Carpenter seems to have used the preparation of her paper as a way to sustain herself in the unfamiliar territory of an imposed ending. We know that writing about an experience can deepen both our observation and reflection on events, so this seems a particularly apt way to contain the feelings which the multiple endings bring up. Some retirees have found it worthwhile to go back into therapy at this stage, whether for a brief or longer period. Supervision provides the space for processing clinical challenges, but occasionally the personal issues around retirement mean that therapy would also be useful.

Countertransference as information

As contributors were appropriately guarded in their anecdotes about clients, I have been grateful for the clinical narratives which Boyd-Carpenter (2010a) provides. She describes the transference/countertransference dynamics which helped her to sense how each patient was responding to the news and particularly which stages they were going through in the process of separation.

> I have watched the tears, the terror, the numb denial of feeling of the client/ child faced with the loss of parent and felt the complementary ache at the thought of never seeing that child again. I have both observed and felt the intensely ambivalent, adolescent anticipation of independence and freedom from this parent-child relationship.
>
> (2010a: 89)

Denise shared an example of her countertransference serving as a window into her patient's disengagement. She described her numbness with one particular patient.

> She distances herself and of course I feel distant from her. I have no sense of how it may be for her after we finish, whereas I do with other clients.

This response might suggest an avoidant style of attachment where the individual learned from a young age to disguise their protest about separation and their need for proximity. The complete blankness in the countertransference could also point towards a more disorganised pattern, with an element of control and aggression and an extreme switching between self states. Whichever pattern best describes this actual client, the impact on the therapist is marked and as Denise conveys, such a guarded defence can evoke a matching countertransference of numbness. This would be challenging at normal times but would be more so when the clock is against us and other patients may be presenting more demanding versions of separation anxiety. Like the well-behaved avoidant child, the adult patient is no trouble and their silent loss may not stand out among the more colourful ambivalent responses of other patients. We need to be alert to the possibility that some patients let us off too easily. A variation on this theme of denial would be cases where the therapist and patient embark too eagerly on finding a new therapist. A premature focus on the referral on could serve to protect both patient and therapist against the negative transference reactions.

Other feelings

Perhaps the most pervasive feelings for the retiring therapist are those arising from the losses she is facing, and these have been considered throughout the book and are addressed in most detail in Chapter 7. A number of contributors spoke of the link in their minds between retirement and death. Perhaps these concerns about mortality are not strictly part of the countertransference, but they were a common part of the emotional experience for those coming to the end of their working life. Denise was one who was in the midst of the process and who commented that part of her feared that retirement could bring illness and death. It is interesting to put this awareness of mortality beside Freud's (1915) assertion that we never believe in our own death:

Our own death is quite unimaginable, and whenever we make the attempt to imagine it we can perceive that we really survive as spectators. Hence the psychoanalytic school could venture on the assertion that at bottom nobody believes in his own death, or to put the same thing in a different way, in the unconscious every one of us is convinced of his own immortality.

(1915: 291)

Contemporary perspectives tend to see awareness of mortality as a sign of maturity, and Becker (1973) points out how costly it is to defend against the all-pervasive threat of death. If we can allow death to have its meaning without being overwhelmed with fear, we will have most chance of growth. Death anxiety and our defences against it can clearly impact on clinical work at any stage, but the therapist's retirement could increase this apprehension about ageing. If the upsurge of thoughts about mortality can be tolerated, the therapist will have more psychic space and flexibility for the work with patients. A developmental question from Waddell (2002: 219) seems as relevant to this life stage as to earlier ones: 'can emotional experience be engaged with or does it have to be fended off?'.

Several contributors did not know any other therapists who had retired and this meant they were quite alone with whatever feelings came up. Denise articulated what many retirees say, that they would have valued more help with retirement, perhaps from their training organisations. She spoke warmly of the article by Boyd-Carpenter (2010a) and its role in naming the experiences she was having:

The paper almost allows you, like therapy, to think it's OK to have those feelings and that you're not alone.

Her comment conveys that more than information or guidance on retirement, affirmation and support may be what is most needed. Another common ingredient in the countertransference appears to be relief. This can itself become a cause of guilt, meaning that there may be guilt both about abandoning the patients and about the relief of getting away. Clementine was one who conveyed her relief at the ending of her stressful work with one very disturbed patient whose attacks had contributed to her decision to retire.

For some there is guilt about abandoning the profession and leaving colleagues at the grindstone. Carol and Beatrice both mentioned the issue of financial privilege: being comfortably off meant they could plan their retirement without being constrained by concerns about money. Carol anticipated that this could be a cause of envy in some colleagues.

Walcott (2011) writes about a similar dynamic but in a less personal way. He reports a global type of guilt in relation to closing his practice, and he voices this in terms of abandoning the profession rather than the patients or close colleagues:

> Renouncing my mistress of almost forty years makes me sad and even regretful. Yet that is only part of what I feel. I can best describe my feelings as those which would accompany the end of a love affair which one himself has concluded [sic].
>
> (2011: 216)

Martinez (1989) writes about the risk of focusing on guilt at the expense of other countertransference messages. She noticed herself compensating for her guilt by focusing on the abandonment and over-interpreting the negative aspects of the situation. She writes that at times she overlooked the sincere gratitude patients wanted to express. She found it even harder to acknowledge the positive feelings that some patients had about her leaving, such as one patient's excitement about being able to work with a male therapist.

Retrospective countertransference

In a paper in which he recounts experience from several retired therapists, Hampton speculates that therapists 'are likely to be left with a great deal of retrospective countertransference, much of it too unspecific to be easily accessed' (2006: 1). This seems a useful concept to describe the considerable feelings which a retiring therapist may find themselves processing in the period after they see their last patient. If the retiring therapist timetables her final supervision sessions for the weeks after she has seen her last clients, there will be some space to process these residual feelings. Where the ending has been made in an emergency, this need to process retrospectively is even more important. I believe that participants' experience of our interviews had some overlap with their experience of supervision and at times they used our conversation to reflect on their work. For the seven contributors who were already retired when I met them, it could therefore make sense to think of them as processing their 'retrospective countertransference' during our meeting.

Countertransference to training organisations

Several contributors mentioned their training organisations. Most often this came up in the context of their concern not to disadvantage a training patient by their retirement, and this was mentioned in Chapter 2. This led me to consider the therapist's relationship over time with their training body, and I wondered whether this conscientious treatment of training patients reflected an unacknowledged need to remain in good standing with one's organisation. Possibly their concern owed something to an identification with trainees. It surprised me because it seemed to imply a greater duty of care to training patients, whereas one might imagine that they are in fact better equipped to deal with an imposed ending than regular patients who often have no one in their life who understands therapy and thus no one who could appreciate what it might mean to lose a therapist. Hampton (2006) has an interesting reflection on the question of loyalty to organisations and suggests that orthodox practice is instituted and maintained by training institutions. He wonders whether orthodoxy is 'subject to decay the further away from them one travels' (2006: 8). He goes on to ponder what this means in terms of a generational battle and whether it might be a creative rather than a destructive development. These questions of loyalty and deviation were also discussed in Chapter 1, where Emma criticised herself for drifting off the psychoanalytic pathway, and they have been explored by Colman (2006). We might understand these anxieties about conforming too little or too much as fuelled on the one hand by our need to belong and on the other by our need to be distinct. It makes sense that this issue of attachment and separateness would carry extra weight when, in retirement, we are facing such a significant separation from colleagues.

Chapter 6

How helpful is supervision?

It's one of those areas where you are going ahead of your supervisor and I think the fact that she was slightly older than me made it a bit strange . . .

(Clementine)

Colleagues Jan and Nina are chatting after Nina's supervision session:

J   Did you tell her then?

N   What?

J   About retirement?

N   No . . . no, I want to get clear in my own mind and work out when to tell people.

J   Isn't that what supervision is for – for weighing things up?

N   Mm, but you haven't met Dorothy have you? I think she's about ten years older than me and I don't think she is going to like me retiring. I think she's going to see me as a light-weight for bowing out.

J   That's about your fear of her criticising you, but how about *her* fear of you?

N   As in?

J   Could she feel threatened? – That you can afford to retire, that you are young enough to relish retirement?

N   [Sighing] Oh god . . . Well probably some of that fits because something is making me cagey with her – and we've never had much success in talking about 'us'.

Attachment implications

Bowlby's theory describes how feelings are regulated within an attachment relationship and how this in turn supports curiosity and exploration.

This essential connection between felt security and readiness to learn makes attachment theory particularly relevant to supervision. We may identify attachment dynamics between a supervisor and a supervisee without going so far as to claim this as a full attachment relationship (Watkins and Riggs, 2012). If attachment understanding can support the supervisor's capacity for attunement, this will in turn enhance containment and thus the value of the supervisory space as a resonating chamber where ideas can be creatively exchanged.

Whether it is the supervisor or the supervisee who is retiring, the supervisory alliance (and thus the secure base of supervision) will be impacted by the process. We know from anecdotal evidence that the loss of a supervisor (through retirement or illness) can be quite troubling to a supervisee. In my sample, some participants mentioned a considerable degree of protest from their supervisees and others spoke of themselves having been very challenged by the loss of a much-loved supervisor.

Mander (2002) writes about the dependent bond which can develop in supervision and how this can be just as pronounced with senior clinicians. These therapists may have long ago ended their own personal therapies and may particularly appreciate and rely on the containment from supervision.

Denise's comments illustrate how retirees may be mentally prepared for protest from patients but be taken aback by distress in supervisees. One contributor recalled a supervisee who had tried to change her mind about ending, pressing her to make an exception and to continue to supervise her. Issy, who was taking a sabbatical, also spoke of protest from supervisees. She reflected both on her supervisees' attachment to her and also on the contribution of her own supervisor:

> I think that our supervisors end up holding a particular part of our psyche – our working psyche . . . This person has been holding up my practice, this is the person who legitimises the way that I work and that's about the relationship. How to replicate that?

Even though we expect supervisees to be relatively robust, an imposed ending still needs to be planned and contained. The issue of retirement touches on possible rivalry in the supervisory dyad, and this is mentioned by Clementine below. When the supervisor steps down, the supervisee could experience an Oedipal triumph or, contrastingly, a disappointment in the 'parent' for giving up their responsibility. Perhaps there may be both. In other cases the supervisee's identification with the supervisor might lead them towards premature thoughts of their own retirement, and possibly this was Patsy's experience. When her own supervisor was retiring she made the decision to do so too and she began working towards an ending before realising she needed to reconsider that choice. Other early dynamics may be evoked in the supervisee – for example, fear of surpassing a parent or an anxiety about rejection and abandonment. It is helpful if the supervisor can facilitate exploration so that the therapist can resolve these kinds of transference tangles before going on to find a new supervisor. A critical factor in such discussions will be the degree of acceptance which the supervisor has achieved in thinking about their own mortality. Just as a therapist's own unprocessed fears of ageing may limit how much she can allow patients to explore their anxiety about dying, so a supervisor's own anxiety will limit her capacity to help supervisees air their concerns about ageing.

When it is the supervisee who is retiring, the supervisor will be helping her through a transition which is unfamiliar to her and there could be envious feelings in either direction. Where there are pre-existing difficulties or inhibitions in the supervisory pair, then retirement of either supervisor or supervisee could exacerbate these and make fruitful exploration more difficult. One of the ways that communication and defensiveness can pass around the supervisory triangle is through reflection and parallel process (Searles, 1955/2012). At best this will serve as information about the dynamics happening in the therapy room and will provide material which can be fruitfully explored in supervision. If a supervisor finds herself on the one hand unwarrantably concerned about the supervisee's fragility, or on the other hand underestimating the challenge being faced, this could be an enactment of a dynamic from the therapist–patient relationship. However, when there are tensions in the supervisory relationship, there can be a temptation to reach too quickly for the ready-made explanation of parallel process and to assume that the difficulty is coming from the therapy room. Stimmel (1995) warns supervisors about this, noting that the concept of parallel process may be used defensively. Sometimes difficulties originate in the supervision room itself – whether in the transference or the real relationship.

In Chapter 1 I considered the fit between the therapist and the patient in terms of their attachment patterns. In a corresponding way we can think about the fit between the supervisor and supervisee, as well as the interplay between all three individuals in the supervisory triangle. If we imagine an avoidant client and a retiring therapist who also has some avoidant traits, we can see that they could collude to understate how much the imposed ending means to this client. If the supervisor in the case also had a residual dismissing pattern, this could make it hard to spot the patient's defensive communications. A further difficulty arises because attachment insecurity can make it hard for us to use supervision effectively. If we lack a sufficiently secure base, then the state of unknowing which we try to allow in supervision is too threatening. Supervisees with avoidant patterns may be most at risk from defensiveness, as people with avoidant traits are particularly uncomfortable with curiosity and uncertainty (Mikulincer, 1997).

Some peer supervision groups have worked together for years, establishing considerable sibling attachments and seeing each other through many life changes. A number of contributors were very attached to their peer groups and had been invited and encouraged by colleagues to continue to attend the group after retirement. In some cases this seems to have worked, but it does pose boundary issues. Annette made a useful distinction between a local therapy support network, whose meetings she was continuing to attend as a retiree, and her peer group. She resigned from her peer supervision group because, having no clinical work, she could not have been a fully participating member though they had urged her to stay.

In those rare cases where a supervisor feels obliged to raise concerns about a supervisee's fitness to practice, there will be a very challenging dynamic for both parties. I am thinking here specifically about age-related deterioration and a situation where a supervisor might want to encourage a therapist to consider retirement. A strong supervisory alliance will provide the best hope of working through to an appropriate outcome, but there is a likelihood that the supervisee will feel shamed and hurt, believing that her attachment figure has turned against her and perhaps seeing this as an envious attack. The dyad will have a huge challenge to work productively. In effect the supervisor is saying, 'You may not be good enough to do this work' and yet, if this frightening possibility is to be thought about, the pair have to trust each other's capacity to reflect on this. A relational approach allows the supervisor to make this dilemma more explicit, naming the joint challenge to keep listening and empathising when the pair is having to handle such a painful dilemma. An example of this dynamic between supervisor and supervisee is described below. At such times it may help the supervisor to be mindful of the supervisee's attachment pattern and thus to attune to their particular defensive style. Failing to keep attachment dynamics in mind can fuel an enactment in the supervision, and an example of this is described in a paper which looks at an impasse in my own supervision work (though this case is not related to retirement; Power, 2014).

Supervision seems to be the part of the work which retirees find hardest to let go and often they find ways to hold onto this role, whether by remaining involved in a peer group or by continuing with supervision work after their last patient has left. This may provide a gentle way to wind down and allow a great depth of experience to be available to another generation of supervisees. On the other hand there are ethical questions to consider, and these are discussed below.

Supervising a therapist who is retiring

In its function as a container and a generative space, supervision can potentially support the therapist through the various challenges of retirement: the decision itself, the clinical challenges once patients know an ending is being imposed and the supervisee's own discomfort about leaving the profession. As well as helping with containment and exploration of these parts of the experience, the supervisor needs to keep the supervisory relationship in mind and to enable the supervisory couple to think about their own interaction. When an issue is taboo, the figure 'in charge' carries particular responsibility for making sure it is aired. If supervisors can become more familiar with the issues which retirement tends to throw up, they will be better equipped to anticipate the kinds of challenges their supervisees may face.

Although supervisors are in a position to offer crucial support with retirement, few of the contributors had had supervisees who retired. One participant suggested that this might be because many older therapists go only to peer supervision and thus leave their individual supervisors before they reach retirement age. I asked Annette whether she had ever had a supervisee retire and she retorted:

> No, I've worked with someone who I felt should retire, who was not prepared to let go. I don't think he was doing any harm but I don't think he was doing much good either. I felt, and said to him, that I felt he was hanging on to it for himself rather than for his patients.

When I asked Rosemary this question, she pondered how 'tact' might prevent a supervisee from mentioning retirement plans to an elderly supervisor.

> I think that's quite funny. No, nobody did. I wonder if that was tact. Tact is not a thing I have. I can see it would not be tactful to go to someone who needed to retire to talk about your own retirement.

She also cautioned that if a supervisee mentioned some preliminary ideas about retirement, it would be important to explore this in a tentative way rather than jumping to endorse it:

> if the supervisor takes it up in a heavy-handed kind of way it becomes reality rather soon.

Patsy told the story of her first aborted retirement, which she had begun to undertake while working with a supervisor who was herself retiring. It is possible that the dynamic of which Rosemary warned was impacting in Patsy's case:

> My supervisor retired. Just before she retired I decided not to retire, I decided to change my decision.

She added that the decision not to retire had been supported by her therapist, whom she had quite recently started seeing.

There seem to be many reasons why in practice supervision rarely provides optimum support for retirees. One factor is the supervisor's ignorance: by definition the supervisor has no first-hand experience of the journey that her supervisee is contemplating. Another factor is the issue of difference. Difference in age and financial circumstances may cause tensions which interfere with the creative exchange of ideas. These issues of power and status may need to be acknowledged, and this aspect of the relationship is discussed in greater detail below.

When therapists, like the contributors to this book, are making a planned retirement, supervision will provide essential space to reflect on the patients' response to the imposed ending. I have written elsewhere (Power, 2012) about the supervisor's tasks in this stage of the work, but a key one is helping the retiring supervisee to access and manage her feelings about leaving. Boyd-Carpenter (2010a) makes the point that the retiring therapist needs to process their own feelings about loss if they are to be sufficiently available for doing the work in their final months. In some supervisory dyads this will be very difficult. One supervisor told an anecdote about this. For months she had tried unsuccessfully to enable a retiring supervisee to connect to her own grief about ending; eventually, in the penultimate session the supervisee burst into tears and acknowledged how hard it was for her to come to the end of her working life.

Imber (1995) writes about her work as supervisor to a number of pregnant therapists, one of whom needed to close her practice entirely in order to relocate as a result of her partner's new job. This is the cascade dynamic apparent in quite a proportion of retirements and closures – the therapist is imposing an ending on her clients because her life circumstances are imposing an ending on her. In such cases supervision has an important role in helping to tease out the different sources of resentment, and Imber explains that on this occasion she found herself becoming more directive than she would usually be, in order to assist the supervisee to own her difficult feelings about the imposed ending. This therapist described one of her clients as being fine about ending, but added that he had lost control of his car when driving and had narrowly escaped serious harm. The supervisee was not showing any curiosity about this contradiction until Imber pushed her to do so. Once a space was opened for them to acknowledge the client's anger, the supervisee could get in touch with her own dismay at being forced to relocate. This in turn increased her capacity to tolerate the client's hostile response.

The supervisor's role in the supervisee's decision to retire

If an able supervisee is wondering whether they want to retire, the supervisor's role in supporting the exploration of the decision is likely to be fairly straightforward. If the supervisee is wondering whether they *should* retire, the supervisor's role is more delicate and the supervisory pair has an ethical dilemma to explore. An anonymous letter to *Therapy Today* seems to indicate that some supervisors may be unprepared for this. A supervisee in her early 70s writes about the difficulty she has in knowing whether her work is diminishing with age. Her account of her conversation with her supervisor indicates how the subject can be avoided, even when one party is brave enough to raise it. 'My supervisor of four years expresses confidence in my work and when I asked her if I should thinking of retiring, she laughed; I took that to mean – not yet' (Anonymous 2011: 18).

In this anecdote the therapist and supervisee in question may have been working to a high standard, but her readiness to consider whether her age was telling on her work deserved a more thoughtful response. The task of facilitating this important exploration is certainly a challenging one, but there will be times when it is ethically necessary. There may be some conflict of interest between the needs of her patients to receive effective treatment and the therapist's need to work, either because income or a sense of meaning will be lacking without it. Traesdal (2013) anticipates the risk of a therapist feeling compelled by financial hardship to keep working beyond her capacity. She proposes that it is a professional duty, 'as far as possible, to arrange ourselves in a responsible way financially so that our

survival will not become a burden that our patients will have to carry'
(2013: 87).

Most challenging for a supervisor is the situation where a supervisee is
not wondering whether she should retire but her supervisor is. In this case
the supervisor is holding the ethical dilemma which has to be faced by the
two together. This is a situation which occurs relatively rarely, though we
can never know how many cases may get fudged, where supervisors find
a way to withdraw from the work rather than go through the emotionally
demanding task of confronting their supervisee and working through to an
ending. The following anecdotes come from one supervisor who had been
prepared to engage with the task on two occasions. The first case concerns
a therapist who had been a very able practitioner but who began to show
clear signs of memory loss and consequently was very stressed by the work.
In supervision she became tearful when the supervisor, empathising with
her anxiety, said she felt the time had come for her to retire. The supervisee
was able to appreciate the concern and to say she would finish soon.
However, her insight would evaporate and when the next supervision came
she would have done nothing towards closing her practice. Eventually, with
sustained encouragement, she was able to set an end date and to stick
to it:

> She required a lot of patience and sometimes I would feel very sad
> seeing a colleague who used to be so 'on top' of her work behaving
> in such a way. At other times I felt angry with her that someone with
> so much experience could be so unreliable – a real conflict of feelings.

In another case this supervisor was working with a less able supervisee.
As the therapist had always timetabled her sessions in a slightly *ad hoc*
way, it was harder for the supervisor to identify how much her memory
loss was also impacting on her clinical work. The supervisor found her
own supervision of supervision very helpful because she was able to
recognise how some of her anger with the supervisee was arising out of
aspects of her own life which were feeling chaotic. The supervisee still
needed help in preparing for retirement, but the supervisor was now able
to find a more empathic and more effective way to work with her.

In her study of older therapists, Jaffe (2011) expressed confidence in
supervisors' ability to provide quality control should it be needed. I agree
that supervisors have this responsibility, but I think this can be a tough
task and they could fulfil it better if the profession itself were holding
retirement in mind. In cases like that above, where the therapist has found
it difficult to acknowledge the reality of their decline, supervisors have had

to invest considerable effort into supporting and encouraging a process of retirement. The anecdote above indicates how supervision of supervision can assist supervisors in this task, but perhaps this safeguard would be more reliable if registering bodies were a little more involved. One possibility might be an explicit requirement for annual reviews in supervision, including an age-related component. This would give supervisors a stronger platform on which to make challenges when they are needed.

How useful is supervision to therapists going through retirement?

Most contributors had not looked to supervision to help with the decision itself. Denise made a clear distinction:

> I don't think I took it to supervision for discussion first, but I have needed to make use of supervision for the various feelings it's evoked in me.

And Clementine:

> Not very much. She was supportive – it was useful to talk about the sessions where we'd looked at ending.

I wondered whether Clementine had thought that her supervisor, older than her, should be retiring:

> I don't think I thought that but sometimes there was perhaps some envy on my part, because I don't think it's easy to be completely wholehearted about such a life change.

Although contributors recounted that supervision had not helped very much with the process of retirement, there is some evidence that supervision has a part to play in helping older therapists adapt and develop. Clementine shared an anecdote about one of the practicalities of ageing that cropped up when she was in her 60s. Because she was not always hearing what was being said in the supervision group, her supervisor suggested that she get her hearing tested. When she did so she discovered that she needed a hearing aid. Clementine recounted that she had not liked the intervention but clearly she saw its value and, being resilient, was able to make use of it. I thought it was significant that this psychoanalytic supervisor had made no bones about offering this practical advice.

A different example of supervision being important in the peri-retirement stage comes from a correspondent (Russell, 2011) to *Therapy Today*. She describes her aspiration to achieve optimal cognitive ageing (Powell, 2011) and explains the strategy she has adopted to achieve this: 'I have chosen to increase the quantity of supervision I receive as I get older, and also to work with a supervisor who has a different model to my own, psycho-analytic as opposed to humanistic/integrative' (Russell, 2011: 40). Russell explains that this is less about policing herself and more about challenging and energising her work.

A couple of participants had attended pre-retirement seminars. Annette had attended a very useful series of meetings when she was still considering the possibility of retirement. She appreciated hearing from others who had made the decision, and these discussions had supported her belief that it would be unethical to just go on and on. While a number of contributors expressed a strong wish that there had been more help with the process, others had managed to find support, or like Beatrice felt content for it to be an individual experience. She describes it not so much as a lonely process, but a personal and private one which she seemed not unhappy to have tackled alone.

Several retired therapists had noticed that colleagues who were still working had a great eagerness to talk to them about retirement. It seems that for those who are beginning to feel their way towards retirement, a former therapist who has closed her practice represents an aspiration and also a resource. There appears to be a degree of envy or surprise about how the person has pulled it off. On the retiree's side there may be reluctance to distil a complicated and possibly painful journey into a neat answer, and also some feelings of resentment towards those still working. One colleague in her 60s described a chance meeting with a retired therapist. The colleague had been eager to hear about the retiree's experience and particularly to learn *why* she had retired, but the retired therapist had not welcomed the enquiries and my colleague had felt rebuffed. Perhaps this rather sticky encounter is a microcosm of the discomfort in the profession and its organisations, and also demonstrates how the wisdom about this transition can get lost.

Containment of the supervisory relationship itself

The ending of the supervisory relationship can itself involve significant dynamics. Some older therapists may have been with their supervisors for longer than they worked with their therapists. Mander draws a picture which many of us can recognise, describing a positive transference to the supervisor with whom the weekly meeting has assumed the nature of a cherished routine and where a plateau of colleagueship has been reached that is creative and nourishing.

(2002: 149)

Supervision always has some degree of power difference, and if the supervisee is older than her supervisor this differential could be exacerbated by the social stigma of age. Where additional power imbalances are operating this could have a significant impact on the dyad. If we imagine the supervisor as being male, younger, richer, whiter and of more elite education and the supervisee as having less of these privileged characteristics, we can expect that power dynamics within the supervisory dyad will need attention. If we neglect to contain these kinds of discomfort, the clinical work may be affected (Power, 2009). When the supervisory couple are discussing the supervisee's retirement, the issue of their relative ages may need to be acknowledged. In the rare cases where a supervisor feels the need to encourage a supervisee to retire, issues of power and privilege are likely to be particularly significant. Whether the supervisee is younger or older than the supervisor who is urging them to consider retirement, the dynamic is likely to be tense and acknowledging the difference may be important.

Another factor impacting on how much can be discussed in supervision will be the theoretical position of both parties. This will indicate where the teach/treat boundary is drawn and how much the dyad feel it is appropriate for the supervisee to explore her feelings about retirement. At one end of the spectrum, Langs (1994) advocates a very rigorous frame intended to enable the decoding of unconscious material which the supervisee is bringing. At the other end of the spectrum, Frawley-O'Dea and Sarnat (2001) encourage the dyad to pay attention to the supervisee's experience of the supervisor and they suggest this is particularly important when uncomfortable feelings are present.

Jacobs, David and Meyer (1995) look at ending a supervisory relationship, from a general rather than a retirement perspective, and they address the question of possible contact between supervisor and supervisee after their final session. They describe the possibility of transition to a new type of professional collegial relationship, but warn against anticipating this shift because the supervisee will need the supervisor to remain available in role to the very end of the work. Given the likely challenges in the final months of clinical work, this seems wise though we might think of the final supervision session, which will be taken after the clients have all departed, as a point of transition where any future contact can be thought about.

The supervisor's role in forced or emergency retirement

Sometimes there will be no dilemma about whether the therapist should retire – she may simply be too ill to carry on. Often it will not be so clear, and Galatzer-Levy (2004) describes the grey area where a therapist who is unwell may function at a level where the harm from cutting short the work could be greater than continuing. In these cases the supervisor is balancing the needs of the patients, as best as she can make them out, with the needs of a vulnerable supervisee. The supervisee, unwell and distressed, will need help to contain her experience as she weighs the risks of either closing a practice unnecessarily or possibly exposing vulnerable patients to inadequate therapy.

In a personal paper, Culliford (2011) poignantly charts the illness and forced retirement of her husband, with whom she ran a joint practice. Her reflections on the crises they faced and the learning she took from the events give us an opportunity to benefit vicariously from the nightmare they lived through. While Culliford's husband was critically ill in hospital, she worked closely with her husband's supervisor to manage first the temporary suspension of his practice and subsequently the full closure. The supervisor and Culliford conferred on the key issues of how much to tell patients at each stage, and they jointly composed letters to send out. Her paper provides a unique account of the practical and emotional steps which may be involved for supervisor and therapeutic executor when a practice has to be closed under very painful circumstances.

Removal from the professional register for being unfit to practice is a very different kind of imposed ending, but perhaps worth mentioning because supervisors may need to help a supervisee who is in this position. Where a complaint has been upheld in respect of one clinical relationship it is common for other clients to feel loyalty to their therapist. This means that the endings imposed on them are particularly complex and painful; they are living through a clinical disaster and supervision may have a role in containing the turmoil and bringing some thinking to bear on the abandonment and enforced separation these patients are facing. Though such a closure would usually come after months of uncertainty, the ending for clients may be sudden. The therapist who is being sanctioned is likely to be feeling intense shame or rage, or both, and these emotions are liable to compromise her capacity to work effectively with patients who are facing an exceptionally challenging emergency ending. Therapeutic executors, supervisors and registering bodies have a profound respons-ibility to support these clients in their decisions about seeking further help.

Emergency endings are not covered in detail in this book, but the Appendix provides a few ideas. A clinical will provides instructions for executors to carry out, but there may be situations in which we are suddenly unable to continue work but are not at the point of handing over responsibility for our practice. It may be useful to have a list to ourselves detailing who we would need to contact and what we need to sort out in such an emergency.

Boundary issues

Retirement is likely to present unfamiliar dilemmas around boundaries, and supervisors will be called on to help think these through.

Questions about disclosure

When supervisees are unwell there is often a need for reflection on how much to disclose about their illness. Writing about her own cancer, Pizer (1998) provides a cogent case for disclosing what would otherwise become an elephant in the room. She suggests that we need to distinguish 'between what we keep private and to ourselves and what is in danger of becoming a withholding secret that distorts analytic process and progress' (1998: 209). Supervision may help us arrive at this distinction.

A supervisor usually helps best by holding open a thinking space, but occasionally supervisees are very grateful for guidance. This was illustrated by Alice, who closed her practice in order to relocate. She had always seen her clients in a therapy room in her home, but during the months when her partner was dying she decided to move clients to an office nearby. She was unsure how much to explain to patients about the change of room and she was very grateful to her supervisor for his direct guidance around this boundary. He said, 'You don't have to tell them anything if you don't want to – you have a right to your privacy.'

Galatzer-Levy (2004) reminds us that patients have a right to give 'informed consent' to treatment and argues that this would include knowing if their therapist was at increased risk of illness and death (2004: 1021). He suggests that just as a surgical patient is entitled to *assume* a clean operating theatre (rather than needing to double-check this point), an analytic patient would assume that the therapist will have a good chance of remaining in sufficiently good health to carry out the treatment for as long as it is needed.

Questions about the boundary in the period after retirement

Having retired very suddenly when diagnosed with pancreatic cancer, Shernoff (2009) made a degree of recovery and lived for another couple of years. Once he was over the initial chemotherapy and was feeling stronger he reflected deeply on the unsatisfactory endings he had been forced to make. He felt drawn to telephone his clients to offer a one-off session in order to make a better closure, but on exploring this with his supervisor he realised that it had more to do with his needs than those of his patients. He describes his supervisor as holding a position that was both firm and empathic.

> He insisted that, difficult as this was, I needed to mourn the loss of my career, accept that it was over, no matter how inelegantly I had been forced to end it, and, like my former patients, move on.
>
> (2009: 112)

Some months later he heard from one of the patients with whom he had had to terminate abruptly. This email, asking for a meeting, came from one of his favourite patients about a year after his retirement. After reflection in his own therapy, he decided to agree to a single further meeting. The former patient reported a sexual relational issue which he was finding hard to discuss with his new therapist. Shernoff was able to encourage him to speak to his therapist, if not about the issue directly, at least about the fact that there was something he found it hard to broach. Shernoff did not charge a fee for the session, citing the fact that he was receiving disability benefits. This question of a fee reminds us what a grey area this is if the former therapist is no longer registered or insured.

Questions of post-retirement boundaries rarely cropped up for my interviewees, but clearly these could pose a dilemma. The issue was most apparent in Emma's story. As she was making an emergency ending she decided to offer clients some opportunity to contact her post-therapy. She did this by giving them her mobile and email details and then by exchanging brief messages in the months after she stopped working. Various writers have addressed the issue of boundaries with former clients (Gabbard and Lester, 1995; Novick and Novick, 2000), but they were looking at therapists who continue to practice. Once a therapist has retired, if she is no longer accountable to a registering body then her contact with former clients will be guided solely by her own ethical compass.

The boundary with a supervisee's own therapy

From contributors and colleagues I have heard of a number of cases where a supervisee had let her supervisor know that her much older therapist was not functioning effectively. In most cases supervisors had been able to contact the training organisation where the therapist was registered and appropriate action was taken, though sadly this often involved an emergency retirement. When, as in these cases, a therapist works with training patients (or with clients who are qualified therapists), this does provide an indirect monitoring function with a channel of communication via the therapist's supervisor. When an ageing therapist is working simply with 'members of the public', this particular avenue of help is not available and clients have less protection.

In a paper drawing on her personal experience, Noak (2011) tells of a case where supervisors were sadly unwilling to act. She recalls events from 20 years earlier when, as a training patient, she had become anxious about the failing health of her analyst. She first tried unsuccessfully to speak to him directly about this. She then raised the matter with both of her training supervisors but they dismissed her concerns, saying 'You know how stubborn he is' and 'This is none of your business' (2011: 3). Noak believes that her analyst, who died while still seeing patients, did not have supervision, 'since he belonged to a generation, which considered supervision unnecessary after a certain point in time'. Unsurprisingly she makes a strong case for supervision having an additional monitoring function for the older therapist. She explains why this can only work if training organisations recognise a 'responsibility to create a culture where this can happen' (2011: 4).

Peer supervision groups

Comments from contributors indicate varying levels of help from peer groups. Clementine had found her peer supervision very helpful for thinking about patients' response to the ending, and as she spoke warmly of this group it was clear that she was connecting to very poignant memories. Annette also found her peer supervision very effective at this stage of her career:

> They were mainly helpful in asking me how I felt about it, and making me talk about it, and supporting me as I worked with him [her final patient].

Annette explained her view that peer supervision had been more appropriate for her at this point than an individual supervisor would have been. She argued that she had had more freedom to bring her own feelings to the peer group. I wondered whether this opportunity to explore feelings was less a factor of whether the supervision was individual or peer and more a reflection of how much validity is given to the therapist's own feelings by the theoretical model used.

A case from the literature also describes how peer groups can sometimes provide exceptional levels of containment and support. Noak's (2011) account of a supervision group that supported a member who was terminally ill shows how peers can sometimes provide support and challenge even under the most distressing circumstances. Just as some supervisors perform better than others, some peer groups are more able to confront and process these existential challenges. The issue of quality control is in the hands of members and it can be helpful to get occasional supervision of the group from a consultant (Power, 2013).

Other contributors spoke of the inherent limitations of their peer groups even though in every case they rated their colleagues very highly and had done years of fruitful work together. Perhaps the emotional closeness of the group can be a disadvantage at such a time. Speaking about her cancer, Emma reported that peer supervision had not been sufficient to contain the exceptionally challenging material she was bringing:

> Funnily enough the peer group wasn't much help. I think it was really too much for them you see – to have somebody sitting in their midst with cancer, talking about the effect it had on the ten [the patients who were ending]. I think that was a bit too much. I felt as though they edged away from it.

To fill the gap, Emma arranged occasional sessions with her former therapist and used these sessions both to think both about her personal situation with the cancer and about the patients. Celia also conveyed that her peer supervision was not providing what she needed in the very challenging process of her forced ending. She offered the insight that the difficulty might lie more in her projection than in the actual limitations of her peers:

> I think that paranoia has made it less helpful than it could have been, because actually with my intellectual self I can see that people are more than willing to explore situations with me. I perhaps am not as willing to explore with them.

Emma and Celia were both facing forced retirement, which is likely to present the peer group with the difficult experience of survivor guilt. Mary's experience suggests that peer supervision can struggle to provide containment for retirement, even when the circumstances are not clouded by life-threatening illness:

> Peer supervision group has been supportive at times, but one is also caught in the fact that people don't like you leaving!

The contrast between individual and collective supervision is mentioned by Susannah in Chapter 9, where she talks about her experience of being supervised in a group during her first pregnancy. In her case this was not peer supervision and her comments relate to the contrast between a space for oneself and a shared space. She had not found the group satisfactory and in her second pregnancy she had been glad she was seeing an individual supervisor. Her experience indicates how hard it can be for group supervision to attend to the exceptional needs of certain members. Just as Susannah's group did not provide optimal containment for a pregnant supervisee, in a similar way it might be difficult for the supervisor of a group to offer enough space to a therapist who was closing her practice in order to retire.

The question of retired therapists continuing their work as supervisors

Five of the contributors had either continued with supervision work or intended to do so. For some this was on a relatively small scale, for others it involved a sizeable commitment and Rosemary had actually increased her supervision work when she stopped seeing her own patients. This meant that when she was obliged to retire from supervision she felt the gap in her life more severely than she had when ending her therapy work. The training organisation within which she supervised had set an age limit for supervisors, and this obliged her to stop.

This intention to continue to practice as a supervisor after ending with clients is very often mentioned by therapists considering retirement, and it came up in Pointon's (2004) interviews with retirees. There may be both organisational and clinical dilemmas to consider as some registering bodies specifically require that supervisors must themselves be practising as therapists. Other codes of ethics and practice leave this matter to the clinician's own discretion. While there is some variation on how this issue is handled, the point on which registration bodies in Britain are very clear is that in order to renew accreditation a member must be under regular supervision. When there is no client work to be supervised, some organisations may permit renewal on the basis of supervision of supervision.

Quite apart from these procedural considerations, there is a clinical question as to whether a supervisor who no longer sees patients might in time lose her sensitivity to the work. There may also be a fitness to practice issue: where the individual has retired from seeing patients because they felt their age was beginning to tell, there may be a question as to how long they could appropriately work with supervisees. Is the work of supervision really that much less demanding? If memory and cognitive capacity is reduced, can the supervisor generate the ideas and connections which are needed? How will the supervisees and their patients fare if the supervisor becomes ill and has to withdraw at short notice?

Beatrice shared her reflections on these dilemmas. She explained that she had given up supervision of students who required a guaranteed length of contract but would continue to supervise colleagues, believing that the aspects of ageing which might put patients at risk were not as concerning with supervisees. With the latter she would feel free to cancel a session if feeling only mildly unwell and also to give much shorter notice of a final end date:

> I do a bit more supervision, but I am watchful there too because one needs to be pretty 'on the go'.

Rosemary also had clear ideas about the distinct competencies needed for supervision. She believed that the difficulty in recalling names and people, which had caused her to retire as a therapist, was not a handicap as a supervisor since it was not out of order for a supervisor to ask when they want to be reminded of details.

The supervisor's own retirement

Like the older therapist, supervisors who are ageing will need to weigh up the risks of becoming seriously ill or dying. While the sudden incapacity or death of a supervisor is not likely to be as critical to a supervisee as the sudden loss of a therapist is to a patient, such a rupture would be significant even for an experienced therapist. It is unsurprising that the sudden loss of a long-term supervisor would be distressing, but anecdotal evidence suggests that even when a supervision relationship is of shorter duration, a sudden death can be traumatic.

When supervisors fail to recognise their decline, the harm can be significant. It is a mistake to expect supervisees to supply quality control by either leaving or seeking support from the relevant body. Their loyalty to the fading supervisor may not permit this at all and at best they will only take that step with dismay. Such a destructive ending risks filtering through to the work with clients. As Murdin (2000: 170) writes: 'Therapists will stay with elderly supervisors to keep them alive, just as patients will stay to heal and repair and keep their therapists going.' The contributors and other therapists have shared a number of anecdotes about ageing supervisors, including one who was unwell enough to need to lie on the couch during supervisions.

A number of contributors indicated that they would expect to give less notice of an imposed ending to a supervisee, naming three or six months as compared with the year or more that most returnees gave to their patients. Denise was working through six months' notice for both patients and supervisees and she had a high number of supervisees who had been with her for many years. She described how troubled they had been by her impending retirement and how directly they had voiced feelings of abandonment and anger.

A number of stories pointed to the meaning that supervisors may have for their supervisees. Annette had experience as a supervisee of her supervisor withdrawing rather abruptly – seemingly due to a change in his employed work. After the ending she describes here, she chose not to seek out a replacement individual supervisor but opted for peer supervision from that point:

> It must have happened over a period of a month – it was a case of, 'I'll know next time you come' and then, 'look I'm sorry I won't be able to see you'. I didn't really have a final session with him. And that was the sort of thing that I was obviously determined not to do, although that was supervision.

A reflection from Rosemary also points to the meaning a supervisor can have in our internal world. At 84 she had tears in her eyes as she recalled the death of a former supervisor whose teaching had been so containing at the start of her career:

> We weren't in touch particularly but it's nice to have her in the world so to speak.

Nicola was one who felt she had learned from a former supervisor's retirement. She had experienced both a supervisor who died very suddenly and one who had retired in a careful managed way, with a year's notice. She felt that the latter had been a good role model for her. She was also clear that she would want some final sessions with her supervisor after seeing her last client:

> I want that process for two things – the ending with clients but also the ending with her.

Boyd-Carpenter (2010a) writes of her supervisees coping well with her retirement. While they expressed shock, sadness and loss they were not overwhelmed by the ending and set about thoughtfully finding new supervisors. Boyd-Carpenter describes their kindness towards her as resembling 'the protectiveness that the young adult often feels to the ageing parent' (2010a: 94). Even though the vulnerability of supervisees is generally less than that of patients, it is important for supervisors to take retirement planning seriously. We know that clients often respond to changes and turbulence in supervision. When a supervisor has to bring their work to a sudden ending there could be a pyramid effect, with the rupture filtering through the handful of supervisees to the much higher number of clients beyond.

Chapter 7

What is lost?

If we have chosen this work to meet our need to be useful, then it will be very hard for us ever to feel that we have done enough.

(Patsy)

So many of our anxieties can recede a bit . . . It's a great sublimator work – so many neuroses and anxieties find a better place rather than becoming prevalent. It's partly an identity thing but I think really it's the connection to people which is so important.

(Clementine)

Eventually the day of our final session will come. For the last time we will receive a client in the therapy room and sit for 50 minutes hoping that our understanding and comments can make a difference to how this client manages herself. For the last time we will scan our internal world for the express purpose of tuning in to the experience of a patient, linking back our thoughts to months and years of sessions, dreams and early memories. Finally we usher the client from the room and turn to face the empty space, the rows of books knowing that our professional need of them is over.

Attachment implications

As a developmental stage, retirement may bring significant changes in addition to the ending of a working life. The retiree's health and that of their partner may be compromised, the home may be downsized, grandchildren may be born and elderly parents may die or need more intensive support. Alongside such tangible changes will be the emotional adjustment to the alteration in status, and in each case our way of meeting these challenges will be coloured by our attachment stories. Even for older people who retain good health and feel internally robust, society's attitude makes it hard for them to be recognised as strong, capable adults. Woodward (2004) recalls the Victorian dictum about children and observes that it is now old people who must be 'seen but not heard'. She suggests that 'This attitude to elderly people not only denies their attachment needs, but by and large makes it impossible for them to be met' (2004: 53).

Whether or not a retiree enjoys good health, there will be a recognition, conscious or unconscious, that the next transition will be the final one of death. The question of the therapist's own death came up in my very first interview. Rosemary quoted a Latin formula used by many mediaeval poets: *Timor mortis conturbat me* – 'fear of death disturbs me'. In our interview Rosemary also spoke about death in her own words, but it was interesting that she reached for this ancient liturgical phrase to reflect on a taboo area. It reminded me of Freud using Latin to refer to his mother's nakedness which he had glimpsed on an overnight train journey (Gay, 1988). As well as threats to the therapist's own health, retirement may bring concerns for loved ones. Clementine tells of losing two of her closest friends and of the impact of age on her immediate circle:

> Retirement is hard but so is getting older, particularly losing friends through death. Older family members and friends also become less available as their energies lessen or they become ill. It is important not to confuse the experience of retirement with the experience of getting older and what that entails.

If we think of mourning as a process of adaptation to loss, we could also see it as a kind of learning, a discovery of what has been taken away and what remains. Following the initial shock, the first manifestation of mourning is the urge to search for the missing person, until the fruitlessness of this gives way to disorganisation and despair (Bowlby, 1980). In an early paper, Murray Parkes (1971) says grief is

> a process of 'realisation' by means of which affectional bonds are severed and old models of the world and the self given up. It tends to be avoided and accounts for resistance to change and depressive reactions to change.
>
> (1971: 101)

More recently attachment theorists have put less stress on severing bonds and are explicit about the value of continuing bonds. There is an understanding that the bereaved can accept the death of the lost person and also remain emotionally attached (Juri and Marrone, 2003). The issue of continuing bonds has been researched by Stroebe, Schut and Stroebe (2005), who propose a dual-process model of mourning in which loss-oriented coping alternates with restoration-oriented coping. Individuals with preoccupied patterns are at risk of being stuck in the former and dismissing individuals in the latter. Those with a disorganised orientation are at risk of the kind of sudden fluctuations in state and intrusive thoughts which could indicate post-traumatic stress syndrome. Stroebe and colleagues (2005) found that bonds can be continued without the negative effects previously expected and that some degree of avoidance (not relentless positivity) is adaptive. Bowlby himself revised the name for his last stage from 'detachment' to 'reorganisation' (Fraley and Shaver, 1999).

Many therapists count 'Mourning and melancholia' (1917) as their favourite of Freud's papers because he movingly explicates the dynamics of chronic grief. The idealising of the lost object prevents the essential steps of grieving and adaptation. For individuals who cannot bear to know their resentment towards the dead person, melancholia offers a way of diverting their anger from the abandoning other and redirecting the punishment towards the self. Quinodoz (2010) indicates the aggression involved in this splitting and projection:

> Whether we reject someone for having caused us pain or consider that person to be perfect in order not to feel the pain caused to us, in both cases we attack our relationship with that person.
>
> (2010: 64)

Bowlby (1973) also points out the importance of anger as an element in mourning. When someone dies we hold an unconscious hope that the lost person can be recovered. Like the mother who loses sight of her toddler and on finding them scolds them fiercely, we protest in an attempt to discourage the deserter from doing this again. Bowlby suggests that mourning happens when the individual accepts both the change which has happened in the external world, and that they need to make a corresponding change in their internal world (1980).

We know that any ending or death can reconnect us to earlier losses, and Alan's final comment conveys this poignantly. He was old enough that in his early life in a rural community, cars had been a rarity, but the intervening decades gave no protection against early losses flooding back:

> Every month I get a new disease. That links up very unfavourable aspects of childhood – like my mother going off in that horse and cart

that the hospital had sent out to get her – and I thinking, 'Where the hell is she going?'

Denise's recollection of the ending of her own therapy also describes this echo from earlier losses:

> I remember being devastated in the last session – not because I wanted to carry on but because it connected to all the other losses of the past and separation.

In the course of working on this book I was surprised by my own experience of loss. I gained a sense of what the contributors were facing when I realised I could not get the book written without cutting back on my own clinical work. For a year or so I had to turn away new referrals and this felt almost like poetic justice. Contributors had told me how sad they felt to turn down the opportunity to work with new patients. I felt I had been quite empathic in how I had listened to their experience, but now I was being made to understand this at first hand, if only as a temporary measure.

Retirement as a reminder of our mortality

Boyd-Carpenter wrote that at times her impending retirement had felt like a death:

> even a suicide or a murder. And indeed, as with the truly dying, I have had to contemplate the lives of my clients continuing and flourishing without me.
>
> (2010a: 89)

By forcing us to think about our own ageing and death, retirement may serve as a creative force, but if we cannot cope with our own fear of death then defences may become more rigid. As well as our fear, there will be sadness at the global loss which approaches and we may have to deal with our envy: can we bear that others carry on living? The sense of what it feels like to become redundant is conveyed by words that Tennyson (1842/1933) gives to Ulysses at the end of his long journey.

> How dull it is to pause, to make an end,
> To rust unburnish'd, not to shine in use!

Later in Tennyson's poem Ulysses rallies his mariners with the line, '*'Tis not too late to seek a newer world'*. This urge to seek new projects could refer to the creative and productive roles which retired therapists are performing, but could also indicate a manic defence. Another poem about Ulysses' voyage stresses not the idea of setting out on a new venture, but the acceptance of what this journey to Ithaca has meant:

> and once you're old, cast anchor on the isle,
> rich with all you've gained along the way,
> expecting not that Ithaca will give you wealth.
>
> (Cavafy, 2007: 5)

I have used lines from two poems about Odysseus to speak of the experience of the retiring therapist and perhaps, the same myth can illustrate the client's story if we think of her as the one who is left behind. Atwood's retelling of the myth in *The Penelopiad* (2005) gives Penelope a voice and chronicles her experience of being left to cope; it also covers the reconnection of this couple after 20 years apart. This re-engagement might represent the experience of clients who come through a long break for maternity or sabbatical. For clients who are 'being retired' the story is bleaker as there is no opportunity for re-engagement. Moreover we might feel that Penelope perhaps had more clues as to what she was getting into, for Odysseus was never the 'stay at home type'.

The theme of life as journey is also explored by Shernoff (2009), who was forced to make an emergency retirement from a full practice when he was diagnosed with pancreatic cancer. He reports that his dreams were full of his longing for his former health and ability to travel. Another analyst who was writing close to the time of his death is Grotjahn (1985), who demonstrates the capacity to both protest and accept the losses:

> I know dying is unpleasant, for to be dead is Nothing. I like that even less. Sure, I am a narcissist. Who in our profession is not? I think of all the investment I have made in myself: the analysis, endless training, the continued self-analysis, the drive to understand, to give insight, and the wealth of knowledge accumulated in a life-time. All this I should give up?
>
> (1985: 301)

We are very familiar with the metaphor of a journey for the passage of the years, so it is intriguing to learn of a very different metaphor for time. Quinodoz (2010) refers to a South American tribe who think of themselves not as moving forward into the future, but of being immobile while time moves up on them from behind. This metaphor seems so apt because it has us facing the past, that is the part of our experience which we can see, while the future is still out of view 'behind' us.

'Old' is a relative term, but wherever we place the marker, becoming a retired person will bring us closer to it. Neugarten (1968) observed that our life stages and role changes create a kind of social rather than a chronological clock. In this social clock retirement may signify to the person, and to those around them, that they are now 'old'. Cath (1997) proposed useful terminology to clarify what we mean by 'old': the 'young-old' refers to the group aged 65 to 75 and the 'old-old' refers to those who are over 85. This leaves the term 'old' for those aged 75 to 85 (1997: 147).

Perhaps in a practical way we could define 'old' as that time of life when death comes into clearer view, as the people just ahead of us and around us begin to show a pattern of dying. This is one of many reasons why the death of a parent in adulthood can feel very disturbing. With that generation gone, the next one in the coffin will be me. The prospect of our death presents us with the most challenging version of separation anxiety in the whole lifespan: we will lose our self and all of our others. As Waddell puts it, 'it is often during the last decades of life that the capacity to sustain a mature state of mind is most severely tested' (2002: 218). The truth of her comment seems to be affirmed by Alan's pronouncement on retirement. He had put off closing his practice until his late 80s and his health had declined very swiftly from that point. For him the loss had felt 'global' and he was emphatic about its impact:

> Retirement is one of the biggest events in life. It's a gigantic event, a gigantic turn of events. It makes one into an old man or old woman straight away and that takes some coping with and it leaves you frail.

He voiced the heaviness of a loss which for him, with his declining health, was powerfully evoking earlier grieving and disappointment:

> It raises all the problems of all the things that one has to give up and gave up in life. And it's like you are called upon to give them up again, and go through the whole thing again about giving up everything.

Writing from his experience as a hospice doctor, Kearney indicates the risk that our defences against death anxiety can alienate us from deeper parts of the self (1996). The individual tries to defend against approaching death by cutting off from her internal world where profoundly difficult emotions are stirring. Kearney describes the ego as 'happiest when in control of a familiar and predictable world but . . . profoundly threatened by the approach of death which it sees as utter chaos and the ultimate unknown' (1996: 13). Quinodoz (2010) makes a similar point, indicating how boredom can be the price we pay for denying our anxiety about death. If we live in denial about our own end and imagine that we have all the time in the world, we will be spared death anxiety but will lose the interest we could have had in each moment. This echoes a general observation by Waddell: 'Development, at whatever age, is founded in the capacity to go on engaging with the meaning of experience with imagination, courage and integrity' (2002: 217).

In the year or so that most therapists work with retirement in view, these challenges of managing feelings about their own death could inhibit exploration with the client. Writing about the impact of ageing on the analyst, Eissler warns us:

> As long as death has not been integrated as a necessity of life but is represented in the ageing analyst's psyche as a conflict-arousing enemy, he will not be able to give his best to his patients.
>
> (1993: 325)

Loss of role

The pace and structure of the therapist's work provide experiences which are intense and exciting within a formal and contained setting. Ogden has described the analytic relationship as 'intimacy in the context of formality' (1992: 175). If this is a way of relating what therapists particularly enjoy, where will the retired therapist find such intensity? Weiss expresses this bluntly: 'Other activities, whether vocations or hobbies, are just not as rewarding' (1997: 472).

The point is illustrated in comments from contributors. Here Clementine indicates the unique sublimation she found in work. She had a particularly full life in retirement but she conveyed the loss she felt a couple of years after ending work:

> It's left quite a gap. I think work has always been important to me – work and study have been a solace . . . a feeling of engagement . . . a very good feeling of satisfaction, clarity, focus . . . I thought today when I did some reading in preparation for this interview, that I really miss this and I've not found something else which absorbs me in quite the same way.

Two years further into retirement I was able to ask Clementine for follow-up reflections, and she indicated that she still misses the sublimating function of work:

> I have had grievous worries about some family members and know that if I had had to work this would have helped because there would have been less time to dwell on these. Also I would have felt more confident because I was achieving through work. Reparative drives can be satisfied to some extent in practising therapy, they can be very frustrated with family members. It is easier to put boundaries on pestering phone calls when one is working and not be at people's beck and call.

This theme is echoed by Barratt *et al.* (2012), who suggest that one particular satisfaction of our work is its challenge and rigour. 'It brings an external discipline, more than just a structure, to the working day' (2012: 111).

Giving up our professional caring role is all the harder because of the way this role has met our need to achieve repair, and to be valued for that. As therapists we may be vicariously gratified and consoled by the care we offer. Studies such as Barnett's (2007), into therapists' unconscious motivations for the work, affirm what we know anecdotally, that most of us were led towards this work through our own losses and wounds. Among the contributors, Patsy was particularly explicit about the meaning that our role as therapists has in our internal world:

> Anthony Storr says that a high proportion of therapists had depressed mothers. I think it's something about trying to get in contact with them and to stop being a therapist feels like to stop trying to make contact.

Clementine's experience also suggested anxiety about losing touch with her mother when she stopped working with clients. In her case she understood this from her dreams. As a child in boarding school she could bank on receiving a weekly letter from her mother who was a most reliable correspondent. In retirement she dreamed that her mother had stopped writing to her, leaving her feeling cut off and rejected.

Viorst's (1982) summary of what the therapist loses in regular endings is daunting enough, but this catalogue of losses would be multiplied when a full practice is being closed down:

the loss of a whole, real object; the loss of some identified-with part of the object; the loss of a healing symbiotic relatedness; the loss of some especially pleasing role; the loss of a host of professional and therapeutic ambitions; and the loss of the analyst's dream of his or her own perfection.

(1982: 416)

Viorst suggests that loss in the countertransference is sharpest when we have a particular identification with part of a patient, or when we are losing 'some especially gratifying role that the work permits the analyst to play' (1982: 407). This struck me as a very significant loss, and the illustration she goes on to provide indicates how important certain client relationships may be for the therapist. She cites the example of a therapist who recognised how much he enjoyed having the role of the loving son to one of his patients, and that in playing this role he was doing what he had never been able to do for his own devalued father. This case gave the therapist a prompt to work through his anger and disappointment towards his own father, and I think it illustrates another significant loss at the point of retirement: opportunities for the therapist to grow in insight and to repair her own internal world.

Like Clementine, Mary, a therapist with a classic pattern of retirement, also articulated the extent of the loss very fully. Again her sad feelings were certainly not due to emptiness in her lifestyle. She explained that she was involved with her grandchildren, she painted, and she also relished the cultural life of London's theatres and museums:

So a lot of positives but they don't completely make up for the dark side . . . yes it feels like falling off a cliff sometimes . . . what it means to be a psychotherapist and what the patients do for you. The projections – what do we do with them when we are coping on our own? And the structure, having this thing to do that matters and gives meaning to everyday life.

Carol also articulates a sustaining or healing function which the work can have for the therapist:

For me it's been an existential loss . . . I think this is why I got quite depressed. It's about saying goodbye to a huge part of one's life . . . and I think that's been really hard . . . Loss of identity, loss of feeling worthwhile, that you're contributing and offering . . . all those things that would make one feel quite good . . . I used to feel quite good about myself after seeing a client . . . I found being a therapist really creative.

In a comment that closely echoes Grotjahn (1985) above, Carol named the reluctance to give up something which had been hard won:

Part of that was about giving up something; something that I'd worked really hard towards.

Speaking two years into her retirement, Emma conveyed that she was not pining after her former role, yet her attachment to the couch itself speaks of a powerful symbolic meaning which it continued to hold:

I haven't wished that patients were on the couch, though I wouldn't want to move the couch – it's too dear.

I have quoted from several contributors who spoke of sadness about the loss of role and the opportunities which being a therapist give us. Patsy voiced what must be a deeper unease for many of us – the fear that our labour has been in vain, that our years of patient listening have made little difference. She indicates that part of the loss we face at retirement is the loss of our fantasy that we can change the world:

I think my ambivalence is not just about retirement, I think it's about being a therapist – about whether it's possible to really believe I have helped people . . . People you sit with for years and years, and what have you done? – moved them on a few inches. It's easier to retire when you feel you've done a good job. Perhaps staying on and on and never retiring is because therapists are after that elusive feeling of doing good, rather than have to face what they haven't done.

Loss of the 'incidental' benefits of the work

Just as incidental factors in therapy can significantly help the patient, there may be value and meaning attached to many incidental elements in the therapist's working life. Jaffe's (2011) research, like mine, suggested that contact with colleagues is of huge significance to therapists. Mary reflected that for some of her peers the therapy world was almost like a family. She spoke of a former colleague who, in retirement, had kept up with attending lectures but had felt rebuffed at one event when a younger colleague had asked what she was doing there. Clementine and Annette both mentioned collaboration with colleagues as something they missed keenly. These were not people who lacked friends or social contacts, but they had found the exchanges between colleagues in the service of the work to be a particularly rewarding form of connection. Patsy also spoke of the importance of colleagues and of missing the intense focus of the work.

> I think there are two things I miss. I miss the space – going down and being in my room and being with someone where you can only focus on the present, and you are there for that hour. And I miss gossiping with my colleagues. I can forget about whether I've bought the supper or whether the roof's got a leak and you can only focus on what is happening to you now.

Carol missed the social experience of learning:

> That's quite a loss actually – that sense of belonging to a community . . . not going on training modules and ringing my colleagues up and saying, 'Which one shall we do?' I am going to miss that sense of belonging.

Boyd-Carpenter indicates the range of losses and the ways they became apparent:

> Writing letters of resignation, shredding paperwork and watching the diary pages become emptier . . . In essence it has been the loss of the intimate and profound links with the other in the room.
>
> (2010a: 94)

Another retiree echoed this loss of 'the other'. She explained that her keenest loss was not the loss of status but of hearing endlessly fascinating stories. She would miss hearing about myriad other walks of life, careers and cultures that she could never inhabit herself – that window on other lives would be closed. In a similar reflection, Alan recalled the task of closing down his office and shredding the notes:

> Throwing away all these notes was like throwing away the people as well.

Factors which determine how we experience the losses

The majority of contributors had had long careers as therapists and for many this followed an earlier career in another caring profession. This raised a question for me as to whether there might be some correlation between length of time in the job and the degree of loss felt. Horner (2002) suggests that coming late to the work means it is not our entire identity and is therefore easier to let go, but I think this would seem to depend on multiple factors. A therapist interviewed by Russell and Simanowitz (2013) had an experience of retirement which fitted with Horner's thesis, but my contributors Hannah and Carol both mentioned a contrary perspective – their sadness that their carefully chosen second career had not had a chance to grow and mature.

There is a belief that people who are totally immersed in their work are more prone to burnout and that this group will find retirement harder. This idea might be supported by Vaillant's (2002) finding that retirees gain most satisfaction from activities which have been long-term interests as opposed to those taken up as new pastimes for retirement. This would seem to imply that a therapist who has been wholly wrapped up in their work, without outside interests, will find the transition harder.

Annette and Rosemary both reflected on a coping style learned from their mothers. Rosemary referred to hers as stoic, and Annette described hers in the following way:

> My mother was always, 'Look forward, never look back'. I suddenly saw that I'm doing it again – I'm looking forward, I'm not looking back. That's in a way . . . how you move on. I'm not doing it in the same way as I did then because obviously I've got a lot of support, a lot of help to deal with it and I know a lot more now than I did then. Nevertheless the old patterns still lurks there, so the future is always brighter.

Emma felt that she had adjusted cheerfully to retirement because of her re-engagement with her earlier career as a writer. She had worked for about a year on a reduced practice before making a full retirement and recalled being very bored at that point because she was used to working much harder. Once fully retired she enjoyed herself:

> I thought I was going to suffer terribly, from a loss of daily intimacy, a loss of consequence in my organisation – which of course has

happened – but that hasn't mattered either really. None of it has really mattered as I expected it to.

For some contributors retirement served to evoke earlier losses. When Nicola's supervisor asked how other endings might be resonating with the closure of her practice she became more aware of her angry feelings:

> I realised at that point, though I hadn't been conscious of it at the time, that most of the endings I've had have been triggered by my husband's moves, they haven't always been my own decision, so I've had to sort of adapt. I was suddenly quite shocked and thought 'Am I retiring because he's retiring?' And then I felt quite angry and I recalled this feeling when I ended with my therapist. [Nicola had explained that she had had to end with her own therapist when the family had moved for her husband's work.] So I've had to be clear that I'm retiring now partly because he is retiring but also because I am choosing to right now.

An anecdote from Rosemary illustrates how relationships with others can help or hinder us with the transition. At a point where she was feeling very low at the prospect of her therapy work ending, she happened to meet an older colleague. Her feelings were inflamed to resentment when faced with his casual confidence about his own skills and his implicit denigration of Rosemary's:

> I remember a beastly person . . . who shall be nameless, when I was feeling it [that she was preparing to retire]. I met him at the theatre, or somewhere, and I said I was feeling a bit droopy 'you know because I'm not taking on any new patients' and this idiot, who was, who will always be, eight years older than me, and way past it in my opinion anyway, said, 'Oh no, I can always help them in some way' . . . I was cross . . . a sort of silly optimism that by sheer personality you could somehow be useful to people.

Analytic thinking on ageing and death

Although Freud's (1905) remarks about ageing are likely to find little support nowadays, his comments about death anxiety and our denial of our mortality continue to have resonance (1915). A therapist in peri-retirement said she agreed with Freud that no one believes in their own death, commenting, 'We can't imagine our not-being but we are gripped, from Oedipal stage onwards, by fears of not having amounted to very much'. Jaques (1965) suggests that in midlife our perception of death changes as we begin to see our own death coming into view:

> Death – at the conscious level – instead of being an event experienced in terms of the loss of someone else, becomes a personal matter, one's own death, one's own real and actual mortality.
>
> (1965: 506)

The strongest critique of psychoanalytic thinking about death comes from existential therapists who understand death anxiety as the primary fear which becomes encoded in our daily anxieties. From an existential point of view, maturity and emotional health depend on coming to terms with our mortality. Thus recognition of our finiteness is key to the meaning-making which gives value to our lives (van Deurzen-Smith, 1988).

All the contributors mentioned death in some form during their interview. Hannah was one who spoke very directly about anxieties over ageing and death:

> What is interesting is that my own mortality has been much more on my mind since I retired. Is this to do with approaching seventy or that somehow [when] working I was more occupied with the present than the future?

Patsy identified the existential anxiety which all retirees face:

> That's one of the things that I find really, really difficult – is not knowing whether I've got a short time left or . . . and I have a feeling it's the opposite and I'll be . . . a hundred! [laughs]

Most psychological theories describe a life-long process of revisiting developmental tasks which were first encountered in infancy, and consequently maturity depends on our coming to terms again and again with developmental challenges. In Kleinian terms this means that the depressive position has to be re-achieved throughout life because each life stage throws up anxieties which we are tempted to manage with a schizoid defence of splitting. According to Klein (1963/1988), the capacity for gratitude is a blessing at any life stage, but we might wonder whether it becomes even more precious in old age. This belief and trust in the goodness of the other and the self are key to contentment at each life stage, and in Bowlby's terms we would say these are evidence of secure attachment. When the inevitable restrictions of ageing (loss of faculties or loss of relationships) reduce the effectiveness of life-long defences, some of our half-tamed inner demons may again threaten us. Hess (2004) neatly describes the challenge of old age: 'growing old tests the security of our internal world, the balance of love and hate, envy and gratitude, good and bad, inside us' (2004: 27). Alan's comments affirm this truth: the task of managing one's inner world becomes ever harder when death is steadily claiming those dear to us:

> That is one of the dominant things about the end of life – that everyone is gone. The witnesses who could say 'Yes this is true' or 'No it isn't' are all gone. So these important parts of me – my witnesses are gone.

According to Storr (1973), Jung, like Freud, was still writing and seeing patients until close to the time of his death at 85. Throughout his life Jung believed in the possibility of development across the life cycle and described the stages of life in terms of times of day, with the sun at noon being seen as the transitional point of midlife (Jung, 1931). He understood the morning of life as devoted to more extrovert tasks and the afternoon as a time for individuation. This time scale is not strictly upheld by contemporary Jungians, but a theory which attributes particular value to the second half of life seems rather appealing. It reminds us that when our competence may be reduced in some areas, our capacity to look for meaning in our life can still be vibrant. Clearly the developmental journey through life does not always progress towards a creative old age, and Stevens (1982) describes the risk of fixating at a certain stage or regressing to an earlier one.

> Jung maintained that development could be arrested and distorted not only by events in the history of the maturing individual, but also by his fear of taking the next step along the path of individuation.
>
> (1982: 148)

Another theory which describes the repeated challenge and opportunity offered by each life stage is the concept of separation-individuation as demonstrated by Mahler, Pine and Bergman (1975). They understood each new separation as challenging our capacity to cope with loss. As the urge to grow ushers in each developmental stage we are obliged to integrate changes in the self. This means that retirement is a point at which our internal world requires a new level of integration, or, if anxiety is overwhelming, defensive strategies may become more entrenched.

Erikson (1980) described his stage theory as epigenetic, meaning that a good enough childhood makes a good enough old age more likely, but at every stage there is a potential for developmental recovery. Erikson sees integrity as the task of this life stage and he defines this as an acceptance of what has been possible, and not possible, for each us over the lifespan. Quinodoz (2010) also indicates the integrative tasks of old age. She emphasises the *work* of growing old, suggesting that those who can consciously recognise the end of their life approaching will feel the need to give meaning to their whole life history and this is done by integrating the different parts. 'The desire to find some coherence in our existence becomes more and more pressing as its end draws near' (2010: 1).

In case we should find these ideas self-evident, Kastenbaum (2000) offers a robust challenge to the value of stage theories, and particularly to the idea of ageing and dying being designated as a task. He suggests that to plot the entire human lifespan as a series of developmental tasks is a bourgeois artistic creation:

> It feels as comfortable as an old pair of bedroom slippers and, generally speaking offers about as much precision and predictive power.
>
> (2000: 22)

Ageism and the stigma of being outside the workforce

A postmodern perspective on ageing suggests that for the rich in our society ageing may be becoming a matter of consumer choice, with people of all ages pursuing 'young' identities and bodies. As the cult of youth is powerfully harnessed by consumer society there is increased pressure on us to 'stay' young, but this may be hard to face without some defensiveness. Some old people may deal with ageing by 'passing' as young, just as some gay or mixed race people might pass as straight or white. The option to 'buy' a younger body makes ageism even more potent: if you cannot manage to look younger than your years with all the options available there really is something wrong with you. This pressure for members of a minority group (in this case the old) to reinvent themselves and demonstrate their credentials for being part of the mainstream is reminiscent of earlier struggles for rights. Mayer (2011) has coined the term 'amortals' for the growing population who arrange to live the same way and do the same things through from teenage to death. Feeling 'young inside' and having a continuing desire to learn and achieve may help to balance out the aches and pains, but it does not solve the stigma of old age. To protect ourselves against the devaluing gaze of the world, we need a strong sense of self built up over the years. Without this we may be drawn into using up psychic resources in a futile conflict with reality.

In a small study of therapists who had retired or cut back their working hours, Russell and Simanowitz (2013) noted the loss of status which can come from not being in work. One interviewee mentioned the social assumptions attached to employment status and felt that those who did not work were seen to be 'of less value and possibly less interesting' (2013: 16). Murray Parkes was interviewed for *The Times* (Bennett, 2011), and his responses perhaps indicate how there may be wider opportunities for those of very high standing in the profession. On the other hand his particularly productive retirement years may simply reflect a dynamic personality. He explained: 'I was basically forced to retire at sixty-five and I got lots of cards with pictures of old gentlemen fishing on the front.' His subsequent years have confounded the image on the cards and in effect he has postponed retirement as he takes bereavement work to new contexts, setting up a trauma recovery programme in Rwanda and leading a team to support British families after 9/11.

Even when a therapist is not yet planning a complete retirement, the experience of simply cutting back on hours can be disheartening. One supervisee who was reducing her hours, with the idea of retirement somewhere in the future, described a disagreeable feeling of becoming 'less than'. She observed the impact on the self of working with fewer patients and said it was as though she were taken back to an earlier life stage. The last time she had had an incomplete practice had been when she was a novice counsellor in dire need of clients, so it took her a little while to become comfortable with this reduction.

While all the contributors were to some degree mindful of ways that ageing and death were signalled by retirement, Celia was one who was facing an immediate loss of capacity. She explained that she might have had plans for retirement but was now having to face letting these go. In the uncertainty about her health she found herself withdrawing from life because it had become difficult to maintain a conversation at the level at which she would like to engage:

> I don't know really what the withdrawal consists of but maybe it is partly a sort of shame I feel because I am not any longer the person that I used to be. Already I can see that now compared to how I used to be.

In earlier generations the transition into retirement and old age may have been eased a little by the greater sense of celebration which was apparent in rituals around the end of a working life. Looking at the role of initiation rites in early societies, Stevens (1982) reminds us that these rites once had a real function of supporting the individual along the pathways expected by their culture. Traditional ceremonies explored separation, transition and incorporation, which are central to our social milestones such as retirement. This is such a core trio of challenges which are no longer contained through the collective attention which ritual provided.

Retirement from an employed post is likely to be marked in some way, even if this is not with the legendary gold watch. Retirement from private practice may happen without any fanfare or celebration. Mary expressed sadness about how little recognition there is of a therapist's work at the point of retirement from private practice. She speculated that this lack of affirmation, the fact that therapists fade away with no mark of acclaim, was an additional factor making it hard for us to opt for retirement. Certainly in those cases where there had been acknowledgement of retirement it was much appreciated. I heard this from Annette, who belonged to a group of therapists who met for social support. These friends and colleagues had arranged an occasion to mark her retirement and chosen a very thoughtful and appreciated gift. The story of a very personal recognition is conveyed in Hannah's account of her last evening's work:

> My partner does most of the cooking and it was always really nice to come down from seeing clients and to find supper ready. On the very last night he'd made a special meal and there was a bottle of champagne.

Gender issues in ageing

The question of differential ageing in men and women is addressed by Jung (1931). He saw older men and women developing complementary gender traits, with men accessing their more feminine capacities and women their masculine side. This is interesting in terms of couple relationships, whether heterosexual or same sex, and such changes could pose a challenge to a partner unless both are developing in tandem. Older people who are single may have more freedom in terms of how they evolve, but with the downside of possible loneliness.

Both genders face a challenge to their sexual sense of self as they age. For women who have derived status from beauty and men who have been invested in sexual potency, ageing may be disheartening. By far the majority of psychotherapists, counsellors and supervisors are women, and so a study by Price (2003) into professional women's adjustment to retirement is interesting. Her qualitative study looking at professional women's adjustment to retirement explores how gender impacts on how well retirees do in reordering their lives. As women's lives have traditionally been marked more by discontinuities, they were assumed to retire more easily. Price reports more recent studies that challenge this and notes that one of the factors which can detract from women's experience of retirement is obligatory family-centred responsibilities. In her small sample, commitment to professional identity during working years was a significant indicator of satisfaction and self-esteem in retirement. This might suggest that therapists who find their work satisfying, and who struggle to let go, may ultimately adjust well to this next life stage.

The experience of gay and lesbian people in old age is explored by Garner and Bacelle (2004), and they propose two hypotheses. On the one hand this group have had to come to terms with stigma and may be better able to cope with the reduced status of age. On the other hand ageing burdens this group with yet another negative societal projection, and for gay men there may be an anxiety about losing their looks which matches the fears of heterosexual women. The current cohort of retiring gay and lesbian therapists would have come of age at a time when heterosexuality was assumed and required by society. Homosexual long-term relationships have only recently had legal acceptance and this will have affected financial planning for retirement. The prospect of ageing and dependency may be particularly daunting for gay people, as anecdotes suggest that care homes and other services for old people often remain homophobic. This group are also less likely to have the possible consolation of grandchildren and for these individuals, as for any who wished for children but were unable to have them, there can be a sadness in hearing so many peers extolling the joys of grandparenthood.

Chapter 8

What is next?

Thinking about having been a psychotherapist, I feel that it has defined very much who I am and this will always be with me.

(Hannah)

For people who have had a less than optimum childhood, if they are successful in education and have a career that satisfies them, there is a kind of interim where they are freed from the worst of the anxieties that came with that childhood, but when the opportunity to be useful in a career comes to an end, then some of those distressing things flood back in.

(Alan)

Picture a page of your diary in the weeks and months after retiring. No longer a series of times and initials, now a completely new set of engagements is evolving. Perhaps there are chunks of time ruled through for mornings at the primary school doing reading support; perhaps there is a regular class for the instrument you always hoped to play, or advanced courses for a skill you already enjoy. Names of friends are scattered through now that lunch, tea and supper are almost always possible. Even early morning swimming dates will no longer clash with regular clients. Perhaps the page has been crammed with activity, or perhaps the page is blank and there is emptiness. A rhythm has yet to emerge.

Attachment implications

In terms of personal circumstances, retiring therapists are a diverse group and so the personal context for this transition will vary greatly. One obviously visible difference is family size. On the one hand is the therapist who lives alone and holds her personal friends as her closest relationships, on the other a therapist who is surrounded by relatives all eager for her attention. Adult children may be queuing up for child care and partners may need time, either because they are frail, needing help or because they are robust, wanting a companion for adventures. Retirement often coincides with a house move, which can mean the loss of lesser attachment figures even if our primary one is moving with us.

The ways a couple negotiate their domestic space and how they use it to regulate their relationship will be impacted on considerably by retirement. This can mean that the formerly safe base of the home temporarily becomes a conflict zone. Quinodoz (2010) writes of a client, Denise, struggling with her resentment towards a newly retired husband: 'In Denise's view, it was quite normal for Sam to have to learn her language, because he was the one who was now "invading" her territory' (2010: 99). Quinodoz's patient was apparently feeling a need to protect herself by controlling Sam, and one of my contributors had experienced something similar. She compared her own retirement with that of her husband some years earlier and recalled his retirement as much more of a challenge for her. She had felt invaded: where the house had been all her own in the daytime, suddenly he had intruded on her space. Another therapist spoke of not wanting to go into retirement ahead of her partner, who was younger than her. Others spoke of partners who were already retired and were impatient for them to catch up. The disadvantages that gay and lesbian retirees may face were considered in the previous chapter, and it is likely that people from other minority groups may also be heavily burdened by ageing. For any oppressed group the stigma of age comes on top of existing prejudice. For this reason, therapists from ethnic minorities or those with disabilities might be doubly challenged by retirement.

As with any novel experience there may be a honeymoon period in the first weeks of retirement (Atchley, 1976). One therapist who was very newly retired told me, 'I say I'm fine and I'm bowling along – but the dreams!' And she then recounted one:

> I was abroad with a group of people and trying to get back home. We were on a bus which broke down and then there was a problem at a train station. Then I became aware that the people I had been with on the journey had gradually drifted away so I was alone. In addition I had left everything (including passport and money) behind in the place where we had been staying. At the end of the dream I was in a strange hotel and couldn't speak the language.

This retiree was quite clear that her dream was speaking to her of the loss of 'home' and the uncertainty she experienced on the threshold of a new country. This colleague was feeling the loss in the weeks after the last client had left, but depending on people's circumstances the impact of retirement may hit sooner or later. One contributor was very committed as a carer to her disabled partner and when she stopped seeing patients she was initially very occupied in caring for him. In a conversation four years after our interview she told me that the full impact was hitting her then in the wake of his death.

Like other developmental milestones, the transition into retirement poses a mixture of losses and challenges. There is anxiety when we embark on any new life stage such as starting school or taking a new job. This fear could be voiced as, 'Will I be any good at this?' In a similar way as a retiree we might also have beginners' nerves. Will I be able to manage on my reduced income? Will I sustain old friends in my new identity and will I be able to make new ones? Without the raison d'être of the work, will I reconnect to empty depressed parts of the self? How will I do at structuring my time when the external demands are reduced? In stepping into this uncertainty the therapist is letting go of a craft whose skills they have honed over decades. Kelly and Barratt write of 'giving up a satisfying skill which generally becomes more rewarding with age and experience' (2007: 200). One therapist remarked with irony, 'I'm retiring at just the point where I've got the hang of it.'

As retirement progresses the nature of attachment bonds may evolve. Bowlby (1973) predicted that attachment patterns would be relatively enduring across the lifespan but responsive to new inputs. Studies on children and younger adults have supported his hypothesis (Fraley and Brumbaugh, 2004), but the picture for older adults is less clear. Magai (2008) raises the possibility that the 'attachment glove' that nicely fits infancy and stretches to accommodate young adulthood might need rethinking to accommodate the developmental changes of midlife and beyond. The few studies that exist on this age group show a different distribution across the range of attachment patterns, with much higher numbers of dismissing individuals, lower numbers of secure and many fewer preoccupied individuals than in younger populations (Magai, 2008). Differing hypotheses have been suggested to explain this distribution. First, this increase in avoidance could be a response to the multiple losses experienced by older people. Second, this could be a reflection of the child-rearing practices prevalent when this cohort was raised. Third, this difference in distribution could be a methodological error: studies may have identified avoidance in behaviour that would be better understood as the effort to 'maintain independence and autonomy in the context of the encroaching depredations of later life' (Magai, 2008: 545). Shaver and

Mikulincer (2004) make a suggestion which might specifically explain the decrease in the anxious preoccupied group. They suggest the reduction in anxiety could have a physiological explanation: 'people may become less emotionally or autonomically reactive with age' (2004: 459).

Other writers have commented on how the focus of our attachment may change in old age. Barker (2011) suggests an increasing propensity to form attachments to places, pets and cherished possessions. Hidalgo and Herandez (2001) also found attachment to place was more important in later life. The role of God as an attachment figure for older people is interesting. Cicirelli (2004) found that the group for whom God had the function of an actual attachment figure was relatively small, but that a much larger group said they found comfort from prayer. Some of these phenomena may not qualify as full attachment relationships, but Bowlby pointed to one very real and observable change in attachment behaviour in older people – as power passes from the older to the next generation, adult children are now perceived as being stronger and wiser:

> Finally in old age, when attachment behaviour can no longer be directed towards members of an older generation, or even the same generation, it may come instead to be directed towards members of a younger one.

> (1973: 207)

How do patients fare in the period after the imposed loss of their therapy?

There are studies which look at the experience of patients following regular endings (Conway, 1999; Craige, 2002) or at the impact of sudden ending through the death of the therapist (Lord *et al.*, 1978), but perhaps the experience of patients whose therapist makes a planned ending falls in between these two groups. The experience of ending was shown to be a challenging one even for trainees who understand the process (Craige, 2002), but in the general population of patients the loss could be more problematic as these former patients are less likely to have anyone who would understand their sense of bereavement. I recall an anecdote from a social worker which illustrates how challenging this loneliness might be. He had been approached by a friend of his, a woman in twice-weekly therapy who was missing her therapist badly over a long break. It seemed that this patient had wrongly expected that her friend from a helping profession would provide support. The social worker had been highly irritated about the request. Lacking knowledge or faith in the developmental pathway of a long-term therapy, he damned the therapy for infantilising the patient and causing her to feel worse than she had at the start a year earlier. There may have been very valid reasons why he avoided becoming over-involved with his friend (who possibly had a strong preoccupied pattern), but his attitude illustrates how little patience the uninitiated may have for those who mourn the loss of a therapist. For patients who are isolated from informed support, the loss of a therapist would be a very lonely experience.

Relief and gains

In her paper written just after retirement, Boyd-Carpenter (2010a) mentions the sense of release which retirement brought. She felt free of the responsibility of a caseload and the close involvement with people's deep struggles. Some retirees have expressed how this relief came as a surprise. It was only after they had finished seeing patients they realised what a burden they had felt in having people dependent on them. It is natural that this sense of liberty is much stronger in the period just after retiring. Quoting from a journal entry shortly after closing his practice following a 46-year career, Walcott wrote, 'I am so happy I am still not accustomed to retirement; it makes it all the sweeter when I remind myself I am free. I will be sorry when I take retirement for granted and no longer have the pleasure of freedom' (2011: 220).

In a personal communication three years into her retirement, Boyd-Carpenter sets out some of the losses and gains (2010b). She indicates that while she has enjoyed studying, reading and being very active at home and with her large family, she still misses the work:

> Life is very good at the moment but I do occasionally feel the sadness of the loss rather as I sometimes miss and remember a few dear friends who died more than 20 years ago . . . And I miss being part of the work force and the stimulation of the contact with people from so many walks of life.

In a follow-up communication to our meeting, Annette also named the relief in contrast to her earlier reluctance to let go of the work and to forego tempting new referrals. One month into her retirement she could say:

> Having done it I'm very pleased I have – no more getting up for early mornings.

Nicola described a very specific relief which was shared by a few contributors:

> There will also be things I'll be really pleased not to have to do: BACP re-accreditation and CPD and goodness knows what else. I won't miss all that's been going on over the years about regulation.

Since closing her practice, Emma had re-engaged fully and successfully with her earlier career as a writer and she speculated that retirement had made this possible, and not just by making time available:

> This thing about somebody having . . . I hesitate to call it a talent – a capacity, a vein of creativity within the self which is actually squashed down by the work and can spurt up when the work stops sitting on them.

This creative 'spurting up' is also indicated by Boyd-Carpenter (2010a), who writes enthusiastically reclaiming the counselling room for other purposes. She describes being 'startled by the energy released for other things and rejuvenated by time for activities long neglected' (2010a: 94).

In a similar way Clementine appreciated having time and energy for personal development, even though she also explained that she had not felt burdened by the disciplined commitment of the work as she had grown up in a very formal home. As I had interviewed Clementine at the start of the study I was able to ask her for her further (written) reflections two years on when she had been retired for nearly four years:

> I think a lot about delaying the ageing process and particularly that aspect of it which means not staying in one's comfort zone. As a retired person I have more scope to do that than I would have if I continued to work . . . That is a definite plus to retirement.

Contrary to the popular fear, her health had improved with retirement. She reported having fewer colds and viruses, and she attributed this to her getting more rest and fresh air as well as having less stress. Patsy also spoke about gaining vitality:

> I'm just beginning to see that actually it might be youthifying [sic]. I hadn't seen it like that at all. I went out to supper with friends and they said 'You look ten years younger'.

Feelings of guilt and ambivalence

Speaking two months into her retirement, Patsy conveyed how feelings of ambivalence do not dissipate overnight:

> Even though I'm retired, I can't quite say whether I've done the right thing or not. I'm still ambivalent . . . Several times I've been really quite depressed . . . and wondered if I've done the right thing.

Alice was looking back three years after her partner had died and she had relocated:

> I still don't know if it was the right thing to do really. And I think if my partner hadn't died I would have re-opened a practice in London and continued to see them . . . I'm not completely happy with that, that I did that. Had circumstances been different . . . but they weren't. I did what I could in the time I had. I did my best – so did they.

A few contributors mentioned anxiety or guilt about leading a life of leisure. Carol said that learning 'just to enjoy not working' was a challenge because of her strong work ethic, yet at the same time a growing part of her was feeling that retirement would be a relief. Clementine also indicated feelings of unease about enjoying leisure:

> There are times when a lack of structure to a day can be wonderful, especially when it is sunny and warm and I can go on the heath and swim when I like and stay as long as I like. I have not found it easy to allow myself to have these days. Habits of doing trivial, time con-suming tasks that could wait, die hard. But I do take them sometimes and then I feel the real benefit of retirement.

In a similar way Patsy, who was two months into retirement, described an internal pressure to be busy and useful.

> Feeling guilty about leading a life that you are just enjoying. That's what would make me go and do something. A sort of puritan ethic. And also I just think it comes from my mother who was a person who never really enjoyed herself.

In a paper reminiscing about the closure of his practice, Walcott writes in a similar way: 'I suspect that the most painful affliction a retiree suffers is guilt. We are plagued by a nagging voice insisting that we must spend the greater part of each day in what are commonly called purposeful, higher pursuits' (2011: 220).

New 'occupations'

Most contributors either intended to offer part of their time in a voluntary capacity, or were already doing so. A study looking at retired occupational therapists (Cole and Macdonald, 2011) found that volunteers felt they were not being fully used and suffered loss of status. This dissatisfaction was not reported by contributors to my study, but perhaps this was because they had been canny in their choice of volunteering roles. Many were involved in quasi-therapeutic voluntary work which included helping with school reading, brief counselling for a local charity and walking the babies whose mothers were in prison. Some were involved in committees and management of local services; several had creative activities, particularly writing. Rosemary described being 'cross' when she was first obliged to stop supervising as she felt it was very wasteful of what she had to offer:

> But then other [opportunities] came along and I was probably writing and the other things I did . . . at some point or other I wrote another book which of course was very absorbing.

Some retirees are involved with grandchildren. An interesting way of theorising the bond between grandparents and grandchildren is proposed by Colarusso (1997). He elaborates Mahler's concept of separation-individuation and sees the grandparent's intense devotion to a grandchild as an echo of the toddler's passionate need for the mother during the rapprochement crisis. He sees the grandparents' investment in their grandchildren and their idealisation of them as both defensive and developmental, providing 'a narcissistic buffer against the stings of old age and the inevitability of death' (1997: 90).

Practicalities of closing a practice

The mixture of loss and relief, mentioned by contributors, is apparent in how the retiring therapist deals with the concrete tools of their trade: the room, the books and the couch. Horner writes vividly of this: 'I sold and donated my entire professional library – not unlike an amputation' (2002: 326). She recalls some early anxiety about how to fill the days until she discovered 'the pleasure of an alarm clockless awakening, of a leisurely breakfast, of reading the paper, and a second cup of coffee' (2002: 326). One new retiree conveyed how the tangible tasks of disassembling the room were a part of the adjustment to the loss, and she recalled thinking: 'I suppose I may as well take those glasses out of the consulting room'. There would be no more patients wanting a glass of water. A similar poignant comment from the domestic life of a newly retired therapist was made by Hindmarch (2009), who wrote: 'Business cards, letterheads, appointment slips are now used for shopping lists' (2009: 25).

During the period when I was interviewing retirees I moved to a new therapy room, leaving one which I had used for over 10 years. I was glad when a client said in his final session in the old room, 'I bet these walls have seen something'. We needed to think about what this meant for him in terms of the work he had done in that space, but it also gave me permission to recognise how much I was leaving behind. It was not only the patients' pain and challenges but mine, my formation as a therapist. I had given a lot of myself in that room.

Patients' notes are another tangible item and one which needs careful handling in view of legal implications. In a paper about access to records for the British Association for Counselling and Psychotherapy, Bond and Jenkins (2009) discuss the length of time that patient notes should be kept after the end of treatment. They report that the time limit for personal injury claims is normally three years, while that for breach of contract is six years. They do not address the issue of retirement, but as a complaint could be brought against a retired therapist, retirees may wish to consider the permitted time spans for bringing complaints when they decide on the disposal of notes. The question of liability insurance also needs consideration. Therapists should check with their insurers whether they will continue to be covered after they have retired and ceased payments. Run-off cover is designed for these kind of situations and can usually be arranged but needs to be negotiated.

Another reminder of how legal and ethical responsibilities continue beyond the last session comes from Trayner and Clarkson (1992). They are writing about good practice in emergency endings, but their paper is relevant to planned retirement. They draw on codes of ethics from various therapy organisations to demonstrate that some professional responsibilities continue after the client work is over. They particularly stress the maintenance of confidentiality and the avoidance of any exploitation of the former relationship. The retiring therapists in this study were mostly based in London, but for retirees living in smaller communities where they used to work there could be a considerable need for continuing thoughtfulness around boundaries. In small towns, as in minority groups in large towns, there will be more chance of retired therapists crossing paths with former clients and this will make the importance of lifelong confidentiality particularly apparent. One can picture many scenarios where an unforeseen meeting could arise. Picture a retiring therapist who has been looking forward to joining the choir in her home town, a community just large enough to support this one musical society. What an unwelcome dilemma she has when at her first choir practice she finds herself standing next to a former patient.

What can general theories of retirement tell us about how we will experience life after work?

I will refer to two psychoanalytically informed studies of ageing and retirement which may help interpret the sample presented in this book. Neither of these studies draws explicitly on the work of Bowlby, but I think in both cases their results are compatible with attachment theory, particularly in the way they recognise the interface between the environment and the internal world. Like attachment theory, these studies indicate a considerable stability in how people manage themselves over time: 'those who felt a need to keep busy had always tried to keep busy; those who blamed others for their frustrations and failures had always done so' (Reichard, Livson and Petersen, 1962: 163).

The Harvard Study of Adult Development

Initiated in 1939, this longitudinal study continues to follow participants with regular face-to-face psychological assessments. Vaillant (2002) has been a key author in the study and he suggests four circumstances in which retirement is stressful: (1) when it is involuntary and unplanned; (2) when the retiree has no financial resources; (3) when home life is unhappy so that work has been an escape; and finally (4) when the retiree is already in poor health at the point of stopping work. Like other writers he challenges the myth, unsupported by research, that poor health is caused by retirement. This debunking is echoed by Clementine in Chapter 9. Vaillant's contention about involuntary retirement is supported by comments from Rosemary and Celia. Questions of financial resources and relative happiness in home life are a significant area not covered in my study. My contributors all appeared to be entering retirement with reasonably secure finances.

From the abundant data produced by the Harvard study, Vaillant identifies four elements that contribute to a rewarding retirement. The first is the replacing of work colleagues with a new social network. The second is play, 'for play permits a person to maintain self-esteem while giving up self-importance' (2002: 224). The third is creativity, which he argues requires protected time and hence may not have been possible in earlier years. Vaillant's fourth element is lifelong learning. He acknowledges that play and creativity lie on a continuum, but believes the difference is important and I like the image he conjures to make the distinction:

> Picasso worked tirelessly to be sure that the whole world was watching. In contrast, a kitten performs acrobatics never exactly performed before . . . retirement play, like the kitten's gambols, is less inhibited, more confident, freer from convention, less approval seeking, and with less performance anxiety than publicly recognised creativity.
>
> (2002: 230)

The last of his criteria, lifelong learning, is strongly represented in the contributors' stories. Vaillant's first element, the establishing of a social network outside of work, will depend on many personal ingredients. Clementine mentioned some very tangible factors which could make this harder: loss of friends through death, reduced energy for socialising and the fact that some friends have much of their time committed to grand-children. Vaillant's other two elements – creativity and play – seemed present in many contributors' lives though clearly these are very hard to measure. Carol and Patsy and Clementine all recognised how their life-long work ethic made it very hard to play. Emma's resurgence of creativity in retirement seemed to fit with Vaillant's contention that creativity thrives on protected time.

Ageing and personality

A smaller study set out to explore the role that personality plays in adjustment to ageing, using a psychoanalytic framework to think about personality styles. Reichard and colleagues (1962) looked at the transition from middle to old age in a homogeneous sample of 87 white men and arrived at an intriguing typology. They indicate that their five groupings owe much to early relationships with parents, and in this way their findings are aligned with attachment theory which was emerging contemporaneously (Bowlby, 1969).

Many of the findings of Reichard *et al.* are supported by the experience of my contributors. Their observation that retirement can lead to a revival of the identity conflicts of adolescence is poignantly confirmed by Alan in Chapter 7. Their comment that 'retirement signifies, perhaps more dramatically than any other single change, that one has become old' (1962: 10) was echoed by a number of contributors. Similarly their contention that 'retirement was most stressful for our respondents just before it took place' (1962: 169) might resonate with the contributors I spoke to in the months just prior to retirement.

Like Vaillant, Reichard *et al.* assert that retirement does not cause deterioration in health and suggest that in those cases where health becomes poor, retirement may have been the result rather than the cause of the ill health. This might explain the construction of Alan's narrative which tells of his health deteriorating very fast at the point of retirement. The study suggests that successful adjustment depends on carrying over existing interests. 'Whether retirement activities are productive or useful seems less important than whether they provide continuity with the past and satisfy lifelong needs' (1962: 92). This observation was particularly endorsed by Emma's fulfilment in retirement despite a forced retirement and cancer.

Reichard and colleagues identified five groups with differing levels of adaption to retirement. They dubbed these: *mature, rocking chair, armoured, angry* and *self-hating*, with the first three able to cope with ageing much better than the last two. The mature group were perceived by the study to be well adjusted and able to enjoy life. Excerpts from their interviews indicate speakers with good reflective function who are comfortable considering and commenting on their own narratives. This would seem to be a clear indication of secure attachment, and the mature group do give happier accounts of their childhood, although of course happy stories can also indicate idealisation and an avoidant attachment.

How do my interviews correlate with the groups that Reichard *et al.* identified? I think it makes sense to understand my contributors as largely corresponding to the mature group, as in my view they demonstrated a strong capacity for reflective function. In my study I did not ask about childhood, but some contributors did allude to it and the images were not all happy. A proportion of psychotherapists come to therapy precisely because they did not have happy childhoods, but many of them have achieved *earned* security through their own therapies (Main and Goldwyn, 1998).

The rocking chair men were seen as oral characters who were passive and dependant. They adjusted well to ageing because they valued the chance to take it easy and welcomed the permission that society affords the old to slow down. This is a fascinating observation: that provided that care is available, the dependency of old age might be a positive transition for some individuals. I doubt that this grouping is represented in my sample as my contributors, like most therapists, are active, relatively autonomous people.

The armoured group had quite rigid defences and as long as these manic defences could survive they were not troubled by old age. They postponed retirement at all costs and tended to be compulsively busy, as though trying to ward off ageing through their compulsive busyness. This is in contrast to the activity of the mature group, which appears to be less desperate and more enjoyable.

The armoured group were more prone than either the mature or the rocking chair group to feel envy towards the young. While some members of my sample referred to the temptation to become overly busy, I felt that they were distinct from the armoured group because of their insight into their busyness. In contrast the armoured group had no insight into their defence and were reluctant to look inside themselves. The willingness to make the decision to retire at an appropriate age (shown by my contributors) is itself an indicator of not belonging to this group.

Reichard and colleagues' final two groups had a very poor adjustment to ageing and retirement. Both of these groups looked back with resentment, and the difference between them was whether they blamed others or themselves. The angry men tended to project their hostility onto others and their aggression appeared to be a cover for depression. Their difficulty in sublimating meant they had few hobbies and very little consolation in retirement. The self-haters were also painfully immersed in resentment, but they turned their aggression against the self and their masochism led them to flaunt their shortcomings and miseries. I do not believe that these two groups are represented in my sample.

Reichard and colleagues' typology is fascinating because it explores a deeper level of functioning than my study was able to access. The data they collected permitted these researchers to identify defensive strategies and personality types. My categories are descriptive of more obvious characteristics. I think this makes them less interesting in psychoanalytic terms but perhaps more immediately applicable in day-to-day life, and they may offer an accessible way of thinking about retirement in ourselves, our colleagues and our supervisees. My initial groupings of older, younger, classic and forced indicate the motivating factors in each therapist's retirement. In terms of correspondence with Reichard and colleagues' typology, I would like to think that contributors belonged to the secure group while each may also have had some residual traits indicating an original attachment style which might match with one of the less secure categories.

One of the factors which will greatly influence our experience of retirement is the way in which being a therapist has supported our own functioning. For some of us our half-conscious need as therapists has been to heal our mothers or other family members. For others it is above all the self which is projected into the patient, and then the focus is more directly on repairing and nurturing ourselves. Still others might have used work as a way to justify our place on the planet and have wanted to contribute to reparation and transformation. Whichever of these or other unconscious agendas is most true for us, if we experience hope as linked to ongoing endeavour then we may struggle with despair when we stop labouring.

Chapter 9

How similar are other imposed endings?

There was once a young boy whose father went off to the war and never returned. His mother struggled alone and she scolded her son for not being the man she was mourning. Many years passed and the woman also died and the grown man made his way to the city. He met a wise woman there who agreed to accompany him on his journey.

She was in many ways a difficult travelling companion and sometimes he regretted her being there. For whole days they didn't speak and sometimes he saw on her face the cruelty he had known in his mother. But after a long day's hike through alien country, he often found her presence a deep comfort. Sometimes when she looked at him and spoke of what was understood between them, he felt as though a frozen part of him was beginning to thaw. At those times he felt he was travelling with a different mother, one he had longed for. Then he felt hope.

One morning when they were ready to set off along the track, she told him she was taking the other path. She was leaving now, she said, on her own journey to find her own fortune. She would look for him when she passed back this way.

Attachment implications

The stories in this chapter could speak of the archetypal story of the hero/traveller who goes off to seek his fortune, or in my adaptation, of the 'wise woman' who leaves her clients while she attends to her own concerns. Therapy itself is very often likened to a journey of discovery, in which the client travels inwards, but in the therapy sagas explored in this book, the therapist has become the traveller and in a sense the status of the client has been usurped by the therapist. We might see childbirth or sabbatical as a project from which the therapist will return changed and enriched by a profound new experience. At these times of the therapist's absence, the client is not only left alone, they are also missing out on an adventure and their own journey is put on hold. As the therapist strides off to climb the mountain, the client is left to wait by the wayside, or perhaps to fall back down.

Some years ago I needed to take five weeks off work for planned surgery. I noticed that the three-stage process of first telling my clients, then actually leaving and finally returning, gave us an interesting experience of separation and reunion with some parallels to the strange situation test (Ainsworth *et al.*, 1978). I wrote about my experience (Power, 2003), likening the period between telling the news and actually going away to the stage where the researcher has come into the room but the parent has not yet left. The five weeks that I was gone had in some ways corresponded to the few minutes that the infant is separated from his parent. In a similar manner this chapter looks at periods of absence from which the therapist will return. This is in many ways very different from retirement, yet some of the dilemmas and challenges are similar. As with retirement, a key factor will be the stage that the work has reached and the age that the client currently experiences themself in the relationship. As with all imposed endings, provided the intrusion to the frame can be survived, the work may be enriched by the challenge.

We will follow the stories of two therapists who took maternity breaks (Flora and Susannah) and two who took sabbaticals (Issy and Paula), as well as that of Simon, who found a different solution to his need for more time out from clinical work. I have covered maternity breaks in more detail as the experience is widely relevant and also because there is a rich literature on which to draw. In terms of a very long break being imposed on clients, the two processes have much in common and the two parts of the chapter are thus complementary. These temporary breaks share certain clinical dilemmas about whether clients can sit out the break or whether they need to be referred on but they are different. In the case of pregnancy the client is witness to a profound change in their therapist and will experience their place being taken by a real child. Paula's summer sabbatical of 10 weeks was much shorter than would normally be taken for maternity, and the issues which it poses may be closer to those which occur for a regular long summer break.

Decisions about how to manage a long break have to be thought through with attachment needs in mind. Many therapists who need time off for illness or bereavement manage this by giving patients the details of a colleague who can be approached for basic information about the therapist's health and likely return date. This arrangement could also be relevant for planned breaks. It means that while clients still have to tolerate uncertainty, the essential need for *access* to the attachment figure is not completely thwarted, even if that attachment figure is not currently being as responsive and reliable as she usually is.

Maternity breaks

Of all the types of imposed ending, the one which is most likely to be repeated is pregnancy. While it would be a very normal thing for a woman to have a second or third baby within the space of five years, if she is seeing long-term clients this could result in erratic therapy, with some of them being left more than once. This experience of multiple pregnancies which is challenging for both therapist and clients, has been written up by Lazar (1990). While she was working at Chestnut Lodge with very disturbed patients she had seven pregnancies, five of which she lost. Browning (1974), a child psychotherapist, also writes of having multiple pregnancies and she describes the responses of three of her young patients. She charts their denial, displacement and fear of abandonment while arguing that the pregnancies served overall as a catalyst, enabling each client to work on what was most necessary for them. In some cases this was an attachment theme (their fear of abandonment), in other cases the child was more concerned about siblings or sexuality. Browning suggested that birth order had an impact on how the news was received, and this observation is likely to hold for adults too. The responses of these children are striking and immediate, and may help us to decipher the more veiled responses of adults. One seven-year-old boy responded with bravado: 'That's okay if you want to have a baby because I'm not coming back!' (1974: 475). This client's next line of defence was to say that he would bring diet pills for the therapist in order to deal with that swelling waistline.

Many of the papers about pregnancy which I reference here were written in the twentieth century and many are American. These early writers were thinking of breaks in terms of weeks rather than months (Fuller, 1987), whereas in the UK today most women want longer breaks and the impact on clients is therefore likely to be more significant. Susannah's breaks were also relatively short – just four months. She explained that she felt alright returning that soon after the birth because her practice was very small and she was working for just a few hours a week.

Flora had opted to close her practice completely when she was expecting her first child. Her plans were then tragically overthrown when she lost that baby at the end of the pregnancy. She went on to have another child and then established a new small practice before becoming pregnant a third time. For this final birth she took a six-month break. Her memories of these two closures – one complete and one temporary – were shared with me 30 years later. I interviewed Susannah two years after her second maternity leave. Her pregnancies were two years apart and one client was with her for both of these breaks. Like Flora, she had experienced a perinatal emergency as her second child was critically ill during the first weeks but happily recovered.

As in retirement, when a pregnant therapist closes her practice, her own life is intruding into the client's process. As in retirement, the client is likely to feel at some level rejected and the therapist to become less anonymous. In the past the therapist's pregnancy was seen as a sign of her being a sexually active woman; with fertility treatment and donor sperm this assumption is not as accurate but is still likely to be present. Susannah laughed as she recalled clients' responses to the news: they had all smiled in a slightly knowing way and this seemed to be about her revealing something about her sexuality:

> I think the smile was around that kind of . . . So before there is nothing about it and you do come into the room as a sexual being and I was quite uncomfortable with it and I think in some ways I had always used the anonymity – I quite liked it.

Like the retiring therapist, the pregnant therapist is likely to face challenges in the transference just at the point where she is vulnerable about her own process. Even in a choice as personal as the timing of a pregnancy, the needs of clients may be factored in. In order to minimise disruption from a maternity break, a woman in private practice who was hoping to have a child might decide first to reduce the number of clients she sees and to avoid taking on more seriously troubled people in the years prior to becoming pregnant. Most of the retirees I spoke to had exercised this kind of advanced preparation in order to ensure that they would not be working with highly vulnerable clients at the point when they wanted to close their practice. In a similar way, later in this chapter Paula emphasises the care she took in screening new clients in the year prior to her 10-week sabbatical.

Women in other professions may be able to delay their choice about when or whether they will return to their former jobs. Therapists in private practice have to be very clear about whether they will return to work with these clients or whether they will take a complete break from the profession and afterwards build up a new practice. If they opt to resume work with their patients then they face the clinical task of managing a long break. The fact that childbirth and the early weeks of a child's life do not follow tidy predictions and can sometimes involve tragedy puts an additional strain on the pregnant therapist. She has to contain uncertainty for clients at a time when she may be struggling to manage her own fears about the birth and her mothering of the baby. In this practical respect a maternity break is similar to illness as there may be doubt about when the therapist will be available again, or whether she ever will be.

Some pregnant therapists will have a choice between closing their practice entirely or taking time out. Flora looked back on the decision she came to for her first baby, who had been conceived after some difficulty:

> I suppose because it had taken me so long to get pregnant ... there was a bit of me thinking that I didn't want to have split loyalties between the baby and the patients and I guess in a way I came to feel the priority was the baby ... And I was in the fortunate position of my partner earning enough.

When she became ill and lost this baby, she felt in some ways relieved not to be returning to her clients.

> And the clinician in me was thinking, 'Thank God, I have finished with my patients', because, especially the client who was always attacking, she would have thought that her fantasies had materialised.

Cullington-Roberts (1994) lost a pregnancy while still in practice. She wrote about her 12-week absence when she became unwell and ultimately miscarried the baby, and she describes how the patients' pain of separation is augmented by fantasy. Exploring the experience of her patients during separation and reunion, she reminds us of the primitive responses of internal attack that patients are likely to face. The infant does not experience the absence of the good breast so much as the presence of the bad breast. This latter is made bad by the child's projections of her own hostility towards the missing breast. We can therefore expect that those adults who are strongly defended against knowing of their resentment towards the pregnant therapist are likely to be suffering an internalised attack.

Breaking the news

The tension between the needs of client and pregnant therapist is very apparent in the question of 'when to tell'. While we like to give clients ample warning of our breaks, for obvious reasons patients cannot be given much advance notice of a maternity break. Most therapists would not want to reveal a pregnancy before the fourth month and some chose not to disclose at all, wanting to understand how the client responds in their own time to this unusual Oedipal event. The risk with this approach is that clients who are reticent or in denial will not mention the pregnancy and could be left with just a few weeks to work on what this means to them. Baum and Herring (1975) point out that the client's response cannot be seen as happening in a vacuum: 'Why is it that in some instances all of the therapist's patients react early and are able to communicate something relative to the pregnancy, while the patients of other therapists say nothing for months or not at all, unless they are asked?' (1975: 420). In each case there will be myriad factors which permit a client to notice the pregnancy, and Baum and Herring's comment reminds us that some of these factors lie within the therapist herself and her own feelings about her transformation.

Most therapists nowadays probably want to hold in mind both attachment and Oedipal dynamics, even though the literature on pregnancy is weighted towards the latter. It was precisely this split which erupted when Bowlby presented Robertson's documentary showing the distress of a little girl who was separated from her family while staying in hospital (Robertson, 1952). Many psychoanalysts present attributed her distress to the fact that her mother was pregnant at the time (Holmes, 1993). In their reading of the film, the child was disturbed by her hostile fantasies towards the unborn child rather than by separation from her mother. The decades of hostility between these two camps are thawing now, but perhaps pregnancy is one of the points where it is hardest to keep both aspects of experience in mind.

My contributor Susannah was mindful of how challenging both of these factors can be:

> It's like a double whammy – mostly you don't have to deal with your therapist being off and also being pregnant.

Both my interviewees started their maternity leave well before the due date because of the risk of a sudden departure if the therapist continues working close to the time of the birth. Clearly there is a tension between keeping the break as short as possible and allowing a safe margin of error on the date. Clementel-Jones (1985) advocates stopping work early because of the likelihood of being tired and emotionally vulnerable at this stage of the pregnancy. She does not mention the attachment issues around the timing of the break.

Both contributors were aiming for a way of offering containment of an imprecise process. Susannah felt it was helpful to give a firm date for resuming work, even if it had to be revised. Flora used a more flexible formula, saying that they would resume in six months and she would write a month before that. Susannah acknowledged that the uncertainties around childbirth meant there was a risk in being so precise, but she felt it was containing both for the clients and for her:

> If I could say 'I'm leaving on this date, but I'm coming back on this date' and I stuck to it, that was helpful for me and a way of managing and containing what was going on.

How clients respond to being left

Reactions to the therapist's pregnancy have been richly explored in the many psychoanalytic papers mentioned throughout this chapter. Their focus is on clients' experience of the growing baby and how they respond in fantasy and behaviour to this intruder in the room. Flora voiced the essential Oedipal experience of exclusion, which would have a unique meaning according to each patient's attachment story:

> It wasn't just the baby intruding but almost me saying 'the baby is kicking you out'.

One of the clearest remonstrations from a patient is reported by Fuller (1987) in the case of a 16-year-old boy, the oldest of five siblings. His protest at separation took a very explicit and illuminating form, and he responded to his therapist's pregnancy saying:

> I won't stand for it! Not again! Enough is enough! Get me a man to see!

A case which clearly reflects the combined attachment and Oedipal dynamics thrown up by pregnancy is told by Dufton (2004). She became pregnant while working with a mixed-race woman who had been born into a white family. This client had subsequently been displaced by a sibling who, being white, was clearly the father's own child rather than, like the client, an accident from a denied affair. The client found the displacement in favour of the therapist's own baby very challenging. Strangely, in a paper which is in many ways very sensitive, the author does not discuss her own skin colour and the intense meaning that this must have had for the client.

Whatever Dufton's ethnicity, this omission reminds us of the risk that clients from oppressed minorities who are facing an imposed ending may be additionally disadvantaged if power dynamics within the room are neglected.

Most writers comment that the reactions of clients to an imposed ending are in line with their customary responses: while the transference may become more charged, essentially the process gives more focus to what was already there. Flora describes this:

> So the way they expressed their feelings about the pregnancy very much represented what they were struggling with anyway. There was quite a spectrum, from the focused attack to a couple of clients who got really concerned about whether I was alright, whether they were too much for me. Then in the middle were those who denied. It was quite a spectrum.

She then said more about the focused attack:

> Another client spent the time between telling and ending in expressing her anger which I hope was cathartic! And I think that's when I realised that that conflict between, 'Is my focus on the baby or the client?' was already there. When clients start attacking you, verbally, or attacking the baby, expressing their anger about the baby – then in a way I felt that I had to protect the baby. You're right in the middle of that conflict and where is your loyalty?

Browning (1974) gives a powerful example of hostility towards her baby from a five-year-old girl whom she was seeing. I will quote this in full as the directness of attack from a child may inform us about the struggles that some adult patients have in accepting the pregnancy:

> Her anger toward my baby was quite dramatic as one day she proceeded to make 'baby soup' out of water, dominoes, and baby dolls. When I innocently asked if she was making soup for the baby, she replied, 'Soup made out of babies!'.

(1974: 473)

Another response mentioned in the literature is the fantasy that the baby is eavesdropping and inhibiting what can be said. This way of experiencing the intrusion is reported by Fuller (1987) and came up in Susannah's story as she recalled a client who was worried about swearing in front of the baby. She listed the issues which came through in sessions:

> competition, rejection, the worry about the harm mothers can do to babies in the womb, the harm they could do: one of my clients used to get worried about swearing.

While recounting these fantasies, it seems appropriate to acknowledge that there is some basis to these fears of harming the child. We know that a mother under attack could experience a rise in levels of blood cortisol and this could impact the baby. Lazar (1990) describes how she became more vulnerable to patients' attacks after she lost successive pregnancies. During her first pregnancy she was more confident of managing the aggression. 'From my naively optimistic and innocent position, I felt I could contain the patient's envious attacks, secure in my sense of safety' (1990: 213).

Another response reported by Susannah was denial:

> I was also aware that on a conscious level they wanted to block it. It felt like they did try to block the bump.

This very common response is also noted in Bassen's (1988) study where one contributor acknowledged a lack of hostility from her patients and speculated that they must have sensed the limits of what she would tolerate because they had been 'extremely well behaved' (1988: 291). The literature acknowledges how difficult it can be for the pregnant therapist to facilitate disappointment and envy in clients and how reluctant clients are to own these feelings, preferring naturally to stay with the benign attitude which they usually also hold.

Provided the feelings can be sufficiently contained, a pregnancy offers great potential for understanding more about the client's internal world, but sadly the experience of being both left and displaced is too much for some clients. Susannah spoke of the client who left prematurely eight months after her return from her second maternity leave. She speculated that this client may have left in order to protect her from his negative feelings about the breaks. It seemed that he may have felt he was about to reach a new layer of aggression, though in addition there was also some evidence that he carried anxiety about a third pregnancy. Lazar (1990) reports that several patients left prematurely, just before or just after the birth of her second child. She interprets this chiefly in Oedipal terms and does not directly mention that their protest may also have been about the threat to their attachment bond: 'it seemed clear that the rivalry and anger were too intense to analyse and instead were rationalized and enacted' (1990: 224).

Managing the separation and reunion: different kinds of temporary arrangements

Flora took six months for maternity leave while Susannah took four; in both cases their clients managed the break by themselves. Susannah had arranged a holding therapist for one client but he only attended for a couple of sessions. Flora wrote to her patients when it was nearly time to resume, while Susannah's clients had the precise date in advance. All her clients had returned to see her on the appointed day.

When the leave of absence is going to be many months, therapists face a dilemma about whether a client will benefit most by being placed with a holding therapist or by bringing the current work to a close and referring on to a new therapy. These very nuanced judgements are often being made under the shadow of financial pressures, and so ethical decision making is clearly important if clients' needs are not to be compromised. An interesting paper by Chiaramonte (1986) reflects on his experience of being the holding therapist for patients whose own therapist was away on maternity leave. He suggests there are three categories of client: those who are well enough to bring forward their ending; those who can cope with the break but will be helped by having a named individual whom they can contact; and a third group of the most troubled clients who need to see a replacement therapist. Susannah had also thought in terms of three categories but her options were slightly different: to wait for her return, to see a holding therapist or to make a permanent transfer to a new therapist. Browning (1974) describes finding different solutions for her various young patients, including maintaining telephone contact with one six-year-old boy through her six-week break.

Chiaramonte suggests that in a six-month temporary contract, much of the time will be devoted to resolving the loss of the therapist. I think it is important to hold in mind the double loss that these clients face. There is a parallel between their experience and that of the child who is left with grandmother in the home country when parents go ahead to a new one. Later when the parents send for this child she will experience a second fracture in attachment. Despite this risk, a holding therapy may still be the best option for clients who are very well established but cannot manage alone.

Some of the complexities of this decision are described by Gibb (2004) in a detailed study of a client who had suffered early abandonment and poor foster care. The pregnancy and its possibility of a good family life re-evoked this client's early trauma, and Gibb faced an acute dilemma about how to manage the break when this patient desperately and aggressively demanded that she arrange a locum therapist. Gibb believed that to do so would be to deny the personal meaning of the relationship and to re-enact the institutionalisation of foster care. It was a powerful bind:

> I was either in the position of acting out an institutional response to care, giving a replacement, therapist or by not doing so being experienced as a really sadistic figure preoccupied only with myself and my baby, leaving her starved.
>
> (2004: 74)

She chose the middle option of arranging for a colleague to be available during her absence. The patient struggled but the therapy survived. Looking back, Gibb had some doubts about this limited provision: 'It may indeed have been too much to expect of her to contact us in time of need, which was the arrangement that was made' (2004: 83). This observation would be particularly pertinent for clients with a dismissing attachment style, who tend to have less capacity for care-seeking.

When referral is made to a holding therapist the arrangements for the transition need care. Stockman and Green-Emrich (1994) recommend holding conjoint sessions to facilitate the transfer at the start and at the end of the maternity leave. Chiaramonte (1986) details the transference and countertransference tangles that can arise around the re-transfer to the original therapist. He names the possible fear of another separation, the idealisation of the new therapist and the devaluing of the original one. Some therapists arrange a holding therapy for clients with the understanding that at the end of the break the client may choose to stay with the new therapist. This approach affords respect to clients' autonomy, but clearly gives scope for complex dynamics with clients potentially feeling they are rejecting one or the other of the therapists. Chiaramonte's model does not allow for a client to stay on with the temporary therapist, and he considers that that desire should be resolved through ongoing work with the original therapist. He sees a major obstacle in the countertransference of the substitute therapist whose own competitiveness is likely to operate: 'Fuelled by the patient's flattering idealisation, the interim therapist may enter into collusion with the patient's wish to avoid re-transfer' (1986: 346–7).

These writers are all grappling with the dilemma of how best to allow both for the client's conscious choice and the unconscious dynamics provoked by the distortion of the frame. When the original therapist comes back into view, how can these conscious and unconscious parts of the client's experience be honoured? There will sometimes be a risk of privileging either the client's overt preference or the therapist's interpretation of the client's internal world. For example a client might opt to stay with the new therapist whom she finds 'warmer', but her original therapist may hypothesise that the temporary arrangements have encouraged a split. If the projections are accepted at face value and made concrete rather than being understood, then the opportunity for repair will be lost. In this case if the original therapist were carrying a transference of the client's withholding mother, the temporary therapist stands a good chance of being experienced as the kindly grandmother. If both therapists can hold this in mind alongside the need to respect client autonomy, the imposition of temporary arrangements can become a catalyst for growth.

Both Flora and Susannah related that on return from the break, clients were wanting to get on with 'business as usual'. Flora commented:

> When they returned they almost carried on where they left off, almost as though they denied what had happened in the break. I suppose it's something about how ruthless clients can be – their right to come back and get on with it.

When I met with Susannah she echoed this:

> It was almost like by the time they came back they wanted to get on with working and not think about me. I think that's the thing – a bit like 'You're back and can we not have to deal with you and your pregnancy?'

As she returned just three months after the birth, Susannah was mindful that clients might see the new mother as vulnerable and hold back on their resentment about the break. She commented:

> I think it helped that when I came back I was quite healthy and strong; I was exhausted but not showing it.

Disclosure

Each type of imposed ending throws up particular dilemmas around disclosure. When a therapist has a baby, even the provision of basic information needs careful thinking through. As Clementel-Jones points out: 'Telling the patient "a baby girl was born" sounds fine, but what about "a stillborn baby girl"?' (1985: 87).This was an issue which Flora had to face when a former client asked to return to therapy with her. She knew he would ask about the baby and so she reflected in supervision and decided to let him know that the child had died but she had since had another. A case reported by Fuller (1987: 24) illustrates how disclosure can be enriching to the work. A patient had asked whether the therapist felt it was appropriate to let her know the baby's name, and when the therapist shared the name the patient replied very quietly:

> You trust me to know your baby's name? You trust me as someone who is concerned and not dangerous. If you can trust me that much, I can only trust myself more.
>
> (1987: 24)

Browning (1974) considers the issue of disclosure from the point of view of a child therapist. She acknowledges that it can be hard to know where to draw the line, but she proposes that since the baby, unlike other aspects of the therapist's personal life, has in a sense been part of the treatment, the patient deserves to know more on this. She found that children in treatment often wanted to know who would be caring for the baby when the therapist was at work and she felt it appropriate to answer this. Perhaps her experience points to the value of considering these frame issues on a case-by-case basis, as the meaning of a certain piece of information will vary according to each client's story. This approach in comparable to Aarons (1975), who chose to withhold details about his relocation from most patients but felt it right to share more information with one who had been raised to be 'seen and not heard'.

The therapist's own emotional journey

Flora recalled how her capacity for the work was affected by difficulties in the pregnancy:

> I became very ill in the latter part of the pregnancy so by the time we got to about 26 weeks I was still working with them but I was desperate for them to finish. We finished at 28 weeks and I think if I'm honest I really couldn't keep them in mind after that. It was like I've just got to get through what I've got to get through. I think the fact that I don't know what happened afterwards was almost like I had to let them go

so that I could focus on what was happening with me. I think there was a real conflict around that.

Birksted-Breen (1986) regrets the tendency to think about pregnancy as an illness from which one recovers and gets back to one's old self. She argues that pregnancy is a developmental opportunity, perhaps another stage in separation-individuation, and therefore the mother will not be the same after the birth. Susannah affirmed this sense of growth and development particularly in relational to the birth of her second child, who was critically ill at birth:

> I had suffered more than I ever had before and that opened something up in me. I know I felt quite different going back.

She recalled her return to work after the break and how she had enjoyed being with clients and having time away from her children. It had been a relief to immerse herself for those few hours in the clients' worlds. She spoke of being determined to achieve some semblance of her life before the babies, but at the same time,

> It was quite hard to do and I was always questioning whether I should be doing it . . . I always had in my mind, what if I had taken a proper break and just said, 'Right I'm going to give myself over to being a parent for the first year'.

As well as these developmental gains, Birksted-Breen (1986) emphasises the losses for the mother: the loss of the replete, pregnant state, the loss of the companion-baby inside and the loss of the phantasy-baby in favour of the real baby. This made me consider the loss to the client who has been allowed to sit in intimacy with mother and unborn baby but is then excluded from that relationship once the baby is born.

Several writers mention the challenge of managing enhanced transference from the patient at a time of vulnerability. Lax (1969: 363) is direct in naming how pregnancy inevitably stirs up in the mother 'some echoes of topical childhood conflagrations'. She argues that if the therapist has not had a chance to work through her own early conflicts around pregnancy, she will be more vulnerable to the transference communications of patients and more likely to react from her countertransference.

We might expect that like many retirees, a pregnant therapist may feel she has betrayed the principles of her contract with patients. This is indicated by Stuart (1997: 354), who suggests that the pregnant therapist 'has introduced action where, by her own arrangement, only talk is allowed'. My impression from the literature, from my contributors and from personal anecdotes is that pregnant therapists may not consciously feel the same level of guilt in the countertransference as others who are imposing an ending or a break. In a study which draws on her own pregnancy and also on the stories of 12 other analysts, Bassen (1988) found some instances of guilt in the countertransference but also some clinicians who recalled being more affectively available during pregnancy. Where guilt was named this was in relation to the reduced availability of the therapist, both in terms of tiredness and distraction, and in terms of the disruption of the maternity leave.

A reflection by Susannah perhaps indicates guilt which is camouflaged within a hypothetical idea. She was pondering the possibility of eventually having another child and imagining how that would be for a client:

> I think I'd feel terrible telling someone about a third pregnancy.

There were other points where she de-emphasised the impact on clients and stressed the continuity:

> It felt like I never really shut down. [A few minutes later] In my mind I never finished.

Speaking with the hindsight of many years, Flora was reflective about the limitations that a pregnant therapist may come up against:

> It's not something you can hide, with the bump – it's a very physical presence in the room. We worked with it but I think it was a narcissistic wound which we didn't work through sufficiently perhaps. Looking back now it can be a blind spot, that there were things about the wounding of the client by having a baby that it is quite difficult to really be aware of and work with.

Susannah rounded off her reflections with a comment which points us towards the depressive position:

> None of it's ideal but you have to think hard about that balance and everybody's needs: their needs, the baby's needs and your needs. How can you do that in a way which is fair to everybody at a time when you probably don't want to think about anybody's needs other than yours and your baby's?

Thinking in terms of disruption to the frame, Dufton (2004) is positive about how a good enough outcome may be achieved despite the intrusion of the therapist's pregnancy. She acknowledges the significant impact of pregnancy on the external frame, but reminds us that essentially the setting is not a set of rules which must be obeyed but 'ultimately a mental attitude within the psychotherapist' (2004: 112).

Supervision

When a supervisor and therapist are at different life stages, perhaps when one or other is pregnant or retiring, then either envy or fear of envy may arise. This potential for difficult feelings in the supervision comes at a time when a trusted supervisor is particularly needed because the shakiness in the frame means that containment from a supervisor is all the more necessary. A paper by Simmons (2011) looks specifically at the dynamics arising when supervising pregnant therapists, and she stresses the importance of the supervisor being able to hold the mixed feelings which therapist and client may be tempted to deny. Clearly it is imperative that the supervisor also recognise and contain any hostile feelings of her own because we know how damaging negative supervisory countertransference can be. Anecdotes of enactments between supervisors and pregnant supervisees tell of overzealous intrusive attention as well as more overt hostile interventions by supervisors (Baum and Herring, 1975; Butts and Cavenar, 1979).

A whole paper is devoted to supervision of pregnancy by Imber (1995). She argues that 'The supervisor of an analyst in special circumstances may need to function in ways that are out of the ordinary to help the supervisee cope with the added stress set off by a special life event' (1995: 282). She illustrates this with a case where she judged it right to be more directive than she usually would. In another case, Imber (1995) discusses the teach/treat boundary and demonstrates containment of the supervisee's feelings which were interrupting her thinking about her countertransference. This supervisee was expecting her third child and she was feeling burdened by one particular client's implicit demands for love and attention. She had often felt criticised by this patient and now she felt guilty that her pregnancy was disrupting his treatment. Imber's intervention was important in helping to separate out the therapist's own self-blame from the patient's projection of guilt. The therapist was then able to recognise how much of this dynamic was about this client's bullying demands, which had been evident prior to the pregnancy.

Susannah reflected on different experiences of group and individual supervision at the time of her first and second pregnancies. She indicates how much can go unnoticed and uncontained when members of a supervision group have competing needs:

> I think it was easier having individual supervision whilst being pregnant. I was very conscious whilst I was in a group that there was so much going on and I was also going to be leaving the group and I felt that I took up too much space, literally and physically . . . They felt almost . . . I very much tried not to, but it felt such a big thing to go through.

This comment highlights the challenge that group supervisors face. One way to manage this is to be transparent about the different needs of group members. Another way of addressing this is for therapists who are going through these kinds of transitions to seek extra consultation. Clearly this would need to be from a perspective which is complementary to their ongoing supervision.

Sabbaticals

The number of therapists who take a sabbatical is small, and very little has been written about the experience. Those planning this sort of break may therefore feel quite isolated, and this is especially true because the different reasons that people have for seeking a sabbatical make their experiences dissimilar. For self-employed therapists the financial costs of taking a sabbatical are obvious, but even though this choice is not affordable to many it is worth naming the gains. Issy spoke enthusiastically about the benefits:

> Actually what kind of model are we setting if we don't know our own rhythms and desires and who we are? Do we know loneliness? Do we know those very kind of existential questions?

The idea of taking the seventh year off for rest is built on the scriptural concept of the Sabbath and was first introduced into universities in the nineteenth century (Benshoff and Spruill, 2002). The value of sabbatical leave in supporting creativity and preventing burnout is confirmed in studies (Davidson, Eden, Westman *et al.*, 2010), and the practice of taking sabbaticals has spread to professions outside academia. Therapists and supervisors are familiar with less radical measures which can help protect against burnout. Foremost of these is taking care that our workload is appropriate both in terms of the overall number of sessions and the types of client and their level of distress.

Sabbatical breaks from therapy vary from the 10 weeks that Paula took to Issy's break of over a year. Clearly a longer absence will pose more challenge to the attachment relationships with clients. As in the case of a therapist's retirement, once the news is announced the door is open for speculation and fantasy. Clients' responses will depend on various factors but chiefly on their attachment story, the point that the work has reached and the amount of time that the therapist will be away. There may be a fear of having worn the therapist to a point of exhaustion, doubt that the therapist will return as promised, rage that she would do this or, contrastingly, denial of hurt and an alleged delight that the therapist is taking care of herself and improving her skills.

As it involves a temporary closure imposed by the therapist, a sabbatical has much in common with a maternity break and indeed sometimes a sabbatical is taken to 'give birth' to a book. Many of the challenges are similar in both types of break: how much notice to give, how much to disclose, how to facilitate hostility about the break, how to manage referral to a new or a holding therapist and how, on resumption, to work with feelings about the abandonment. There are also differences, the most notable being that when the therapist is leaving for a sabbatical, the client does not have the additional challenge of sharing the therapy space with the therapist's unborn baby. Their assumptions and fantasies about the break will therefore not involve that particular element of disturbance.

Issy was 54 when I met her six months into her sabbatical. After a year of deliberating and planning, she had taken another year to close a busy practice with the intention of taking at least a year away from the work. As Issy's story has elements of both temporary and full closure it has much in common with retirement narratives. There were various factors which contributed to her decision to take time out, but the most specific had been concerns about her health which had amplified her questions about the meaning and pace of her work. She worked largely with traumatised clients and, as well as a flow of short-term contracts, her practice included about a dozen people whom she had seen for many years. Half of these were coming twice a week.

Paula was 65 when I met her and she had taken her sabbatical the previous year. Having had a full-time practice for many years, at this stage of life she had chosen to work part-time doing 12 sessions a week, with three of these being supervision. Reflecting by herself and testing ideas with her supervisor, she had designed a sabbatical in two halves: she took two five-week breaks with a week in the middle where she was available for clients to have a check-in session.

Simon was 62 when I interviewed him. On turning 60 he had pondered his options about retirement, including the possibility of a shorter working week, but he settled on taking every fifth week off. This was a preventative or developmental step rather than a response to feeling tired or less able. He described it as a 60th birthday present to himself, and he clearly took great pleasure in the chance it gave him to immerse himself in creative work. He felt the result was much more nourishing for him than he could have achieved by reducing the hours he worked each week. He established a working structure which we might think of as a 'monthly sabbatical'. With a two-week break in the summer, he now works 44 weeks of the year so he pointed out that it is the distribution of sessions that has changed more than the overall number. Simon acknowledged that it created an unusual frame but felt this was clinically viable:

> So we are never more than four weeks away from another break. One might ask whether the work ever gets going, gets deep – but I think it does and the material about dependency seems to be very strong.

His solution brings to mind Quinodoz's (2010) idea of retirement 'à la carte'. Many therapists arrange a staged retirement, letting go of different strands of their work one by one.

What is the sabbatical for?

Issy's plan to take a sabbatical had evolved gradually, but the most tangible factor had been illness. Living with this existential anxiety had thrown up a new level of doubt about the work and she committed to making space for these questions.

> Could I legitimately carry on working at the level I was working without stopping to question, 'Is this having an impact on my body? To what level is working on a daily basis with trauma affecting my physicality?'
>
> For me not caring, having been a carer since quite a young age was . . . a big deal. So those are my CPD tasks – about time and space and just being. Yep, all the things I think are quite pertinent to the profession and will I hope enrich my on-going contribution to it, but they aren't really about what I am going to achieve out there in the world. They are about internal, emotional milestones.

Paula's decision to take a sabbatical was based on personal family reasons. She did not give her clients a reason for the break, and most of them assumed that she was taking a break in order to work on a new book. She explained to me that while she had done some writing, her reasons for taking time out had been personal rather than professional.

Caution about retirement had motivated Simon to seek a new pathway with a more gradual transition. He had witnessed his father struggle with the transition into retirement:

> When he no longer had that role to disappear into he sat at home listening to the radio feeling impotent. There is an extraordinary sense in which retirement is payback time.

Simon explained that his change in working hours was not about being tired or having problems with his memory, but reflected an adjustment within himself. He described this in terms of coming to a reconciliation about the work and its meaning to him.

> It's been about changes in my ambition and my will to power and my relationship with questions of status and authority. For a long time I worked in order to achieve recognition and often was thwarted in that, but not always. But you reach a point where that changes and you think 'This is a fool's game and there are much better ways to work and reasons for working' . . . Maybe it is also about saying, 'if I give up the desire to be cock of the heap then why to do work?'

Simon was transparent with his clients about the reason for the changes in the frame:

> In order to stay fresh and to continue to enjoy my work I'm going to work for four weeks and take the fifth week off. Would you be in agreement with working with me in that way?'

Management of the break

Issy began to plan her sabbatical well in advance and she decided that one year's notice for clients would be optimal. She recalled how she broke the news to her clients.

> It was different – it really was individual with every client. There were certain things that I did that were quite formulaic so I made sure that

I put it in writing. I told people verbally but I also put it in writing as the capacity for forgetting is quite something.

She had one or two clients who could not fully imagine her absence and only after she had gone did they realise that, after all, they did want to take the details of colleagues to whom they could go. She suggested that therapists on sabbatical need a policy for this: how will they respond if contacted by clients during the break?

Issy recalled how she had handled disclosure about her health. She had not shared any details but had reassured clients that she wasn't dying. Here she describes the terms on which she ended with clients:

> I was keen not to foreclose on the space that I knew I needed, so I didn't have a specific return date. I said my sabbatical would be 'at least a year'. All my clients said that they would like to know when I came back into practice so I agreed to let them know when I was working again but completely understood that they might well have established an alternative therapeutic relationship that I wouldn't want to intrude upon and that they had no responsibility to me. However they'd always be welcome to continue their journey with me – should they wish to do so.

Like therapists who are leaving for a long maternity break, Issy was seeking to balance the ongoing attachment needs of clients against her need to be relieved of her role as attachment figure to take best care of herself. She had felt it was relevant to offer clients the information about her return to practice as she did not want to prevent them from ever contacting her further down the line if, like many clients, they should feel the need to do further work. The model she describes is similar to that used by some therapists on maternity break, and I have covered the pros and cons of using a holding therapist above.

Paula explained her thinking behind the way she announced her break:

> The reason I used the term 'sabbatical' and gave the exact dates a long way in advance was that I didn't want people to think that I was ill. That was important to me. I didn't want to leave it so wide open that people could fantasise that I'd got a serious illness such as cancer.

She added that she knew some therapists would see such fantasies as enriching the work, but it would not sit comfortably with her to have people worrying when it was not necessary. She described why she felt summer was probably the least disruptive time to take a break: clients are used to a long summer break, a lot of people feel better in the summer and if they are taking a holiday of their own then their sense of abandonment is reduced. In common with the therapists who were preparing to retire, Paula had prepared for her break by closely monitoring potential clients. She explained that in the past she had worked with more fragile people and a sabbatical would not have been possible. Over more recent years she had chosen not to work with such traumatised clients and in the year prior to her break she had been particularly careful to refer on the one or two who had presented. Because all of her existing clients were at a secure stage in their process, she did not feel the need to arrange back-up therapy but she would have done so if she had judged it necessary:

> I suppose you could say that my planning for a sabbatical started a year or more in advance. There were a couple of people who came who I didn't take on but referred on to colleagues because I thought 'it won't be good for them to start with me and then for me to take a long sabbatical'. So I was very selective about who I took on in the run up to the announcement.

The model she devised is interesting because it could be useful to other therapists. She summarises the ingredients of the extra containment which she provided. This attention to the frame was in addition to the screening of new patients and to the work within sessions where the meaning of the separation could be thought about:

> I think I just aimed to provide as much containment in the experience as I could – a lot of notice, a very calm announcement well in advance, a letter with the actual dates inserted, and the optional check-in week, again with the dates given in the letter.

Clients' responses

Issy describes some of the dynamics which arose when she announced her sabbatical. Here she alludes to sibling rivalry along with some ingenious defences, illustrating how one can deflect anxiety away from one's own vulnerability:

> Initially I said, 'I need to let you know that in a year's time I will be taking some time out of practice and we will need to end our therapy' and listening to how people would reformulate that and the fantasy

that I was letting some of them go and not others, and I had to say, 'No, I am closing my practice'. Then some people would become very worried about my other clients! So it was interesting the way people responded to it.

In common with some of the contributors who were retiring, Issy had one client who coped with the imposed ending by leaving first:

There was one client who absolutely could not bear the fact that I was leaving and curtailed very, very quickly and that was quite hard because there was the sense of work left to be done.

All of her other clients were able to tolerate the feelings that came with the abandonment, and Issy described feeling very moved by their commitment to the relationship:

To stay with somebody you know is leaving you, I think the only parallel is death.

When Paula announced her sabbatical she offered patients the chance to book a session during the middle week of her break. She felt patients used these sessions to check that she was still in good health and that they were still remembered. These were not sessions where they were breaking new ground, but some patients were clearly relieved to see her and to share a little of their news. She recognised that the check-in was containing for her as well as for clients, as it gave her a chance to see how they were coping. It offered another opportunity to arrange for a colleague to be available over the second half of the sabbatical for any clients who were struggling to cope with the separation:

They all came in the check-in week – every single one, so there was 100 per cent take-up of the option of a check-in session. And my feeling was that it was really reassuring to them and that it was much, much easier than ten or eleven weeks in a row.

Simon felt that his gradual winding down would protect his clients from too sudden a disillusionment. He makes the case that this gradual evolution in the frame is helpful to clients and spares them the shock of their therapist suddenly switching from being apparently very altruistic to apparently very self-centred:

I've made it a professional habit to be very cautious about my omni-potence. So the fantasy that one is always there, always paying attention and always fantastically disciplined and then suddenly you say, 'I'm going to do something incredibly self-indulgent, I'm going, I'm retiring and you are not to know what I'm going to do but you can imagine that I'm going to go on a world cruise.'

Simon is posing an interesting challenge to the therapist who retires in the more conventional one-off style. Against this we would also want to consider what we forfeit from the analytic space if we opt for increased realism through gradual disillusionment.

The therapist's emotional experience of sabbatical

My interview with Issy conveys the rich opportunities which sabbatical permits for reflection about the work of being a therapist. The comments which she made in the middle of her year off convey a significant process of self-questioning, and she speaks of the impact on her sense of self:

It felt like closing down a whole part of me, not just a business . . . I've had moments of, 'I might never go back to being a therapist, why am I a therapist?' – so that's been part of it. But that was matched by 'I love this profession and it's a vocation for me'.

Paula reflected on her countertransference in the months after she returned from her sabbatical and said that the work had felt fresh. Although her motivation for taking a break had not been based on any sense of being wearied by the work, she felt it had been good for her and that it had enabled her to see her patients afresh. She realised she had been enjoying the work more since the break, and in an email after our meeting she offered an interesting reflection on the previously unacknowledged countertransference elements that contributed to this experience:

It goes without saying that when you take the decision to practice as a therapist, you also take on the restrictions that come with that decision. But, over the years, I think something else can creep in – a feeling of being trapped by your patients and a resentment that, because of them (rather than because of your own decision) you are unable to take off more than three of four weeks at any one time. In my case, this was entirely unconscious and it is only in retrospect, and in the context of our conversation, that I have become more aware of it. It seems to me now that the 'freshness' and the enhanced enjoyment of the work were in large part because I had ceased to feel trapped and had ceased to hold any unconscious resentment against my 'imprisoning' patients.

Simon described how his alternative version of sabbatical, with time for creativity, provided an ongoing refuelling:

In my case, the act of painting is about setting up a mirror to myself. There's a marvellous mirror to the self which counteracts all that I'm giving out when working with anxious people.

Issy echoed this in the value she placed on the opportunity for growth and learning. She said her sabbatical was 'the biggest piece of CPD that I have ever done'.

Conclusion

This chapter has focused on the risks to the clinical process that are posed by a prolonged absence, but it is important to acknowledge the opportunities which a break can bring. Depending on their identification with their therapist, clients might feel inspired by their therapist's adventure. If the break comes at an opportune time in their own process, they could be pushed to grow and develop as a result of being left alone. It is also important to acknowledge that the setting will have a huge impact on the way a therapist's absence is experienced. All the stories in this book have followed therapists in private practice and explored the particular challenges for the solo practitioner when the expected frame cannot be maintained. In the introduction I mentioned the containing power of organisations, where patients can more easily have emergency access to a colleague or benefit simply by knowing that the institution is surviving even though the individual is missing. When patients in an organisation see a holding therapist, the sessions may take place within the same building and this may feel more containing than a referral from one private setting to another. On the other hand, a private setting may have other benefits as self-employed therapists will usually have more flexibility in how they organise their maternity leave. The advantage of this is the scope it gives for the expectant mother to choose arrangements which are as good as possible both for the clients and for her.

An understanding of retirement may inform our thinking about temporary absence and vice versa, and there are also points of commonality with regular therapy work. The dynamics of a sabbatical are closest to those of a normal holiday break, with separation and reunion both evoking distinct responses from clients with predominantly dismissing or preoccupied attachment patterns. The dismissing adult, like the avoidant infant in the strange situation test, is very skilled at keeping anxiety out of view. She will probably appear to cope well and might find it hard to seek help if she were not coping. In contrast, preoccupied adults will at times be overwhelmed by a desperate need to elicit the care which has never been reliable. They are more likely to demand attention, but their way of doing so may confuse us and prevent them from getting the help that they need. We have heard evidence of both of these ways of coping, and perhaps these anecdotes from contributors can help us if we ever need to plan a long break.

Maternity leave is perhaps the kind of absence which elicits the most complicated attachment issues. As in the case of a break for illness or bereavement, a pregnancy presents additional reasons why clients may deny their resentment. We all know that we 'should' feel sad for someone who is grieving or unwell and that we 'should' feel happy when someone becomes pregnant. In the case of pregnancy, clients may be burdened by the pain of being displaced and by their anger towards the baby. They may be even more distressed by their feelings of shame about these primitive responses.

The experience of therapists on sabbatical prompts us to consider how we look after ourselves. Those who become worn out tend to describe burnout or boredom, but the term 'rustout' is proposed by Kottler (2010). He suggests this as a more apt description because 'it better represents the kind of slow, gradual process that eats away at a therapist's spirit' (2010: 181). Perhaps the most dangerous loss for a therapist is the loss of curiosity, and if we lose this we fall into the unfortunate assumption that we think we know what we are going to find. Being in such a state of knowing (as opposed to unknowing) is likely to become very boring and thus further undermine our engagement in the work. Sabbatical is just one way of reinvigorating the therapist's capacity for exploration. We may be encouraged by the solution that Simon devised, as it suggests that there may be creative ways forward outside the normal patterns of working. I heard of another innovative idea for achieving reinvigoration from a therapist who gave himself a six-week summer break in the year he turned 60.

Paula's intention in taking a sabbatical had not been to refresh herself in the work, but this was nevertheless one of the outcomes of her break. In contrast, although prompted by her health, Issy was deliberately creating a space to reconnect with parts of the self which may become invisible in our day-to-day lives as therapists. Without the caring role, the task of translating the internal world of the other, who are we? When we take a step back, what forgotten parts of ourselves may come into view? She asked herself and us:

> What comes out of the woodwork if we can't constantly be projecting our own needs into our client relationships?

Conclusion

When I was setting out on the writing of this book I had the following dream:

> I am visiting a small city in another country. It is a prosperous, rather high-tech city with impressive modern architecture and town planning. I am therefore doubly amazed to learn that each street light has to be turned off individually. I talk to the young man who is employed to do this. He is quietly walking from one lamppost to another and I now see that each carries a text giving the history and details (I think age, frequency of repairs, number of usages) of that particular light. After speaking to him and sensing his relationship to the lights, it makes more sense to me that the turning off needs to be done in this personal way. The young man is a student from the UK on a summer job and the task of turning off the lights is linked to his degree. To do it well he needs to understand the city and how it works.

The reader may recognise many possible meanings in this dream, but it is not difficult to see it as an exploration of the project that I was undertaking and of my own development as a visiting student. Initially as the dreamer I had the crude assumption that it would make sense to mechanise the turning off process, but I then realised that there is more to it than I had thought. This speaks to my own learning during the preparation and writing of this book.

Strengths and weaknesses of the study

The participants in this study shared their stories at different points in their process. At one end of the spectrum, Nicola was still 10 months away from the point of retiring, and at the other, Rosemary was nine years into retirement. While this has added to the rich variety of perspectives, it is not possible to identify how much the stage at which each story was told has impacted on the way contributors shared their experience. If I had been able to interview all 14 therapists at the same stage of the process, I would have heard a different set of stories and we cannot know how the passage of time has coloured the memories. We do know that memories are influenced by many factors, including our emotional needs and our defences. This subjective quality to our recollections is neatly conveyed by Barnes in *The Sense of an Ending* (2012), where he has his narrator make a list of memories and then comment, 'This last isn't something I actually saw, but what you end up remembering isn't always the same as what you have witnessed' (2012: 3).

This study has been conducted on a personal basis rather than within an academic structure. The initial impetus for this research came from my need as a supervisor and peri-retirement therapist to understand what was involved in closing a practice. The momentum was sustained by the curiosity of interviewees, who all showed an appetite for exploring their experience and for using the space which our meeting offered them. I think our shared professional position made it possible to achieve a high level of trust, and the space which we co-created allowed for the kind of reflection that we find in supervision.

Personal factors beyond the reach of this study

As therapists we might expect that one of the most critical factors in how we approach and manage the transition to retirement will be our internal world: how do our defensive styles and our internalised figures govern how we manage loss and challenge? The answer to this unasked question was sometimes given explicitly but often implicitly. Patsy was one who spoke directly of how her need to support a depressed mother had contributed to her work as a therapist, and to her difficulty in letting it go. In this study I neither have sufficient material about unconscious process, nor the right to interpret it too eagerly. It might be tempting to speculate, but it would be foolish. For example, where retirees appear most relaxed with the transition we cannot know whether they owed that comfort more to internal or external factors. Of these latter perhaps the most significant might be having supportive family and friends, financial security, good health and the opportunity for developing ourselves in retirement. When it comes to internal factors which could impact on how we handle this transition, it feels even harder to make a short list. Perhaps some key areas would be: the degree to which work has contained and affirmed us; our capacity to mourn; the effectiveness of our defences; how we manage our envy; and how much appetite we have for developing ourselves in retirement.

Are there clinical lessons we can learn from contributors' experience?

The role of the frame in psychoanalytic work means that when a therapist steps outside of the expected boundary to announce her retirement, there are parallels with an actor who breaches the 'fourth wall' and steps down into the audience. In both cases there is an illusion, or convention, to which both parties had willingly subscribed and then this is broken. How much might this study help us to manage that fracture? Or, as in a concept used by Anna Freud, can these stories help us recognise 'the least detrimental alternative' (Goldstein, 1972: 626)?

One of the most specific correlations to emerge in this study was that between the motivation for retirement and the period of notice given. Where pull factors are strongest, as for Denise and Hannah, the winding down with patients was done over a shorter period. Where a push factor was the main trigger, as in Rosemary's case, a more organic process over a longer ending period was allowed. When retiring therapists are deciding how long a period to allow for the process of ending with patients, they might find it helpful to bear in mind that this tendency could be operating. The experience of this sample would suggest that where therapists are anticipating the next stage more eagerly, they may opt for a shorter retirement process and where therapists are most reluctant to say goodbye to patients, they may opt for a longer period of notice.

In some ways Rosemary's organic process could appear to be an optimum solution from the patient's point of view as it avoids intrusion or, in Winnicott's terms, impingement. However, when we take unconscious process into account, this conclusion is not so convincing. We might picture a scenario where one or two remaining clients are keeping a therapist in harness while they each amble towards the end of a long therapy. If the therapist never announces her retirement there could be scope for some difficult dynamics: will the last patients sense that they are keeping the therapist waiting, or will they believe they are keeping her going? What if the final patient decides to end but at the 11th hour suffers a traumatic bereavement and wants more time?

In terms of gauging how individual patients fared in the wake of an imposed ending, this study has focused on therapists' anecdotes, vignettes and perceptions and, almost by definition, it has not looked at the experience from the patient's point of view beyond the juncture of their therapists retirement. Contributors' comments endorse what common sense suggests, that patients with troubled attachment histories were most threatened by the forced ending. The study by Lord *et al.* (1978) into patients' reactions to the death of their analyst may be the piece of research which comes closest to informing us about how different types of client respond to the retirement of their therapist.

What answer have I found to my initial question, 'How hard is retirement?'

While retirement represents a challenge for most adults, therapists seem equipped to observe the process and make sense of what they are going through. This means that many retiring therapists will engage in this transition as a developmental opportunity. The degree of stress they experience with this depends on factors within individuals as well as on their external circumstances, and in my sample there was a wide range in how stress was experienced and communicated.

As I did not use a formal instrument to assess stress in my retirees, I can only make a subjective comment about how I experienced their relative degrees of comfort with closing their practice. The small size of my sample means it can have no predictive power, but I hope my observations can help us think more intelligently about the wider experience of retirement from the profession. Having in mind the question 'How hard was it?' and thinking of my group of 13 retirees, I see the spectrum of experience as falling into four clusters: those who appeared to retire with ease; those who experienced the greatest sadness and loss; those who felt the most ambivalent; and those who conveyed the most stress. We could call these: *high comfort*: Beatrice, Emma and Hannah; *high grief*: Mary, Clementine, Annette and Rosemary; *high ambivalence*: Patsy, Carol and Nicola; and *high stress*: Celia, Denise and Alan.

How did each of the original subgroups fare?

How does this scale of comfort-versus-stress correlate with the original groups that I identified according to their motivation for retirement? These groups were the younger, the older, the forced and the classic. The principle distinction between them was the mixture of push and pull factors which had led the individual to the decision to retire. There are two points where these reasons for retiring seem to overlap with the degree of stress experienced: those with high grief were clustered in the classic group and those with high ambivalence were clustered in the younger group. In contrast, those with high or low stress were distributed throughout the four motivational groups. Clearly there were multiple factors operating for each individual which this study has not been able to track, but from the experience which was gathered and analysed we can make broad observations. The classic group seemed to weather the transition better than they expected. The forced group had a difficult path, but in some cases this was balanced out when other factors were within the control of the retiree (I am thinking of the solace that both Emma and Rosemary found in writing). The young group was highly diverse, but a noticeable trend was the added challenge of taking such a step when the choice was entirely voluntary. The older group, representing just two enormously different experiences, reminds us of the cruel diversity in our development at the age of 88.

Classic

Retirement is hard for this group, but in my sample they weather it well. Clementine, Annette and Mary represent a large number of older therapists, in that their reluctance to leave the work they love was balanced by their fulfilment in other parts of their lives. They are conscious of being challenged by the transition, they adjust well but remain aware of what had been lost. While all the contributors had a strong commitment to their work, these three conveyed the strongest sense of grief at the loss of this role and the ending of their careers. Their loss was great because their attachment was great, but I sensed that their regret about ending was different from the ambivalence of Patsy and Carol.

Forced

Rosemary, Emma and Celia were all obliged to retire because of physical decline or illness. The experience of being compelled to stop work may add an extra dark layer to the loss, and the way an illness develops may influence how this loss can be grieved. Where Emma had to some extent recovered her health and was able to re-engage very fully with her intellectual and creative strength, Celia was facing ongoing uncertainty and the imminent loss of cognitive capacity. The sense of bleakness about her retirement was focused on this loss of health which threatened to overwhelm the more specific loss of work. Rosemary was in good health for her age and was living through retirement with some frustration: she was quite well enough for most of the activities which she wanted to do, except for being a therapist.

Younger

Hannah, Patsy, Denise, Carol and Nicola represent very varied experiences of retirement. Hannah expressed the most comfort with the step. Denise was interviewed at the point when she was under most pressure, so her story gives a snapshot of the struggle which may be faced in clinical terms but tells little about how this therapist may adapt to retirement in the longer run. The most distinctive feature of this group was the higher degrees of ambivalence in Patsy, Denise, Carol and Nicola. Possibly this fits with the fact that they were making the decision without pressure, free either to continue working or to stop. Writing about the retirement of psychologists in private practice, McGee (2003) suggests that feelings of anxiety, vulnerability and ambivalence are often more marked in voluntary retirement than when a therapist has less choice about stopping work. Hannah's relative lack of ambivalence is very interesting, especially given that she had trained in psychotherapy late in life, with the intention of practising for many years. Her readiness to change her long-term plans is notable.

Older

Since his retirement at 88, Alan's health had deteriorated very steadily, leaving him with a reduced lifestyle. Beatrice, also retiring at 88, was interviewed six months before she stopped seeing clients and was in very good health. Her attachment to the work was reflected in the length of her career, but at the same time she conveyed a readiness to let it go and did not communicate a heavy sadness about losing it. This grouping confirms what we know – that chronological age is a poor predictor of the capacity to work.

Comparing the different types of closure

The various endings surveyed in this book are alike in the challenge they pose: the disruption of the frame and the threat to the client's attachment relationship with the therapist. In each case of an imposed ending, the therapist's action shakes the secure base of the relationship. In each case there is a question as to whether trust can be sufficiently restored for the pair to work productively on the ending or on the impact of a temporary closure. A therapist who is retiring or relocating will be hoping to leave the client with some measure of internalised secure base. As one published first-hand account tells us, when this is not achieved the sense of wounding and grievance may be profound (Anonymous, 2001). For those making a temporary ending, the challenge is to sustain the secure base well enough through the break and then repair and restore trust when the therapeutic couple reassemble. Relevant to all these types of ending is the challenge of engaging with protest from several clients at a time of personal vulnerability. This comment from Flora relates to maternity leave, but could have been spoken by a retiree:

> There is likely to be much more of the negative transference than there has ever been because the clients' needs are being thwarted. And that can be very important material but if you've got that coming from a whole caseload of clients that is very tough.

Within the group of retirees contributing to this book, there is diversity. Among the stories of other endings, that of Alice (who relocated) has most overlap with the retirement narratives. She speaks of the same concerns faced by retirees: questions of pacing, of disclosure, of becoming less anonymous and of managing contact after the closure. Above all these issues is the sadness felt by client and therapist and the clinical challenge of working with whatever the imposed ending means for each client. Whereas retirement is something that all older therapists must eventually embrace, relocation may appear to be more of a free choice. In reality the decision to relocate rests on a number of factors and many of these are outside the therapist's control. This was the case for Alice, whose decision arose from her partner's illness and their consequent joint need to be closer to family. Many therapists who relocate are doing so to accommodate a partner's change of job, and time pressures can be more critical for relocating therapists than for retirees. With relocation the therapist may be juggling significant external factors such as transition between salaried jobs, a house sale and children needing to change schools. Keeping up an income stream while closing one practice and re-establishing another is clearly a big consideration.

While these parallels between relocation and retirement are marked, the similarities with temporary breaks for maternity and sabbatical are not quite so strong. When the closure is temporary the client is spared the complete abandonment of a therapist who is 'jumping ship', but the therapeutic pair is faced with the different challenge of managing a long absence. Pregnancy brings a unique challenge to the therapeutic pair: first the displacement by the visibly growing baby and then the break. The unpredictability of childbirth means that a maternity break, like illness in the therapist, brings doubts about the return date. Like the retiree, the pregnant therapist has to contain difficult dynamics from several patients at a point where they themselves are vulnerable. Whether temporary or permanent, the closure brings loss which needs to be mourned. Issy was speaking about sabbatical leave, but her blunt summary could have been made by a retiree. She said:

> The therapeutic couple was in grief.

Sabbatical stories show younger therapists choosing to address the existential questions which retirement may eventually force on us all. During their leave of absence there is space to reflect on the need in them which pushes them to do this work. If we are able to give ourselves such a breathing space we may ponder how that part of the self will fare when we finally come off the treadmill of clinical sessions.

Money

Financial resources are a key factor in retirement planning, so it seems important to acknowledge that the book has not explored this in any detail. The subject of money did not appear central to the therapists I interviewed. It must have carried weight in their retirement process and I deduce that they did not feel comfortable sharing that with me; possibly this reticence simply reflected the taboo about mentioning wealth. The contributors were by definition in a position where they could live reasonably in retirement without the income which they had once earned as therapists. However, in the wider pool of therapists this will not always be the case and there will be hardship. It is important that people are able to earn sufficiently during their working lives to provide what they need for retirement, but this is a major economic and political question outside the scope of this book.

We know from managing patients' fees that it can be hard to distinguish what is real about money from what is symbolic. The feeling that 'I will be short of money if I retire now' could represent a stark reality, but this sense that 'I won't have enough' could also be a projection. Some contributors mentioned money as a practical factor in decisions which influenced the precise timing of closing their practice: payments of rent on consulting rooms and payments of fees to professional bodies provided an incentive to get on with the decision. Perhaps these practical triggers provided a hook on which to hang the bigger decision. A number of contributors recognised that their relatively comfortable financial position was a privilege, and they spoke of colleagues who were less fortunate and who might like to retire but needed to keep earning.

What's to be done when therapists avoid retirement?

The contributors to this book had approached their retirement with realism and thoughtfulness. When therapists fail to do this, the profession faces the question of how to protect patients. This book has not set out to propose a solution but rather to illustrate the seriousness of the challenge and to follow a group of responsible practitioners as they made the journey into retirement. A subject that has no easy answers naturally divides opinion in the profession. Some would like to see a mandatory system of monitoring from the various registration bodies, possibly with an annual assessment after a certain age. A few people support the idea of an upper limit for working with clients. At the other extreme are those who endorse the right of the therapist to work up to their death. These therapists argue that early retirement leads to a waste of experienced clinicians and that patients can benefit from working with someone who is able to face their own ageing and death. In between are those with different ideas on how quality control might be maintained.

Junkers (2013) is one who has addressed the question very carefully and presents a strong case for action by institutions. Several papers in her book catalogue distressing cases where colleagues did not feel they could intervene despite apparently clear evidence of an ageing analyst losing capacity. From her wide knowledge of these cases she concludes: 'it is the responsibility of the institution to help contain problems that may not be amenable to individual solution' (2013: 31). In recent years opportunities have opened up for retiring therapists to reflect with colleagues on their questions about retirement. A number of organisations are beginning to run workshops and ongoing discussion groups for therapists in peri-retirement. Another way to get support for this stage is to connect with a mentor who has already been through the process, though this latter misses out on the benefits that come from being in a group of peers.

It is sometimes argued that the solution to this dilemma lies in the hands of supervisors. I think that supervisors could be an important link in the chain, but they need more support with this task. We are requiring two difficult tasks of them: first to be sure enough of the problem and second to become the bearers of bad news. In peer supervision or individual paid consultation, both of these tasks require considerable skill and courage. Those therapists who postpone retirement may be more than averagely defended against their ageing process: if we avoid believing what our own senses could tell us about our falling off in acuity, we may be equally unwilling to hear about it from others. So in these cases supervisors, whether peer or individual, would have a particularly challenging task.

Anecdotes in Chapter 6 reflect this reluctance to retire. If we do leave our retirement to a late age then by the time we face it we may already be living with considerable losses, and this could make the additional loss of work a particularly unwelcome step. I had the sense that this may have been Alan's experience, whereas Beatrice's process suggests that not all those who continue working to a late age are fearful of retirement.

Although I have stressed the limitations of supervision as a quality control mechanism, I think this function could be improved if supervisors received additional organisational support. A more demanding framework for assessment might help with this. Occasional reviews are good practice for any supervisory dyads, and it could be possible to formalise this without turning it into a time-wasting exercise. I see this as akin to the challenge that adult, middle-aged children meet when their parents become unreliable as drivers. A difficult conversation needs to be had and the adult child or GP might cope better, if the licensing authority were more demanding about evidence. Similarly a system of formal peer appraisal is used in some professions and could be a way of providing a safeguard and certainly of highlighting the issue. Even if this method is only able to identify the most obvious problems, it might contribute to a cultural shift in organisations.

I think that a useful institutional aim would be to increase recognition of our fragility throughout our working lives. More bluntly put, we need to let go some omnipotence and become more comfortable with knowing about vulnerability in ourselves and our colleagues. My research uncovered too many stories of supervisors and colleagues turning a blind eye – being unwilling to admit that help was needed. As well as our existing ethical guidelines to monitor therapists' performance, it would be helpful to develop more openness to recognising and responding when peers are struggling. This role of the analytic community is indicated in the strongly worded paper about an analyst's relocation (Anonymous, 2001). The writer suggests that we need to understand the analytic situation as three persons – the analysand, the analyst and the embracing community. The writer acknowledges that the latter may not usually have an active role, but 'there might be benefits, in terms of protection of both the analyst and the analysand in seeing the analytic duo as embedded in a larger, protective matrix' (2001: 54).

If we could achieve a shift in how we think about retirement, it seems likely that there would be incidental benefits. Thinking more openly and carefully about closing a practice for retirement would mean that greater support was available to the many therapists who need to relocate or to take a significant temporary break in their working life. Equally, those who have taken maternity leave might become more aware of how much they have to contribute to the thinking about retirement. As the numbers of therapists approaching retirement age is increasing, the problem is a pressing one and if organisations do nothing then more clients risk being harmed by therapists who are unable to recognise the effect of their own ageing.

One route by which we all contribute to the culture around retirement is through our individual responses to our peers who are planning to stop working. I heard many anecdotes from retirees who sensed that colleagues who were not retiring felt threatened by their departure. I have also observed this disappointment first hand in my own feelings when a valued mentor or colleague retires. When the person retiring is older we may tend to feel this as the loss of a parent; when it is a peer who is going, we may feel we are losing a sibling. In addition to resentment there may be envy – 'How did she manage to break free while I cling to the rock?' Carol described this response in herself on discovering that her former therapist had retired while she was still struggling with ambivalence.

A very practical responsibility which may indirectly help increase our understanding of retirement is that of therapeutic wills. This is an area of practice which has improved considerably within the last decade, with organisations now holding stricter requirements for a therapeutic executor to be in place as soon as a clinician starts seeing patients. While this does not tackle the issue of retirement, it may help to loosen our defences around our omnipotence. The task of writing a therapeutic will is considered in a number of papers (Firestein, 1993; Despenser, 2008; O'Neil, 2013), and a short section on emergency endings can be found in the Appendix.

Ending

Florence Hendriks's cover for this book shows us a therapy room with two chairs abandoned in a narrow space. The link that might have existed between this pair is tenuous or broken, with one chair almost turning away. Possibly the therapist is looking at her freedom in the outside world while the client at the front has our attention. Or is it the client who is staring out of the window while the therapist is sitting in the front corner under our microscope? Presently the chairs may be stacked away or put to a new use.

Ultimately the theme which underlies these stories is that of ageing. Shakespeare gives this to us in a relatively palatable form, describing a gradual process in the first person. He conveys the sadness of loss but also the lingering sweetness of what came before:

That time of year thou mayst in me behold
When yellow leaves, or none, or few, do hang
Upon those boughs which shake against the cold,
Bare ruin'd choirs, where late the sweet birds sang.

(Sonnet LXXIII, 1–4)

Being therapists, we will not feel comfortable if we do not keep the shadow in view and this is very present in Larkin's starkly named poem, 'The old fools' (2012: 81):

Their looks show that they're for it:
Ash hair, toad hands, prune face dried into lines.

Being human, we look at the end of the story for redemption. I think we find it in the portable skills which the retired therapist takes with her. However many years we live as retired people, these skills will travel with us in our relationships with others and with ourselves. Three years into her retirement, Boyd-Carpenter (2010b) wrote this:

Finally I have found that I do know myself 'well enough to get by' and I made the right decision in retiring.

I have been a few years working on this book and in cat terms that represents a significant advance in age. My older cat still uses the adventurous exit route I described at the start of the book, but he does so rarely. His first choice is now definitely the sedate one via the front door but, not having a sense of self, he may be spared a sense of loss about this constraint. However, I imagine that his lack of awareness means he also misses out on the sense of achievement which the retiring therapist can gain from surviving loss and transition. In contrast to my cat, the contributors to this study have been keenly aware of their process and this enabled them to reflect with insight upon their retirement. Their generous sharing has created this book.

Appendix

Questions about retirement indicated by this study

How do we gauge whether we need to retire?

Is the idea of retirement coming more from push or pull factors?

If a colleague had a fly-on-the-wall view of your therapy room, what would they notice?

Are there colleagues or supervisors who could bear to tell you if you need to go?

Whatever colleagues say, have they stopped referring to you?

If there was an aspect of the work in which your capacity were declining, what would it be?

How much of your clinical work are you letting your supervisor see? Does she know enough about your responses and interventions to recognise whether your skills have declined? Or is the focus more on the client?

How realistic are you being about your own health and age and the statistical likelihood of sudden illness?

How do we plan the closure of our practice?

At what date do you want to be fully retired?

How much notice do you feel would be useful to clients for working through the imposed ending?

At what point would you cease taking on any new long-term clients?

At what point would you cease taking on any new clients at all?

At what point would you cease taking on those likely to be highly impacted by an imposed ending, such as those with fractured early attachments?

If, in the lead-up to retirement, you choose to take short-term referrals, how will you guard against taking on a patient who would be damaged by brief therapy?

Over what period would you want to inform clients (given the emotional energy needed for this task)?

Over what period would you pace the endings (given that saying goodbye to several long-term clients in one week would be overwhelming and make it hard to attune and respond fully)?

How will you word your announcement? – for example, how precise will you be about the timing?

How much will you disclose – would you answer a question about whether you will be moving away? Would you let patients know where you are moving to? Would you give an address to which they can send a Christmas card?

Have you established what your insurer can offer in terms of run-off cover?

How will you stagger the various associated endings: supervision, teaching, committees and other involvement with colleagues?

Would you inform any former clients, such as those who ended recently and who you felt were likely to re-contact you one day?

How do we work with clients' responses to the abandonment?

Are patients' defensive strategies being identified and decoded?

How does your theory help you to make sense of clients' responses to the news?

What might the imposed ending mean in terms of each client's attachment story?

Which clients may be most challenged by the experience of being left?

Can you recognise how you may be projecting your own feelings about the ending onto your patients? Could you be underestimating the distress of avoidant clients and exaggerating the fragility of others?

What age has each patient reached in the transference?

What stage is each at in their working through?

What are our feelings about ending?

To what extent have you engaged with your own feelings about ageing and death?

What function does your work have in your internal world? How do you feel about losing that source of affirmation?

How might your own attachment story be influencing how you manage the ending and respond to different clients?

What feelings have you recognised in yourself, both in sessions and outside?

How do you feel around colleagues who are not retiring?

What patterns from earlier endings may be impacting on you?

What do we do about referral on?

What criteria do you use when assessing whether a client needs to continue work with another therapist?

Could the therapist's feelings about retirement be colouring her decisions about referral on?

What if a therapist tends towards referring everyone on, or to make no referrals? What would this signify about her feelings?

If you don't refer on, how do you feel about clients doing fine without you?

If you do refer on, is there some fear about other therapists seeing how you worked?

What are your thoughts about the best timing for a patient to meet their possible new therapist? How much information would you think of sharing with her?

How well do we use our supervision?

Can you use the supervisory space to think over the question of retirement, allowing yourself plenty of time to reflect before coming to a decision?

Do you allow your supervisor to see enough of your work that they could tell whether your age was beginning to impact negatively on your clients?

How do you feel about your relationship with your supervisor? How will each of you feel about your relative ages and about her continuing to practice as you wind down?

Could we benefit by other help?

Have you looked for workshops you could attend?

Is there an ongoing discussion group in your area or could you set one up?

Would returning to therapy, whether brief or long term, be appropriate?

Given that closing a practice means being available to clients who all have reason for distress and anger, how can the therapist support herself and remain robust enough to work with this protest?

What do you think about Vaillant's (2002) four predictors of satisfaction in retirement: forming a new social network, playing, creativity, lifelong learning? What ideas do you have for achieving these?

How do we do as supervisors of retirees?

How have you managed the challenging task of bringing a supervisee's attention to the question of her age and performance?

Could you structure reviews in a way that support this function?

How comfortable are you when a younger supervisee wonders whether she will retire? What would help you to facilitate an unhurried exploration?

How well do you do at containing the anxieties which retirement brings up for a supervisee? Are your own anxieties about endings and ageing getting in the way?

How alert are you as a supervisor to the clinical challenges that the retiring therapist faces?

How much do you use consultation to support yourself in these challenges?

Questions about temporary endings – such as sabbatical

If a break is likely, can the therapist prepare well in advance by not taking on highly vulnerable clients?

What clinical factors will influence the decision about the length of the break?

How much choice will there be about when to break the news?

Given the length of the absence, how do you imagine each client will cope and what are your criteria for whether to refer to another therapist?

Does it make sense, in terms of your model, to arrange for a holding therapist?

Which colleagues might you approach to serve as an access and information point for clients during your absence?

Given the possible need for clients to share resentment when you return from the break, how can you best prepare and support yourself?

Can supervision be used to think through issues of disclosure and how to respond to clients' enquiries about the break?

If clients have had sessions, or just contact, with another therapist during the break, how has this impacted on the reunion with you?

Questions about emergency endings

Is your therapeutic will up to date?

Are your therapeutic executors mindful of the responsibilities that they may have to fulfil?

Are supervisor and executors aware of each other?

Who would contact your executors if you were run over, and are they aware of how urgent that task would be?

Have you considered what you might do if you are too ill to see clients for a final session – for example, would you want to write a letter?

Have you considered your wishes in terms of your funeral and the possibility of former patients attending?

What provision has been made for destruction of client records – both hard copies and any data on computers?

What regulating bodies, directories and websites need to be informed?

What online presence would need to be taken down?

Questions about maternity leave

If you hope to become pregnant in the future, what are your thoughts about the number and type of clients you would ideally like in your practice at the point when you leave them?

How can you move towards that optimum level of work?

Do you have a supervisor who will be supportive and containing as you manage the process of separation and reunion against the background of your life-changing events?

At what point would you tell clients of a pregnancy?

What would you tell them?

How long a break would you plan?

Knowing the intended length of break and also your clients' attachment patterns, which of these options would you offer each of them:

- Ending therapy completely because close enough to 'ready'?
- Ending the work with you and going to another therapist?
- Taking time out of therapy but having the name of a colleague to whom they could go for emergency sessions?
- Taking time out of therapy but having the name of a colleague who will provide contact and relevant information, but not sessions?
- Seeing a temporary 'holding' therapist during the break? How will you proceed if the client wishes to stay with the new therapist?

On return from a maternity break, how much information would you give?

As a new mother, how can you best support your resilience so that you will be available for clients to share their resentment about being left and displaced?

If there were serious complications for you or your baby which prevented you returning as planned, what might you communicate to clients and who will arrange support or referral for them?

References

Aarons, Z.A. (1975) The analyst's relocation: its effect on the transference-parameter or catalyst, *International Journal of Psychoanalysis*, 56: 303–19.

Abend, S.M. (1982) Serious illness in the analyst: countertransference considerations, *Journal of the American Psychoanalytic Association*, 30: 365–79.

Adams, M. (2014) *Myth of the Untroubled Therapist: Private life, professional practice*. London: Routledge.

Ainsworth, M.D.S., Blehar, M.C., Waters, E. and Wall, S. (1978) *Patterns of Attachment: Assessed in the strange situation and at home*. Hillsdale, NJ: Erlbaum Associates.

Anonymous (2001) Killing me softly: an analysand's perspective on the ethical problems of relocating a psychoanalytic practice: *Psychoanalytic Social Work*, 8: 41–55.

Anonymous (2011) Letters page, *Therapy Today*, September: 18.

Atchley, R.C. (1976) *The Sociology of Retirement*. Cambridge, MA: Schenkman.

Atwood, M. (2005) *The Penelopiad*. Toronto: Canongate.

Avis, M. and Freshwater, D. (2006) Evidence for practice, epistemology, and critical reflection, *Nursing Philosophy*, 7(4): 216–24.

Barker, M. (2011) Ageing and attachment, in P. Ryan and B. Coughlan (eds) *Ageing and Older Adult Mental Health: Issues and implications for practice*. New York: Routledge, pp. 176–91.

Barnes, J. (2012) *The Sense of an Ending*. London: Vintage.

Barnett, M. (2007) What brings you here? An exploration of the unconscious motivations of those who choose to train and work as psychotherapists and counsellors, *Psychodynamic Practice*, 13(3): 257–74.

Barratt, G., Kegerreis, P. and Wetherell, J. (2012) Thinking about and planning for retirement, *British Journal of Psychotherapy*, 110–116.

Bassen, C.R. (1988) The impact of the analyst's pregnancy on the course of analysis, *Psychoanalytic Inquiry*, 8: 280–98.

Baum, E. and Herring, C. (1975) The pregnant psychotherapist in training: some preliminary findings and impressions, *American Journal of Psychiatry*, 132: 419–22.

Becker, E. (1973) *The Denial of Death*. London: Souvenir Press.

Bembry, J. and Ericson, C. (1999) Therapeutic termination with the early adolescent who has experienced multiple losses, *Child and Adolescent Social Work Journal*, 16(3): 177–89.

Benjamin, J. (1990) An outline of intersubjectivity: the development of recognition, *Psychoanalytic Psychology*, 7S: 33–46.

Benjamin, J. (2004) Beyond doer and done to: an intersubjective view of thirdness, *Psychoanalytic Quarterly*, 73: 5–46.

Bennett, R. (2011) Life is too short for retirement: you use it or lose it, *The Times*, 30 December: 21.

Benshoff, J.M. and Spruill, D.A. (2002) Sabbaticals for counsellor educators: purposes, benefits and outcomes, *Counselor Education and Supervision*, 42: 131–44.

Bernier, A. and Dozier, M. (2002) The client–counselor match and the corrective emotional experience: evidence from interpersonal and attachment research, *Psychotherapy: Theory, Research, Training*, 39(1): 32–43.

Biggs, S. (1999) *The Mature Imagination: Dynamics of identity in midlife and beyond*. Buckingham: Open University Press.

Birksted-Breen, D. (1986) The experience of having a baby: a developmental view, *Free Associations*, 1E: 22–35.

Bond, T. and Jenkins, P. (2009) *Access to Records of Counselling and Psychotherapy*. BACP information sheet G1. Lutterworth: BACP.

Bowlby, J. (1969) *Attachment and Loss: Volume I, Attachment*. London: Hogarth.

Bowlby, J. (1973) *Attachment and Loss: Volume II, Separation, Anxiety and Anger*. London: Hogarth.

Bowlby, J. (1977) The making and breaking of affectional bonds, *British Journal of Psychiatry*, 130: 201–10.

Bowlby, J. (1979) *The Making and Breaking of Affectional Bonds*. London: Tavistock Publications.

Bowlby, J. (1980) *Attachment and Loss: Volume III, Loss: Sadness and depression*. London: Hogarth.

Bowlby, J. (1988) *A Secure Base: Clinical applications of attachment theory*. London: Tavistock/Routledge.

Boyd-Carpenter, M.J. (2010a) Reflections on retirement, *Psychodynamic Practice*, 16(1): 89–94.

Boyd-Carpenter, M.J. (2010b) Personal communication.

Bretherton, I. and Munholland, K.A. (1999) Internal working models in attachment relationships: A construct revisited, in J. Cassidy and P. Shaver (eds) *Handbook of Attachment: Theory, research and clinical applications*. New York: Guilford Press, pp. 89–111.

Browning, D.H. (1974) Patients' reactions to their therapist's pregnancies, *Journal of the American Academy of Child Psychiatry*, 13(3): 468–82.

Butts, N.T. and Cavenar, J.O. (1979) Colleagues' responses to pregnant residents, *American Journal of Psychiatry*, 136: 1586–1589.

Carlisle, E. (2013) Life-long analysis?, in G. Junkers (ed.) *The Empty Couch*. New York: Routledge, pp. 67–78.

Cath, S.H. (1997) Loss and restitution in late life, in S. Akhtar and S. Kramer (eds) *The Seasons of Life: Separation-individuation perspectives*. NJ: Jason Aronson, pp. 127–56.

Cavafy, C.P. (2007) Ithaca, in *The Collected Poems*, translated by E. Sachperoglou. Anthony Hirst, Contributor. Oxford: Oxford University Press.

Chiaramonte, J.A. (1986) Therapist pregnancy and maternity leave: maintaining and furthering therapeutic gains in the interim, *Clinical Social Work Journal*, 14(4): 335–48.

Cicirelli, V.G. (2004) God as the ultimate attachment figure for older adults, *Attachment and Human Development*, 6(4): 371–88.

Clementel-Jones, C. (1985) The pregnant psychotherapist's experience: colleague's and patient's reactions to the author's first pregnancy, *British Journal of Psychotherapy*, 2(2): 79–94.

Cohen, J. (1983) Psychotherapists preparing for death: denial and action, *American Journal of Psychotherapy*, 37(2): 222–6.

Colarusso, C.A. (1997) Separation-individuation processes in middle adulthood: the fourth individuation, in S. Akhtar and S. Kramer (eds) *The Seasons of Life: Separation-individuation perspectives*. NJ: Jason Aronson.

Cole, M.B. and Macdonald, K.C. (2011) Retired occupational therapists' experiences in volunteer occupations, *Occupational Therapy International*, 18(1): 18–31.

Colman, W. (2006) The analytic super-ego, *Journal of the British Association of Psychotherapists*, 44(2): 99–114.

Coltart, N. (1991) *Slouching towards Bethlehem*. London: Karnac Books.

Coltart, N. (1996) *The Baby and the Bathwater*. London: Karnac Books.

Conway, P.S. (1999) When all is said . . . A phenomenological enquiry into post-termination experience, *International Journal of Psycho-analysis*, 80: 563–74.

Cozolino, L. (2008) *The Healthy Aging Brain: Sustaining attachment, attaining wisdom*. New York: Norton.

Craige, H. (2002) Mourning analysis: the post-termination phase, *Journal of the American Psychoanalytic Association*, 50: 507–50.

Culliford, P. (2011) How prepared are we for sudden illness and unplanned retirement? *Supervision Review*, Summer: 8–13.

Cullington-Roberts, D. (1994) The absent psychotherapist, *Psychoanalytic Psychotherapy*, 8: 63–76.

Daly, K.D. and Mallinckrodt, B. (2009) Experienced therapists' approach to psychotherapy for adults with attachment avoidance or attachment anxiety, *Journal of Counselling Psychology*, 56(4): 549–63.

Davidson, O., Eden, D., Westman, M., Hammer, L., Krausz, M., O'Driscoll, M., Quick, J., Cohen-Charash, Y., Kluger, A., Maslach, C., Perrewe, P. and Rosenblatt, Z. (2010) Sabbatical leave: who gains and how much? *Journal of Applied Psychology*, 95(5): 953–64.

Despenser, S. (2008) Have you made a clinical will?, *Therapy Today*, 19(7): 31–3.

Dewald, P.A. (1965) Reactions to the forced termination of therapy, *Psychoanalytic Quarterly*, 39: 102–26.

Dewald, P.A. (1982) Serious illness in the analyst: transference, countertransference and reality responses, *Journal of the American Psychoanalytic Association*, 30: 347–63.

Dewald, P.A and Schwartz, H.J. (1993) Life cycle of the analyst: pregnancy, illness and disability, *Journal of the American Psychoanalytic Association*, 41: 191–207.

Doka, K.J. (ed.) (1989) *Disenfranchised Grief: Recognising hidden sorrow.* Lexington, MA: Lexington.

Dolan, R., Arnkoff, D. and Glass, C. (1993) Client attachment style and the psychotherapist's interpersonal stance, *Psychotherapy: Theory, Research, Practice, Training*, 30(3): 408–12.

Dufton, K. (2004) Somebody else's baby: Evidence of broken rules and broken promises?, *Psychoanalytic Psychotherapy*,18: 111–24.

Eissler, K.R. (1993) On possible effects of aging on the practice of psychoanalysis: an essay, *Psychoanalytic Inquiry*, 13: 316–32.

Erikson, E.H. (1980) *Identity and the Life Cycle.* New York: WW Norton.

Farber, B., Lippert, R. and Nevas, D. (1995) The therapist as attachment figure, *Psychotherapy*, 32(2): 204–12.

Ferenczi, S. (1927/1955) The problem of the termination of the analysis, in *Final Contributions to the Problems and Methods of Psychoanalysis.* New York: Brunner/Mazell, pp. 77–86.

Firestein, S.K. (1974) Termination of psychoanalysis of adults: a review of the literature, *Journal of the American Psychoanalytic Association*, 22: 873–94.

Firestein, S.K. (1993) On thinking the unthinkable: making a professional will, *The American Psychoanalyst*, 27: 16.

Fonagy, P. (2009) When analysts need to retire, in B. Willock, R. Curtis and L. Bohm (eds) *Taboo or Not Taboo? Forbidden thoughts, forbidden acts in psychoanalysis and psychotherapy.* London: Karnac.

Fonagy, P. and Target, M. (1996) Playing with reality: I. Theory of mind and the normal development of psychic reality, *The International Journal of Psychoanalysis*, 77(2): 217–33.

Fonagy, P. and Target, M. (1997) Attachment and reflective function: their role in self-organisation, *Development and Psychopathology*, 9: 679–700.

Fraiberg, S. (1969) Libidinal object constancy and mental representation, *Psychoanalytic Study of the Child*, 24: 9–47.

Fraley, R. and Brumbaugh, C.C. (2004) A dynamic systems approach to conceptualising and studying stability and change in attachment security, in W.S. Rhodes and J.A. Simpson (eds) *Adult Attachment: Theory, research and clinical implications.* New York: Guilford Press, pp. 86–132.

Fraley, R. and Shaver, P. (1999) Loss and bereavement, in J. Cassidy and P. Shaver (eds) *Handbook of Attachment: Theory, research and clinical applications.* New York: Guilford Press, pp. 735–59.

Frawley-O'Dea, G. and Sarnat, J. (2001) *The Supervisory Relationship*. London: Guilford Press.

Freeth, R. (2001) Ending therapy when one's therapist dies, *Counselling and Psychotherapy Journal*, July: 18–20.

Freshwater, D. (2007) Reading mixed methods research: Contexts for criticism, *Journal of Mixed Methods Research*, 1(2): 134–46.

Freud, S. (1905) On Psychotherapy, *Standard Edition*, 7: 257–68. London: Hogarth Press.

Freud, S. (1915) Thoughts for the Times on War and Death, *Standard Edition*, 14: 289–300. London: Hogarth Press.

Freud, S. (1917) Mourning and Melancholia, *Standard Edition*, 14: 237–58. London: Hogarth Press.

Freud, S. (1918) An infantile neurosis and other works, *Standard Edition*, 17. London: Hogarth Press.

Freud, S. (1923) The ego and the id, *Standard Edition*, 19: 19–27. London: Hogarth Press.

Freud, S. (1937) Analysis terminable and interminable, in *Standard Edition*, 23: 209–54. London: Hogarth Press.

Frommer, M.S. (2009) On ending a practice and a life: commentary on Michael Shernoff's final paper, *Journal of Gay and Lesbian Mental Health*, 13: 118–25.

Fuller, R.L. (1987) The impact of the therapist's pregnancy on the dynamics of the therapeutic process, *Journal of the American Academy of Psychoanalysis and Dynamic Psychiatry*, 15: 9–28.

Gabbard, G.O. and Lester, E.P. (1995) *Boundaries and Boundary Violations in Psychoanalysis*. New York: Basic Books.

Galatzer-Levy, R.M. (2004) The death of the analyst: patients whose previous analyst died while they were in treatment, *Journal of the American Psychoanalytic Association*, 52: 999–1024.

Garcia-Lawson, K.A., Lane, R.C. and Koetting, M.G. (2000) Sudden death of the therapist: the effects on the patient, *Journal of Contemporary Psychotherapy*, 30(1): 85–103.

Garner, J. and Bacelle, L. (2004) Sexuality, in S. Evans and J. Garner (eds) *Talking Over the Years: A handbook of dynamic psychotherapy with older adults*. Hove: Brunner Routledge, pp. 247–64.

Gay, P. (1988) *Freud: A life for our time*. London: Papermac.

Gendlin, E. (1996) *Focusing-Oriented Psychotherapy: A manual of the experiential method*. New York: Guilford.

Gervais, L. (1994) Serious illness in the analyst: a time for analysis and a time for self-analysis, *Canadian Journal of Psychoanalysis*, 2: 191–202.

Gibb, E. (2004) Reliving abandonment in the face of the therapist's pregnancy, *Psychoanalytic Psychotherapy*, 18: 67–85.

Glick, R.A. (1987) Forced terminations, *Journal of the American Academy of Psychoanalysis*, 15: 449–63.

Goldstein, J. (1972) Finding the least detrimental alternative: The problem for the law of child placement, *The Psychoanalytic Study of the Child*, 27: 626–641.

Greenberg, J.R. and Mitchell, S.A. (1983) *Object Relations in Psychoanalytic Theory*. Cambridge, MA: Harvard University Press.

Grotjahn, M. (1985) Being sick and facing eighty: observations of an aging therapist, in R. Nermiroff and C. Colarusso (eds) *The Race against Time*. New York: Plenum, pp. 293–302.

Guy, J.D., Stark, M.J., Poelstra, P. and Souder, J.K. (1987) Psychotherapist retirement and age-related impairment: results of a national survey, *Psychotherapy*, 24(4): 816–20.

Hampton, C. (2006) Ending work as a psychotherapist: conversational reflections on the issues of retirement, *Oxford Psychotherapy Society Bulletin*, 43: 1–9.

Hartlaub, G.H., Martin, G.C. and Rhine, M.W. (1986) Recontact with the analyst following termination: a survey of seventy-one cases, *Journal of the American Psychoanalytic Association*, 34: 896–910.

Haynes, J. (2009) *Who is It That Can Tell Me Who I Am?* London: Constable and Robinson.

Hess, N. (2004) Loneliness in old age: Klein and others, in *Talking Over the Years: A handbook of dynamic psychotherapy with older adults*. Hove: Routledge.

Hidalgo, M.C. and Herandez, B. (2001) Place attachment: conceptual and empirical questions, *Journal of Environmental Psychology*, 21(3): 273–81.

Hindmarch, C. (2009) On being open and letting go, *Therapy Today*, 20(8): 24–7.

Holmes, J. (1993) *John Bowlby and Attachment Theory*. London: Routledge.

Holmes, J. (1997) 'Too early, too late': endings in psychotherapy – an attachment perspective, *British Journal of Psychotherapy*, 14(2): 159–74.

Holmes, J. (2010) Termination in psychoanalytic psychotherapy: an attachment perspective, in J. Salberg (ed.) *Good Enough Endings*. New York: Routledge, pp. 63–82.

Hopkins, L. (2008) *False Self: The life of Masud Khan*. London: Karnac Books.

Horner, A.J. (2002) Frontline: is there life after psychoanalysis? On retirement from clinical practice, *Journal of the American Psychoanalytic Association*, 30: 325–8.

House of Lords (2012) Constitution Committee – Twenty-Fifth Report, Judicial Appointments March, ch. 7, para. 191: www.publications.parliament.uk/pa/ld 201012/ldselect/ldconst/272/27210.htm

Howitt, P. (dir.) (1998) *Sliding Doors* [film] UK. Paramount.

Imber, R.R. (1995) The role of the supervisor and the pregnant analyst, *Psychoanalytic Psychology*, 12(2): 281–96.

Jacobs, D., David, P. and Meyer, D.J. (1995) *The Supervisory Encounter*. New Haven, CT: Yale University Press.

Jaffe, S. (2011) The experience of working as a therapists in old age: an interpretative phenomenological analysis. Unpublished MA dissertation.

Jaques, E. (1965) Death and the midlife crisis, *International Journal of Psycho-Analysis*, 46: 502–14.

Jung, C.G. (1931) *The Stages of Life.* C.W.8.

Junkers, G. (ed.) (2013) *The Empty Couch.* New York: Routledge.

Juri, L. and Marrone, M. (2003) Attachment and bereavement, in M. Cortina and M. Marrone (eds) *Attachment Theory and the Psychoanalytic Process.* London: Whurr, pp. 242–67.

Kaplan, E.H., Weiss, S.S., Harris, L.H. and Dick, M.M. (1994) Termination imposed by the analyst's relocation: theoretical and practical considerations, *Canadian Journal of Psychoanalysis*, 2: 253–67.

Kastenbaum, R. (2000) *The Psychology of Death.* London: Free Association Books.

Kearney, M. (1996) *Mortally Wounded.* Dublin: Marino.

Kelly, M. and Barratt, G. (2007) Retirement: phantasy and reality – dying in the saddle or facing up to it?, *Psychodynamic Practice*, 13(2): 197–202.

King, P. (1974) Notes on the psychoanalysis of older patients: reappraisal of the potentialities for change during the second half of life, *Journal of Analytical Psychology*, 19: 22–37.

Klein, J. (2006) When retirement threatens, in A. Foster, A. Dickinson, B. Bishop and J. Klein (eds) *Difference: An avoided topic in practice.* London: Karnac, pp. 65–7.

Klein, M. (1963/1988) *On the Sense of Loneliness, Envy and Gratitude and Other Works 1956–63.* London: Virago.

Klockars, L. (2013) Ageing in European psychoanalytic societies, in G. Junkers (ed.) *The Empty Couch: The taboo of ageing and retirement in psychoanalysis.* London: Routledge, pp. 101–10.

Kohut, H. (1971) *The Analysis of the Self: A systematic approach to the psychoanalytic treatment of narcissistic personality disorders.* New York: International Universities Press.

Kottler, J.A. (2010) *On Being a Therapist*, 4th edn. San Francisco, CA: Jossey-Bass.

Kubler-Ross, E. (1970) *On Death and Dying.* London: Tavistock Publications.

Langs, R. (1994) *Doing Supervision and Being Supervised.* London: Karnac Books.

Larkin, P. (2012) The old fools, in P. Larkin (ed.) *The Complete Poems.* New York: Farrar, Straus and Giroux.

Lax, R.F. (1969) Some considerations about transference and countertransference manifestations evoked by the analyst's pregnancy, *International Journal of Psycho-Analysis*, 50: 363–72.

Lazar, S. (1990) Patients' responses to pregnancy and miscarriage in the analyst, in H.J. Schwartz and A-M.S. Silver (eds) *Illness in the Analyst: Implications for the treatment relationship.* Madison, CT: International Universities Press, pp. 192–226.

Lean, D. (dir.) (1945) *Brief Encounter* [film]. London: Denham Film Studios.

Leowald, H.W. (1962) Internalisation, separation, mourning and the superego, *Psychoanalytic Quarterly*, 31: 483–504.

Lewis, C.S. (1961) *A Grief Observed.* London: Faber and Faber.

Likierman, M. (2001) *Melanie Klein: Her work in context.* London: Continuum.

Limentani, A. (1982) On the "unexpected" termination of psychoanalytic therapy, *Psychoanalytic Inquiry*, 2: 419–40.

Lord, R., Ritvo, S. and Solnit, A.J. (1978) Patients' reactions to the death of the psychoanalyst, *International Journal of Psychoanalysis*, 59: 189–197.

Magai, C. (2008) Attachment in middle and later life, in J. Cassidy and P.R. Shaver (eds) *Handbook of Attachment: Theory, research and clinical applications.* New York: Guilford Press, pp. 532–51.

Mahler, M., Pine, F. and Bergman, A. (1975) *The Psychological Birth of the Human Infant.* New York: Basic Books.

Main, M. and Goldwyn, R. (1998) Adult attachment scoring and classification system. Unpublished manuscript, University of California at Berkeley.

Main, M. and Solomon, J. (1986) Discovery of a new, insecure-disorganised/disoriented attachment pattern, in T.B. Brazelton and M. Yogman (eds) *Affective Development in Infancy.* Norwood, NJ: Ablex, pp. 95–124.

Main, M., Kaplan, N. and Cassidy, J. (1985) Security in infancy, childhood and adulthood: a move to the level of representation, in I. Bretherton and E. Waters (eds) *Growing Points of Attachment Theory and Research*, Monographs of the Society for Research in Child Development, 50(1–2). Chicago, IL: University of Chicago Pres, pp. 66–104.

Malan, D.H. (1975) *The Study of Brief Psychotherapy.* New York: Plenum.

Mander, G. (2002) Timing and ending in supervision, in C. Driver and E. Martin (eds) *Supervising Psychotherapy.* London: Sage, pp. 140–52.

Mander, G. (2010) Leaving: reflections on retirement from psychotherapy, *Supervision Review*, Summer: 22–3. London: British Association of Psychoanalytic and Psychodynamic Supervisors.

Mann, D. (1973) *Time-Limited Psychotherapy.* Cambridge, MA: Harvard University Press.

Martinez, D. (1989) Pains and gains: A study of forced terminations, *Journal of the American Psychoanalytic Association*, 37: 89–115.

Mayer, C. (2011) *Amortality: The pleasures and perils of living agelessly.* London: Vermilion.

McGee, T. (2003) Observations on the retirement of professional psychologists, *Professional Psychology: Research and Practice*, 34(4): 388–95.

Midgley, N. (2006) Psychoanalysis and qualitative psychology: complementary or contradictory paradigms?, *Qualitative Research in Psychology*, 3: 213–31.

Mikulincer, M. (1997) Adult attachment style and information processing: individual differences in curiosity and cognitive closure, *Journal of Personality and Social Psychology*, 72(95): 1217–30.

Milner, M. (1950) A note on the ending of an analysis, *International Journal of Psychoanalysis*, 31: 191–3.

Mitchell, S. (1993) *Hope and Dread in Psychoanalysis.* New York: Basic Books.

Mitchell, S. (2000) *Relationality: From attachment to intersubjectivity.* Hillsdale, NJ: Analytic Press.

Murdin, L. (2000) *How Much is Enough? Endings in psychotherapy and counselling.* London: Routledge.

Murray Parkes, C. (1971) Psycho-social transitions: a field for study, *Social Science and Medicine,* 5: 101–15.

Murray Parkes, C. (1972) *Bereavement: Studies of grief in adult life.* London: Tavistock Publications.

Neugarten, B.L. (ed.) (1968) *Middle Age and Aging.* Chicago, IL: University of Chicago Press.

Noak, A. (2011) When retirement turns into forced retreat, *Supervision Review,* Summer: 3–7.

Norman, H.F., Blacker, K.H., Oremland, J.D. and Barrett, W.G. (1976) The fate of the transference neurosis after the termination of a satisfactory analysis, *Journal of the American Psychoanalytic Association,* 24: 471–98.

Novick, J.and Novick, K.K. (2000) Love in the therapeutic alliance, *Journal of the American Psychoanalytic Association,* 48: 189–218.

Ogden, T.H. (1992) *The Primitive Edge of Experience.* London: Maresfield Library.

O'Neil, M.K. (2013) The professional will, in G. Junkers (ed.) *The Empty Couch: The taboo of ageing and retirement in psychoanalysis.* London: Routledge, pp. 150–60.

Pedder, J.R. (1988) Termination reconsidered, *International Journal of Psycho-Analysis,* 69: 495–505.

Pizer, B. (1998) Breast cancer in the analyst, in L.Aron and F. Sommer Anderson (eds) *Relational Perspectives on the Body.* Hillsdale, NJ: Analytic Press, pp. 191–212.

Pointon, C. (2004) When is the right time to retire?, *Counselling and Psychotherapy Journal,* 15(4): 18–21.

Powell, D. (2011) *The Aging Intellect.* London: Routledge.

Power, A. (2003) Using attachment theory to understand patients' responses to a therapist's medical break, *Attachment and Human Development,* 5(1): 78–93.

Power, A. (2009) Supervision – a space where diversity can be thought about, *Attachment: New Directions in Psychotherapy and Relational Psychoanalysis,* 3: 157–75.

Power, A. (2012) When a supervisee retires, *Psychodynamic Practice,* 18(4): 441–55.

Power, A. (2013) Supervision of supervision: how many mirrors do we need?, *British Journal of Psychotherapy,* 29(3): 389–404.

Power, A. (2014) Impasse in supervision – looking back and thinking again, *Attachment: New Directions in Psychotherapy and Relational Psychoanalysis,* 8: 154–71.

Price, C.A. (2003) Professional women's retirement adjustment: the experience of re-establishing order, *Journal of Aging Studies,* 17: 341–55.

Quinodoz, D. (2010) *Growing Old: A journey of self-discovery* (transl. David Alcorn). London: Routledge.

Rangell, L. (1966) An overview of the ending of an analysis, in R.E. Litman (ed.) *Psychoanalysis in the Americas*. New York: International Universities Press, pp. 141–73.

Rangell, L. (1982) Some thoughts on termination, *Psychoanalytic Inquirer*, 2: 367–92.

Reichard, S., Livson, F. and Petersen, P.G. (1962) *Aging and Personality*. New York: Wiley.

Rizq, R. (2008) The research couple: a psychoanalytic perspective on dilemmas in the qualitative research interview, *European Journal of Psychotherapy and Counselling*, 10(1): 39–53.

Robertson, J. (dir.) (1952) *A Two-Year-Old Goes to Hospital* [film]. London: Tavistock.

Robutti, A. (2010) When the patient loses his/her analyst, *The Italian Psychoanalytic Annual*, 4: 129–45.

Russell, M. (2011) Correspondence, *Therapy Today*, October: 40.

Russell, M. and Simanowitz, V. (2013) Retirement or Renaissance?, *Therapy Today*, 24(2): 14–18.

Sabbadini, A. (2007) On the open-endedness of psychoanalysis, *Psychoanalytic Review*, 94: 705–13.

Sandler, J., Dare, C. and Holder, A. (1992) *The Patient and the Analyst*. London: Karnac.

Sanville, J.B. (2002) When therapist and patient are both in Erikson's eighth stage, *Psychoanalytic Inquiry*, 22: 626–39.

Scharff, D.E. and Scharff, J.S. (2004) *Object Relations Couple Therapy*. New York: Rowman and Littlefield.

Schlessinger, N. and Robbins, F. (1974) Assessment and follow-up in psycho-analysis, *Journal of the American Psychoanalytic Association*, 7: 418–44.

Schlessinger, N. and Robbins, F. (1975) The psychoanalytic process: recurrent patterns of conflict and changes in ego functions, *Journal of the American Psychoanalytic Association*, 23: 761–82.

Schlessinger, N. and Robbins, F. (1983) *A Developmental View of the Psychoanalytic Process: Follow-up studies and their consequences*. Madison, CT: International Universities Press.

Schwarz, I.G. (1974) Forced termination of analysis revisited, *International Review of Psychoanalysis*, 1: 283–90.

Searles, H.F. (1955/2012) The informational value of the supervisor's emotional experiences, in H. Searles, *Collected Papers on Schizophrenia and Related Subjects*. London: Karnac.

Segal, H. (1958) Fear of death – notes on the analysis of an old man, *International Journal of Psychoanalysis*, 39: 178–81.

Shaver, P. and Mikulincer, M. (2004) Attachment in the later years: a commentary, *Attachment and Human Development*, 6(4): 451–64.

Sherby, L.B. (2004) Forced termination: when pain is shared, *Contemporary Psychoanalysis*, 40: 69–90.

Shernoff, M. (2009) Sudden retirement of a psychotherapist due to terminal illness, *Journal of Gay and Lesbian Mental Health*, 13: 106–16.

Siegel, J. (1992) *Repairing Intimacy: An object relations approach to couples therapy*. Northvale, NJ: Jason Aronson.

Simmons, R. (2011) Supervising pregnancy, *Supervision Review*, Summer: 14–16. London: British Association of Psychoanalytic and Psychodynamic Supervisors.

Slade, A. (2004) The move from categories to process: attachment phenomena and clinical evaluation, *Infant Mental Health Journal*, 25(4): 269–83.

Snowdon, D. (2001) *Aging with Grace: What the nun study teaches us about leading longer, healthier and more meaningful lives*. New York: Bantam Books.

Sorensen, B. (2009) And when the therapist or supervisor dies . . ., in L. Barnett (ed.) *When Death Enters the Therapeutic Space: Existential perspectives in psychotherapy and counselling*. Hove: Routledge, pp. 193–206.

Stevens, A. (1982) *Archetype: A natural history of the self*. London: Routledge.

Stimmel, B. (1995) Resistance to awareness of the supervisor's transfences with special reference to the parallel process, *International Journal of Psychoanalysis*, 76: 609–18.

Stock Whitaker, D. (1985) *Using Groups to Help People*. London: Routledge.

Stockman, A.F. and Green-Emrich, A. (1994) Impact of therapist pregnancy on the process of counselling and psychotherapy, *Psychotherapy: Theory, Research, Practice, Training*, 31(3): 456–62.

Storr, A. (1973) *Jung*. London: HarperCollins.

Strauss, H.M. (1996) Working as an older analyst, in B. Gerson (ed.) *The Therapist as a Person*. Hillsdale, NJ: The Analytic Press, pp. 277–294.

Stroebe, M., Schut, H. and Stroebe, W. (2005) Attachment in coping with bereavement: a theoretical integration, *Review of General Psychology*, 9(1): 48–66.

Stuart, J. (1997) Pregnancy in the therapist: consequences of a gradually discernible change, *Psychoanalytic Psychology*, 14(3): 347–64.

Sugg, S. (2011) Letters page, *Therapy Today*, September: 19.

Sussman, S. (2007) *A Curious Calling*. Lanham, MD: Aronson.

Szajnberg, N.M. and Crittenden, P.M. (1997) The transference refracted through the lens of attachment, *Journal of the American Academy of Psychoanalysis*, 25: 409–38.

Tallmer, M. (1992) The aging analyst, *Psychoanalytic Review*, 79: 381–404.

Tennyson, A.L. (1842/1933) *The Poems of Alfred, Lord Tennyson: A selection*. London: Oxford University Press.

Thompson, P. (2000) *The Voice of the Past: Oral history*, 3rd edn. Oxford: Oxford University Press.

Tracey, T. J., Wampold, B. E., Lichtenberg, J. W. and Goodyear, R. K. (2014). Expertise in psychotherapy: an elusive goal?, *American Psychologist*, 69: 218–29.

Traesdal, T. (2005) When the analyst dies: dealing with the aftermath, *Journal of the American Psychological Association*, 53: 1235–1265.

Traesdal, T. (2013) Analysis lost and regained, in G. Junkers (ed.) *The Empty Couch: The taboo of ageing and retirement in psychoanalysis.* London: Routledge, pp. 82–90.

Trayner, B. and Clarkson, P. (1992) What happens if a psychotherapists dies?, *Counselling*, February: 23–4.

Vaillant, G.E. (2002) *Aging Well: Surprising guideposts to a happier life from the Landmark Harvard Study of Adult Development.* Boston, MA: Little, Brown and Company.

Valenzuela, M., Brayne, C., Sachdev, P., Wilcock, G. and Matthews, F. (2011) Cognitive lifestyle and long-term risk of dementia and survival after diagnosis in a multicentre population-based cohort, *American Journal of Epidemiology*, 173(9): 1004–12.

Van Deurzen-Smith, E. (1988) *Existential Counselling in Practice.* London: Sage.

Viorst, J. (1982) Experiences of loss at the end of analysis: the analyst's response to termination, *Psychoanalytic Inquiry*, 2: 399–418.

Vowles, D. (2011) Personal communication.

Waddell, M. (2002) *Inside Lives: Psychoanalysis and the growth of the personality.* London: Karnac.

Walcott, W.O. (2011) Reflections on retirement, *Psychological Perspectives*, 54(2): 208–25.

Watkins, C.E. and Riggs, S.A. (2012) Psychotherapy supervision and attachment theory: review, reflections, and recommendations, *The Clinical Supervisor*, 31: 256–89.

Webster's (1936) *Collegiate Dictionary*, 5th edn. London: Webster's.

Weiss, S.S. (1972) Some thoughts and clinical vignettes on translocation of an analytic practice, *International Journal of Psychoanalysis*, 53: 505–13.

Weiss, S.S. and Kaplan, E.H. (2000) Inner obstacles to psychoanalysts' retirement: personal, clinical, and theoretical perspectives, *Bulletin of the Menninger Clinic*, 64(4): 443–461.

Weiss, S.S., Kaplan, E.H. and Flanagan Jr., C.H. (1997) Aging and retirement: a difficult issue for individual psychoanalysts and organised psychoanalysis, *Bulletin of the Menninger Clinic*, 61(4): 469–81.

Winnicott, D.W. (1949) Hate in the countertransference, *International Journal of Psycho-Analysis*, 30: 69–74.

Winnicott, D.W. (1953) Transitional objects and transitional phenomena—A study of the first not-me possession, *International Journal of Psycho-Analysis*, 34: 89–97.

Winnicott, D.W. (1958/1965) The capacity to be alone, in *The Maturational Process and the Facilitating Environment.* London: Hogarth Press, pp. 29–36.

Winnicott, D.W. (1962a/1990) The aims of psycho-analytical treatment, in *The Maturational Processes and the Facilitating Environment.* London: Karnac, pp. 166–70.

Winnicott, D.W. (1962b/1990) Ego integration in child development, in *The Maturational Processes and the Facilitating Environment.* London: Karnac, pp. 56–63.

Winnicott, D.W. (1969/1989) The use of an object, *International Journal of Psychoanalysis*, 50: 711–716.

Woodward, J. (2004) Attachment theory and ageing, in M. Green and M. Scholes (eds) *Attachment and Human Survival*. London: Karnac, pp. 53–70.

Worden, J.W. (1983) *Grief Counselling and Grief Therapy*. London: Tavistock Publications.

Zevon, W. (1993) If you won't leave me I'll find somebody who will [song]. New York: NBC.

Index